On Moral Considerability

ON MORAL CONSIDERABILITY

An Essay on
Who Morally Matters

Mark H. Bernstein

New York   Oxford
Oxford University Press
1998

Oxford University Press

Oxford   New York

Athens   Auckland   Bangkok   Bogotá   Buenos Aires   Calcutta
Cape Town   Chennai   Dar es Salaam   Delhi   Florence   Hong Kong   Istanbul
Karachi   Kuala Lumpur   Madrid   Melbourne   Mexico City   Mumbai
Nairobi   Paris   São Paulo   Singapore   Taipei   Tokyo   Toronto   Warsaw

and associated companies in
Berlin   Ibadan

Copyright © 1998 by Mark H. Bernstein

Published by Oxford University Press, Inc.
198 Madison Avenue, New York, New York 10016

Oxford is a registered trademark of Oxford University Press.

Library of Congress Cataloging-in-Publication Data
Bernstein, Mark H., 1948–
On moral considerability : an essay on who morally matters
/ Mark H. Bernstein.
p. cm.
(Includes bibliographical references and index.
ISBN 0-19-512391-3
1. Ethics.   2. Animal welfare—Moral and ethical aspects.
I. Title.
BJ1012.B47   1998
179'.1—dc21   97-52259

1   3   5   7   9   8   6   4   2

Printed in the United States of America
on acid-free paper

*In memory of my father, Louis,
and in memory to my companions and friends
Woody, Eli, and Margot*

*For Matilda, Robert, Rachel,
Jedidiah, Jonah, and Knish*

Acknowledgments

I thank *Philosophical Studies* for allowing me to use my essay "Contractualism and Animals" (April 1997). Mike Almeida, Stew Cohen, Bob Kane, Al Martinich, and Peter Singer have read parts, if not all, of earlier drafts of the manuscript and these generous friends and colleagues have my gratitude for offering suggestions that have improved it. To Nancy Daley, in mercifully allowing me both to escape from necessary household duties and to mutter—philosophically and otherwise—for some four years without once calling either the local constabulary or neighborhood psychiatric ward, my sincerest thanks.

Cynthia Read, Jessica Ryan, and Pam Upton, philosophy editor, production editor, and copyeditor, respectively, at Oxford University Press, have my thanks and admiration.

Contents

Introduction   3

PART I   THEORIES OF WELFARE

Chapter 1. Experientialism   9
Chapter 2. The Desire of Theory   37
Chapter 3. Perfectionism   79

PART II   ANIMAL MATTERS

Chapter 4. Animal Patienthood   117
Chapter 5. Contractualism and Animals   147

Conclusion   169
Notes   171
References   181
Index   185

On Moral Considerability

And the gods granted Alessandra just one wish. The only requirement was that the wish be for the destruction of something. Without deliberation, Alessandra wished for the end of suffering.

And even Buddha smiled.

Introduction

This is a work on moral patienthood. In it, I investigate what must be true of an individual so that it deserves moral consideration.[1] After developing an account of patienthood, I argue that we—normal adult human beings—have unjustly disenfranchised some individuals from our moral domain. The argument in the book, then, is not merely "academic"; if it is essentially right-headed, the way in which most of us live our lives ought to be dramatically altered. I hope this work will pave the conceptual groundwork for a detailed examination of the sorts of revisions that morality requires of us.

In a sense, legitimate entry into our moral community is quite simple. If an individual can be morally engaged by us, it ought to be. If we can act in a morally right and wrong way toward a particular individual then, perhaps defeasibly, that individual deserves our ethical consideration. I suggest that all that such an individual requires is a welfare or well-being; there must be ways in which an individual can (prudentially) be made both better and worse in order to qualify as a moral patient. Thus, accounts (theories) of moral patienthood are intimately connected with accounts of welfare. The best way of understanding the latter indicates the most propitious way of understanding the former.

I assume that nihilism is unacceptable. I will not try to prove either that there are some individuals who deserve moral consideration or that we know who some of them are. They are us. It is a criterion of acceptability of any theory that normal adult human beings can be made both better and worse off and so are moral patients. If any reader seriously believes that this already begs contentious questions, so be it; this may be an opportune place to part company. I will argue that our moral borders extend far beyond ourselves, and I hope that those who have a less provincial attitude toward moral personhood will read further.

Part I addresses theoretical concerns. Granting that we have the capacity to be made better and worse off, I examine what it is about us that makes for our modifiable welfare. Three viable theories present themselves; indeed, I show how the latter two can be viewed as a reaction to some disenchantment with the first theory. The first I dub "experientialism"—the view, roughly, that our well-being is solely a function of how we are doing "from the inside." To the extent that our conscious experiences are pleasing, our welfares are enhanced; to the extent that these experiences are displeasing, our welfares are diminished. The second view is called the "desire theory," wherein our lots are improved insofar as our desires are satisfied and worsened insofar as our desires are frustrated. The third account, "perfectionism," claims, roughly, that we are better/worse off in virtue of possessing certain qualities, qualities that extend beyond merely feeling good/bad and having desires fulfilled/thwarted. Although different perfectionists supply different candidates for these qualities, all concur that the status of these qualities as welfare-modifying is a function of the properties themselves and is not derivable from any relationship the properties may have with either an individual's experiences or desires.

I argue at some length that both the desire theory and perfectionism lead to various untoward results. I detail how acceptance of the desire theory commits one to the view that one can be made better and worse off posthumously, and that although this notion is more plausible than it may appear on initial hearing, it ultimately cannot be satisfactorily defended. Thus, we have a powerful reason, among others, to reject the desire theory. I employ a similar strategy against perfectionism, arguing that acceptance of this theory commits one to "deep ecology," a theory of patienthood that allows for nonliving, let alone nonexperiential, individuals to be warranted subjects of moral consideration. Deep ecology, as I show, is conceptually confused, and so we have a strong justification, among others, to dismiss perfectionism. Experientialism, on the other hand, when properly characterized, is defensible against serious attacks. Moreover, any residual worries do not affect the domain of patienthood that emanates from the theory of welfare.

Part II discusses the most significant application of these results. If an experiential life suffices for moral standing, then many nonhuman animals should be included in our moral realm. At least this is so if we accept the commonsense idea that some nonhuman animals have conscious experiences. Some neo-Cartesians reject this commonsense idea. I argue that the reasons for their rejection are spurious. Furthermore, I find fault with the arguments that allege to demonstrate either that no nonhuman animals have desires or that only humans have some special (perfectionist) quality that uniquely confers moral standing upon them. Thus, even were we to accept a desire or perfectionist theory of welfare, we have no good reasons to dismiss all nonhuman animals from our moral sphere.

Finally, I discuss the merits of contractualism toward animals. I argue, as opposed to the received view, that contractualism has the resources to incorporate nonhuman animals as robust members of our moral community in just the same way that it includes normal adult humans. If, however, contractualists wish not to accept this olive branch, they will inevitably flout some of our most entrenched moral beliefs, beliefs so fundamental to the way we conceive morality that their renunciation is all but unthinkable.

(II)

Some brief comments on methodology are in order. I believe that we have ethical intuitions or "considered moral beliefs." I unabashedly make use of mine, and I would be surprised if you do not share most of mine. The use of intuitions is hardly peculiar to ethics. We have epistemic and metaphysical intuitions and, were this book in either of these two areas, I would put them to serious work. Although I will not argue the point here, I believe it impossible to write a work in any of these fields (perhaps in *any* field) without employing some types of intuition. At any rate, I read Descartes's heroic failure in the *Meditations* as bringing into relief the fact that one cannot get something from nothing; even Descartes's genius was insufficient to overcome hyperbolic doubt.

I have tried to restrict technical (stipulative) language. Where I defer to tradition or ease of exposition and employ such language (in fact, the central idea of "moral patienthood" is, admittedly, technical), I make a sincere effort to explain it in nontechnical, ordinary language.

The work is apolemical and ahistorical. My goal is not to attack any philosopher's program, although, naturally enough, some philosophical positions become targets. I do not attempt to put the issues of moral personhood into historical perspective. I trust no one takes this as an indication that I believe either that this problem cannot be traced to the Moderns or even the Ancients, or that their contributions are not insightful.

I

THEORIES OF WELFARE

I

Experientialism

(I)

Normative ethical theories give us guidance regarding the conduct of our lives. In general terms, they supply us with the right and wrong ways to behave or instructions about how we ought to live our lives. These theories would have little practical import were there not individuals who could act in accordance with these precepts and individuals toward whom such behavior morally mattered; we need moral agents and moral patients in order for moral theories to find application.

My concern is primarily with moral patients, those individuals with the capacity to be morally considered and treated, or, equivalently, those individuals with the capacity to be morally enfranchised or engaged. Moral patients or, indifferently, individuals with moral standing are just those individuals who have the capacity to absorb moral behavior; they are the individuals toward whom moral behaviors can be intelligibly addressed. Moral patients and moral patients alone can be the objects of morally right and wrong actions. Accounting for the identity of moral patients is tantamount to circumscribing the scope of morality. To develop an account of moral patienthood or moral considerability is to theorize why particular individuals have substance from a moral point of view, why it is that certain individuals morally matter. This essay is an extended argument for a certain conception of moral enfranchisement, a conception that will help determine which of the world's items have moral significance.

(II)

I have characterized the notion of moral considerability or moral patienthood as the capacity to absorb moral consideration. This characterization was intentionally *descriptive*. There would have been no impropriety in beginning with a normative characterization of moral considerability or patienthood, for, after all, "moral considerability" and "moral patienthood" are terms of art rather than phrases in our ordinary lexicon. My reason for choosing the nonnormative or descriptive characterization is to make explicit a relationship that might otherwise go unnoticed. If one begins with a normative characterization of patienthood, there is a possibility that ultimately one will be satisfied with the account but not know what implications hold for those individuals, if any there be, who have the capacity for moral consideration and yet lack the desert for such consideration. Starting with a value-neutral account of moral patienthood naturally invites a discussion concerning the relationship between having the capacity for consideration and deserving it. Moreover, it presents a forum for discussing some metatheoretical concerns.

Consider the following:

(M) If an individual can be morally considered or treated then she ought to be morally considered or treated.

I suggest that this statement is extremely plausible, especially where "ought" is understood defeasibly. That is, I am minimally claiming that, all else being equal, or "special circumstances" aside, if an individual has the capacity for being morally considered, she warrants (deserves, merits) moral consideration. Moreover, I believe that all parties interested in providing an account of moral considerability at least implicitly subscribe to (M). Still, there may be detractors from other quarters; apologists of Hume's dictum that there is no legitimate inference from an "is" to an "ought" may find any alleged inference from a "can" to an "ought" even less palatable. Nonetheless, although in general one is not justified in drawing normative conclusions from premises concerning possibilities, the inference in (M) should be granted.

Clarification of (M) may begin with some commentary on the notion of capacity. Moral patients have the capacity to be morally considered and moral agents have the capability to morally consider. Although I believe it is true that "capacity" typically carries the connotation of passivity while "capability" typically suggests activity, this is not a matter of any importance; if one wants to interchange the use of these dispositional terms, or use the same term in each description, one has complete latitude to do so. More significant is the recognition of the relationship between capacities and capabilities, however they may be described. In this vein, it is helpful to consider the relationship between solubles and solvents. Solubles have the capacity to dissolve in solvents and solvents have the capability to dissolve solubles; there cannot be a capacity to be acted upon without a capability to act upon and conversely. Salt has the capacity to dissolve in water but not aqua regia, and so it trivially follows that water, but not aqua regia, has the capability to dissolve salt. Aqua regia, but not water, has the capability to dissolve gold, and so it trivially follows that gold has the capacity to be dissolved in aqua regia but not water. The relationship between capacities and capabilities is reciprocal and relative.

Similar considerations apply to the relationship between moral patients and moral agents. Just as salt has the capacity to be dissolved in water but not aqua regia, some individuals may have the capacity to be morally considered and treated by some, but only some, other individuals. Just as aqua regia has the capability to dissolve gold but not salt, some individuals may have the capability to morally consider and treat some, but not all, individuals. This admission might seem to compel another, namely, that the goal of trying to give an account of what makes an individual morally considerable is overly ambitious. At best what I can hope for is an account of moral patienthood relative to some segment of the world's population, where the chances of success are undoubtedly best found if the inquiry were relativized to the normal adult human population. For, to continue the analogy, as salt has the capacity to dissolve in water but not aqua regia, there is no reason not to think that some individuals are moral patients *to us* while remaining ethically inaccessible to beings that are not adult humans. And, similarly, there may be creatures who can be morally engaged by nonhumans but are ethically estranged from us.

If the worry stems from the fact that moral agents and moral patients are identified relationally, we can call upon our chemical analogy for some help. Just as a general account of solubility is not hindered by the fact that certain items are solubles only relative to other items that are solvents (and conversely), a general account of patienthood or considerability is not stymied by the essential relational character of moral patients and agents. There may, however, be a slightly different concern that lurks behind the deflationary caveats. Perhaps the real worry is that this inquiry must, by its very nature, incorporate an anthropocentrism that inevitably vitiates any prospects of success. The idea here is that any discussion of moral consideration is, and must be, seen through very human eyes. Thus any results I may claim to unearth are seen as biased and provincial. Although I, or humans in general, may be incapable of understanding how a certain individual may be morally considered, this is no reason to believe that the individual cannot be a moral patient, *simpliciter*. There may be a host of extraterrestrials who can both com-

prehend and effect this moral interchange. Although we may be incapable of understanding how to morally engage certain individuals, others,
morally and intellectually our superiors, might effortlessly do so.

The easiest way with this point is to concede the anthropocentrism
but deny its malignancy. The concepts of consideration, engagement,
enfranchisement, and the like are the concepts they are in virtue of the
way we use them. But this truism cannot possibly have the proposed
dire consequences. First, acceptance of this trivial truth does not imply
that human beings are the only beings who can either bestow or receive
moral consideration. Acceptance of this reputed implication, a claim I
vehemently reject, is probably based on a sort of "paradigm case" argument, some argumentation to the effect that the very meaning of these
terms derives from the fact that they are truthfully applied only in dealings concerning humans. What actually follows is simply another truism
to the effect that if any creature is morally engaged with another, then
we must be able to conceive of its behavior in human terms. For if its
conduct is literally inconceivable in these terms there is no reason for us
to characterize its conduct under the rubric "moral." Indeed, even this
claim, although true, is misleading because too weak. It may yield the
impression that although the individual's behavior cannot be so characterized, it still may be true that its conduct instantiates moral engagement. But it cannot be; "moral engagement," too, is a concept that,
precisely like all others, receives its applicability from human use. Thus,
second and more important, there is no invidious anthropocentrism assumed in this investigation. Concepts, including the concept "concept,"
are human constructions.

The same point can be made in terms of translatability. An extraterrestrial logically cannot mean "telephone" if he is referring to a small
insect that travels in large groups and frequently disrupts picnickers. Of
course, he can utter the sound "telephone," and so the sound he uses
to name these small creatures might be homonymous with the word we
use to refer to a communication device. This does not imply that our
concepts are unique or that our concepts have some privileged cosmic
standing. It merely means that if we are to translate his language into
our language or if we are to deem his utterances intelligible, then we
must be able to understand or make sense of them, at least in the very
broad sense of understanding how his utterances can be understood by
someone. If this is classified as human chauvinism, so be it. It is benign,
and not because it is inevitable (although it is), but rather, by virtue of
its platitudinous nature, it does not prejudice our moral investigations.

So much for some metatheoretical concerns. Still, I have given no
positive reason for my claim that (M) is extremely plausible. Those who

are impressed either with Hume's diatribe against the possibility of bridging the "is/ought" gap or, more recently, with Moore's "open-question" test purporting to show that normative terms cannot be naturally analyzed are likely to dismiss any putative deductive link for the plausibility of (M). If we are prohibited from deducing "ought" from "is," we surely are not allowed to infer "ought" from "can"; the logical space is presumably larger. Of course, it is open to such apologists to accept (M) on strong inductive grounds. This, however, is not a debate I wish to enter. I am not so much interested in the source of the plausibility as in consensus about it. To this end, consider a scenario that finds you in the presence of an individual who can be morally considered or treated. Outside the rarefied atmosphere of philosophy, are there any persons who would maintain the belief that one ought not, all things being equal, take his moral considerability into account when acting? It is difficult to imagine any proposed ethical theory for which rejection of this belief would not serve as a *reductio*. Accounts may differ in their justification of such a belief, or even in whether any justification is necessary or possible, but acceptance of the belief would be a sine qua non of a theory's serious candidacy.

Acceptance of (M), then, makes the modal characterization of "moral patient" moot. Not only do those parties who dispute the scope of patienthood accept the proposition that an individual with the capacity for being morally considered deserves to be so considered, but the idea seems virtually foundational to any viable theory of ethics.

(III)

I begin my odyssey into the nature of moral standing by putting forward, as an uncontentious formal point, that the capacity for moral consideration requires that the individual have a welfare. To have a welfare or well-being is to have the capacity to be benefited and harmed, to be capable of being made both better and worse off. It would appear to make little sense to claim that an individual can be the recipient of moral behavior—that is, can be acted toward in morally right or wrong ways—while admitting that the individual lacks so much as the capacity to be made better and worse off or to have interests that can be positively and negatively affected.[1] About such purported formal relationships, there can be very little in the nature of argument. I hope that it strikes all of us as immensely odd to be told that there is an individual before us which lacks the capacity for any well-being, possesses no ways in which its existence can be made either better or worse, and yet subsists as an object with whom we can morally engage. This truism concerning the relationship between considerability and well-being, far from being breached, is further confirmed by the fact that we may have particular obligations to individuals who do own welfares to act in particular ways toward welfareless individuals. So if we adopt the common supposition that pencils lack, and normal adult humans have, welfares, then borrowing a pencil normally places moral proscriptions upon what we may do with the pencil. We may not, for example, break it into tiny bits. But this restriction on our actions is not a result of any moral obligation that we have toward the pencil per se (or "directly") but is, rather, a consequence of an obligation that we have toward the welfared owner of the pencil. Once these cases of "indirect" obligation are distinguished from the robust cases of ("direct") obligation, and once one recognizes that the formal thesis is intended to apply to only "direct" obligation (a realization that would strike all nonphilosophers as evident), there should be less reluctance in accepting the innocuous entailment between moral considerability and prudential well-being.

In characterizing my point of departure as "uncontentious" and "formal," I mean no more than I say. I am implying neither that in all cases of moral engagement is an individual being either benefited or harmed, nor that all cases affecting one's welfare have moral import. Nor, of course, am I suggesting a particular conception of welfare or well-being; at this juncture, this would be question begging in the extreme. If we already presuppose knowledge of what sorts of individuals possess welfares,—which individuals, that is, that have the capacity to be made better and worse off—then my proposed neutral starting point would carry with it rather substantive implications. Alternatively, although I am suggesting that having a welfare (having the capacity to be made better or worse off, having the capacity to be benefited and harmed, having interests) is necessary for moral considerability, I am not investing this claim with any material substance. The formal point can be agreed to by advocates of the most disparate views of moral patienthood. The real battle, as we shall soon see, will concern identifying the best account of individual welfare, for these accounts will deeply inform the resulting theories of patienthood.

It is worth emphasizing just how little is conceded when one accepts, as a formal condition, that the possession of a welfare is necessary for moral considerability or moral standing. Serving as an apt analogy is the debate that concerns Berkeleyans and Representative Realists regarding the nature of the empirical universe. Presumably both parties would agree to the existence of such a universe, and that tables, chairs, and blackboards are constituents of it. The disagreement concerns the ontic nature of these tables, chairs, and blackboards, with the Berkeleyan urging and the Realist resisting the idea that these entities are essentially immaterial. The consensus regarding the existence of an empirical world, though not vacuous, amounts to very little; in no way is it intended to prejudge the nature of the world's objects. The substance of the agreement resides in the fact that it rules out the possibility of the world containing nothing that is empirically perceivable, a position that would find few apologists. The agreement also affords us a procedure and a vocabulary in which to intelligibly conduct the metaphysical inquiry. The formal position that moral patienthood necessitates prudential well-being should be viewed in a light similar to the way agreement is achieved by the Berkeleyans and Realists. In like spirit, only the most argumentative should demur. The material question of the constitution of an individual's well-being, just like the inquiry concerning the ontic makeup of the empirically perceivable world, is intended at this juncture to be left completely open.

Although I have suggested that theorists of all stripes will agree that the capacity for moral consideration implies the capacity for a prudential well-being, the converse relationship does not meet with unanimous consent. At least some contractualists, for example, apparently believe that the capacity for possessing a welfare does not suffice for incorporation into the moral realm. I will later devote a somewhat detailed and insulated discussion to contractualism (see Chapter 5), but until that point, we can safely bracket the contractarian's concerns and continue our debate within a framework that meets with agreement from the other theorists. The typical presumption, and one with which I wholeheartedly identify, is that the ownership of a prudential welfare, the mere capacity to have one's life be made better and worse, does suffice for moral membership. The fact that most debates about whether certain individuals merit moral enfranchisement revolves around the question of the correct assessment of what constitutes an individual's well-being and whether particular individuals do, in fact, have this prudential capacity attests to the pervasiveness of this presumption. This would not be the central focus if there were not a general consensus that the capacity to be benefited and harmed *confers* moral patienthood. Thus, the realm of the morally considerable is derivable from the domain of the prudentially welfared. That is, the acceptance of any particular theory of welfare, the acceptance of any theory that tells us what constitutes well-being, automatically yields a domain of moral patienthood. Since it is possible that different theories of welfare may yield the same domain of patients (it may be that, although there are different accounts for benefits and harms, both accounts apply to exactly the same individuals), knowledge of which individuals merit moral consideration does not, in itself, inform us *why* it is that these individuals are morally considerable. Thus, while an individual is a moral patient if and only if she has a well-being, the explanatory direction runs from welfare to considerability rather than the other way around. Moral patients are just those individuals who have the capacity to be benefited and harmed, where what constitutes benefits and harms is supplied by the theory of welfare we employ. Theories of welfare and theories of considerability are, therefore, inextricably linked.

(IV)

These considerations suggest a particular methodology. Let us examine certain theories of well-being with the aim of discovering how the constitution of benefits and harms, of enhancement and diminution of the welfare of an individual, is best conceived. We will not (and probably could not) dispense with our prereflective notions about the domain of moral patienthood, but we will maintain them, as much as we can, undogmatically and therefore provisionally. The best theory of well-being will greatly inform the theory of patienthood that we, at least provisionally, accept. If we can derive a compelling account of how individuals are made better and worse off, then moral patients will be just those individuals who can enjoy the benefits and suffer the harms so understood. To those contractualists (and any others) who take exception to the idea that the capacity for welfare implies moral considerability, I ask indulgence until I can address their concerns in some depth.

Any acceptable account of moral patienthood must meet some minimal criteria. The most obvious demand upon such a theory is that it gives us a principled method of determining which individuals merit moral consideration. This, as we have seen, is derived from a view about well-being, a view about what it is that confers well-being upon a subject. Such a determination must comport, in perhaps imprecise ways, with some of our entrenched moral and nonmoral beliefs. If a theory of patienthood resulted in normal human beings' being excluded from moral considerability, we would have strong reason for its rejection. (This is one example of why it would it would be detrimental, if not virtually impossible, to completely dispense with our prereflective beliefs concerning the domain of the considerable). None of this is intended to imply a prejudice in favor of the status quo, let alone sanctifying our ethical heritage. In fact, some of our contemporary moral practices will be open to serious challenge if the final results of this inquiry are accepted. Still—and this idea will reappear later—we cannot simply begin morally *ex nihilo*, any more than Descartes could successfully found certainty in an epistemic vacuum.

Another pretheoretical concession is that the events classified as benefits and harms should strike us as benefits and harms. We should not be left wondering why a performance of a particular action that is characterized as beneficial toward an individual really makes that individual better off, nor should we be left scratching our heads why a behavior deemed harmful really makes the individual in question worse off. Terms such as "benefit" and "harm" are not terms of art, and presumably the proponent of a theory of moral considerability, a theory that necessarily involves the welfares of individuals, is not employing these terms in a technical or stipulative way. In fact, if the theorist uses these terms idiosyncratically, nothing more than verbal chicanery occurs. All these verbal maneuvers would be without value to the serious issue at hand unless the jargon were eventually connected to the normal use of language. Better we oppose the specialized lexicon from the outset. At best it plays the superfluous role of intermediary; at worst, and more likely, it has the deleterious effect of obfuscating the discussion.

(v)

I want to begin my reflections concerning (our ordinary) concept of welfare by investigating two related properties that are frequently suggested as having ramifications for an individual's well-being. Some have indicated that rarity—and its limiting point, uniqueness—confer patienthood upon an individual. (Some who believe that members of endangered species are more "morally significant" than members of nonendangered species seem, at times, to suggest this.) Uniqueness, per se, raises a peripheral issue of triviality. In accordance with Butler's dictum that "everything is what it is and not another thing," everything is unique, and there is, to the best of my knowledge, no theorist who believes that literally each and every thing (however, exactly, things are to be discriminated and identified) is deserving of moral consideration. More charitably, we should understand those who offer uniqueness (and rarity) as a property that confers patienthood upon an individual as relativizing this property to a kind or species.

Still, this more generous interpretation is mistaken, although instructively so. Consider first an individual who is not a moral patient and so lacks the capacity for being benefited and harmed. Assume that this individual is one of a group of its kind of things. The fact that all other members of the group were destroyed, leaving the individual in question as the unique exemplar of its sort, would seem to have no effect upon the moral capacity of the remaining individual. It is not as though the eradication of other members of the group, in and of itself, can create a capacity for prudential welfare in an individual in whom it was heretofore absent. But we should not read too much into this. It is conceivable that in the course of the destruction of the other members, some *causal* effects might be absorbed by the sole survivor, modifying its status from amoral to moral patient, from being without a welfare to possessing one. But if this scenario were to occur, it would not be the change from being one of many to being unique (or even rare) that, in and of itself, would account for the alteration of moral status. Rather, in the course of effecting this proportional shift, the environment would have been modified in such a way that the amoral patient would have been transmuted into a moral one. The point is that in undergoing the purely relational change—from being one of many to being unique—there is no unmysterious way in which the individual can change from lacking the capacity to be benefited and harmed to possessing this capacity.

The same reasoning pertains to the reverse case: an individual's loss of uniqueness, in and of itself, cannot rescind patienthood. Suppose that a unique individual is correctly characterized as a moral patient. There is no intelligible reason to suppose that it loses this moral status merely in virtue of gaining species partners. The purely relational change in this individual—from being unique to being one of a group—has no nullifying effect on its moral status. The moral impotence of uniqueness and rarity extends further. A moral patient who remains a moral patient after being made one of a group would not have had her moral status reduced, nor would a common moral patient who becomes unique or rarer have her moral status enhanced. It surely seems bizarre to think that my moral status can become diminished merely in virtue of the overnight births of several babies or that my moral status improves in virtue of a few persons suffering mortal gunshot wounds the previous day. These do not seem to be the sorts of events that are appropriate for the modification of personal well-being. The powerful intuition at work here is that moral status is a function of what the individual is deeply, profoundly like. The births of babies or the deaths of adults do not seem to be about *him* in a way that would be required for a change in his moral status. To put the point rhetorically: Why should he count morally less or more merely in virtue of these rather extraneous events? My suggestion is that the failure of uniqueness or rarity to be qualities that, in and of themselves, affect the welfare of individuals resides in the fact that they are purely extrinsic or relational properties. I believe that extrapolation upon these cases yields the significant insight that our ordinary concept of well-being requires that a change in either degree or kind be a product of some modification of the intrinsic or nonrelational properties of the individual in question, properties in the object that persist despite modifications in the relations that the object has with other objects. Welfare itself, then, is a personal attribute that is a function of an individual's intrinsic or nonrelational properties.

Reflecting on other examples seems to confirm that this is implicit in our ordinary understanding of personal well-being. Being the original member of some series is a purely relational property. But it is difficult to see why being the first individual of a certain sort, in and of itself, can make one either better or worse off than being the fifth, sixth, or thousandth, of the set. Being to the right of some object is another purely relational property, but again, it is difficult to comprehend why having a different spatial relationship (perhaps to the left of that same object) can either establish or annihilate a moral status or make a moral patient either better or worse off. Relational changes are just too *tangential*. The motivating intuition is that only in virtue of an inherent modification of an individual—a modification that occurs to the individual per se—can that individual have her welfare either enhanced or diminished.[2]

I believe that the intuition that purely relational modifications cannot make the individual who undergoes those changes either better or worse off (or create or destroy moral status altogether) shares a kinship with the intuition that rails against the idea that so-called Cambridge changes are real changes. Virtually all agree that an individual undergoing a Cambridge change is *affected* in only the most Pickwickian way. I have just thought of Wittgenstein, and so now Wittgenstein has the property of being thought of by Bernstein some forty-seven years after his death. But it is surely odd to think of any change, in any real or robust way, occurring to Wittgenstein. This is not to deny that there are examples that may be difficult to classify as one sort rather than another, nor even to deny that there is a difficulty in providing a perspicuous analysis of Cambridge changes that suffices to capture the intuitively unproblematic cases, but the fact remains that there seems to be something quite ethereal to the idea of an individual undergoing a Cambridge change. In much the same manner, purely relational modifications appear to lack the efficacy or robustness to account for change in the moral status of an individual. To modify an individual's well-being, or, more dramatically, to generate or destroy an individual's welfare requires a state of affairs that affects the real constitution of the individual, and this, so goes the suggestion, can only happen if the individual's intrinsic properties are altered.

This idea gains credence when we recognize that we can apply it to certain of our thoughts about fictional characters. We begin with the belief that, in a literal way, there is nothing that anyone can do to enhance or diminish the welfare of Sherlock Holmes or Batman. Of course, this is not a statement so much about our impotence as it is a commentary on the fact that Holmes and Batman, being fictional characters, lack—indeed necessarily lack—a welfare. On the view just adumbrated, this privation of welfare can be explained by fact that Holmes and Batman have no intrinsic properties; their entire existence (or subsistence) is constituted by their purely relational properties. These relational properties are neither spatial nor temporal, but narrative. Meinongians to the side, all there is to Batman and Holmes are the stories that comprise them.[3] We can, then, think of fictional characters as objects that can absorb only Cambridge changes. This gives some explication for the shadowy existence we attribute to such characters and why they have perennially presented philosophers with ontological perplexities; metaphysically approximating Stein's Oakland, there is (virtually) no there there.

Some might be prone to run the argument the other way around. From this perspective, we begin with accepting the notion that fictional characters are best thought of as objects possessing only purely relational properties. Then, if it is true that both the possession of a welfare and the modifications to a welfare require an individual to own intrinsic properties, fictional characters should be incapable of being benefited or diminished. Since fictional characters do lack the capacity to be made better or worse, we have some confirmation of the idea that modifications to an individual's well-being must affect intrinsic properties.[4] For the purposes of supporting the intuition, both arguments serve equally well. Regardless of the evidential relationships that obtain among our beliefs regarding fictional characters, the set of beliefs themselves are consistent with, and to that extent lend support for, the view that modifications of the welfare of an individual are constituted by changes in its nonrelational or intrinsic properties.

We may use the vocabulary of "value" to express these results. We can say that purely relational properties have no value to their possessors, meaning only that the possession or deprivation of any of these properties has no effect on the welfares of the individuals in question. This amounts to the claim that no modification involving solely relational properties can either change the moral status of an individual—from moral patient to amoral patient, or conversely—or confer benefit or harm upon the individual who is the subject of these modifications. This is consistent with the claim that the recognition (or belief) that an individual's purely relational properties have changed may have value to the epistemic agent even when the epistemic agent is identical to the individual whose purely relational properties have changed. One might hold, for all that has so far been said, that recognizing that his own purely relational properties have been altered, in and of itself, makes that individual better (or worse) off. Because such recognition is itself not a purely relational property, we have no reason to preclude it, a priori, from having intrinsic moral value to its possessor. Such recognition may also have instrumental value to the epistemic agent; it may ultimately help bring about a state of affairs that does, in and of itself, benefit (or harm) the agent.

To think of an individual's welfare as a function of intrinsic properties comports well with our prereflective notion that the concept of moral patienthood is objective, in the sense that whether or not an individual has the capacity to be benefited and harmed is not merely a matter of human arbitrariness or convention. This attribute of objectivity is shared by some, but not all, extrinsic or relational properties. To elucidate this idea, consider a very plausible account of what makes an individual a human being. Many philosophers and scientists would concur that possessing a particular DNA structure is what confers humanity upon an individual. Indeed, there are those in a Kripkean vein who would argue that this relationship between DNA structure and humanity is not a mere de facto relationship, but one that obtains necessarily.[5] Of course what particular DNA configuration bestows humanity is a matter of scientific investigation; no one would suggest that this relationship is discoverable merely by conceptual investigation. It is reasonable, then, to view the claim that "possessing DNA structure D makes an individual human" as a necessary a posteriori truth. Nuances aside, the main point is that this account of the nature of humanity conforms with our prereflective notion that what makes someone human is not some arbitrary or conventional property that a particular individual has. Rather there is something "under the skin" that accounts for humanity, some objective state of affairs whose existence does not depend upon particularly human practices, categorizations, or idiosyncrasies.

On the other hand, we do not believe that there is any similar state of affairs that makes an object a bookcase. For an object to be a bookcase, it must be intended to be used for certain very human purposes. Although beavers may be able to create objects that are virtual replicas of bookcases, and that humans can use as bookcases, they are not generating bookcases. There is nothing "under the skin" that accounts for an object being a bookcase. Rather, what makes an object a bookcase is inevitably associated with our provincial, human practices. In opposition to the aforementioned account of humanity, it is wrongheaded to suppose that there is some property, B, such that "possessing property B makes an individual a bookcase" expresses a necessary a posteriori truth. The existence of bookcases—that is, the existence of objects *qua* bookcases—

is, as I am using the term, not an "objective" fact; were it not for the particular uses that humans make of these objects, bookcases would not exist.

I believe that we think of benefits and harms as objective occurrences in the world. The pretheoretical supposition is that the benefits and harms that befall individuals are not merely matters of convention or arbitrary practice. Whereas bookcases would cease to exist (*qua* bookcases) if human practices were to undergo alterations, major overhauls in the interests of humans would have no effect on the existence of DNA structures, and so would have no nullifying effect upon human existence. I am suggesting that it is appropriate to regard benefits and harms as operating in the latter manner.

Locke's distinction between primary and secondary qualities may help elucidate the point. Primary qualities were those powers that really resided in the external world and caused a perceiver to have ideas that accurately reflected the manner in which these external objects existed. So, for example, the extension and shape of objects were properties that were intrinsic to the external world and so completely independent of any perception of them. Not so for the secondary qualities, powers in the objects to produce ideas in perceivers that did not reflect the actual ontic status of those objects. Objects are not *really* colored or textured. Rather, these ideas that perceivers have of the objects are products of colorless, textureless corpuscles or atoms. Without mindful perceivers, colors and textures would only exist dispositionally in the external world, never to be manifested until and unless some creatures with minds similar in structure to those of humans were to cast their sensory apparatuses in the appropriate direction. To suggest that benefits and harms are functions of the intrinsic properties of an object is to analogize them with Locke's conception of primary properties. As the nature of the existence of primary properties is unthreatened by any change in perceptual situation, the nature of an individual's welfare is impervious to changes that occur in an object's relations with other objects.

(vi)

The attractiveness of the view that only individuals with intrinsic properties are capable of possessing welfares, and that modifications to these properties are what make that individual better and worse off, helps explain the plausibility and popularity of what we may call the "experiential theory of welfare" or "experientialism." Roughly, experientialism proclaims that an individual's well-being is exhaustively constituted by how well or poorly she is faring "from the inside." Welfare is purely and totally subjective: to the extent that the individual feels good, his life is going well, and to the extent that he feels poorly, his life is going badly. To qualify as a moral patient, then, to be the sort of individual who can be morally considered, one needs the capacity for conscious experience. To appropriate Thomas Nagel's phrase from a different but related context, there must be "something that it is like" for an individual to be a moral patient;[6] to appropriate Gerard Manley Hopkins's more graceful language, an "inscape" is required for moral standing.[7] At least on a commonsense level, one would be hard-pressed to think of any property that has a greater claim to intrinsicness than an individual's experiential mental states. While it is obvious that an individual's subjective state of mind can greatly be influenced by external happenings, it surely appears as if the creature's subjective well-being is itself as far removed from being a relational property as possible.

Although experientialism deems the capacity for conscious experience as necessary for patienthood, that capacity alone is not quite sufficient. There are two reasons for this. A subtlety comes to the fore once we realize that we have the concept of an individual with the capacity for (subjective) experience and yet lacking the capacity to have the content of his experience modified. Such an individual never undergoes and can never undergo a change in his subjective life. At least to some, God is an example of such a being, one who exists in eternal conscious bliss, not merely subjectively unperturbed, but unperturbable. Of course, to many of these same people, there are individuals who occupy the opposite side of the ledger; those damned to hell are in an immutably poor experiential state. Nor is there any reason to opt for one of these extremes. As long as the subjective experiential states are not subject to modification, experientialism would seem to preclude their possessors from moral standing. There is nothing that anyone can do, nor is there anything that can transpire, to make these individuals either better or worse off. It may be pointed out, in passing, that these claims about the nature of experience are scarcely inarguable. Some have suggested that the very notion of eternal conscious bliss is incoherent; therefore, if God is alleged to possess this property, so much the worse for His possible existence.

But even the capacity for modifiable conscious experience will not quite suffice, since the capacity must be of a certain sort of modifiable experience. The experiences must be of the sort that are pleasurable or displeasurable to the agent. Only if the individual has the subjective capacity to *enjoy* and *suffer* does he qualify as an individual with a welfare, and so as an individual with moral standing. To see why this addendum is required, consider an individual whose experiences are modifiable but who can feel neither better nor worse from these experiences. This individual is unlike a camera; there really is "something to be like" this individual, but he cannot be made either better or worse off by a change in his experiences. He can experience, robustly experience, a sunset one evening, a baseball game the next, and a fine dinner on the evening after that. He has modifiable experiences, but, from his interior perspective, there are no better feelings attached to one as opposed to any other. As far as enjoyment or suffering is concerned, where this is understood as a function of what transpires from the inside, all of his experiences are identical. Moral patienthood, in accordance with the prescriptions of experientialism, requires the capacity for hedonic experiences. Experientialism, then, is a theory of welfare that tells us that how well or poorly an individual is doing is purely a matter of how well or poorly he is doing from the inside, where benefits and harms are functions of the individual's subjective hedonic states. Experientialism indicates that the realm of the morally considerable is constituted by those individuals with the capacity for modifiable, hedonic conscious experience. If we use "phenomenology" or "sentience" as abbreviations for this capacity, we can say that experientialism dictates that all and only those with moral standing are phenomenological or sentient individuals.

Although experientialism is committed to the existence of certain experiences that make an individual better off and others that make a life worse off, it is not committed to the view that there exists a set of experiences such that if an individual has them, he is better off, and a set of other experiences such that if an individual has them, he is worse off. This is what we should suspect; one's experiential life is essentially subjective, in that experiences owe their identities as good or bad to the way they seem to their possessor. Alternatively, experiences just are how they seem, and it is among the most mundane of facts that the world seems different to different persons. Despite this truism, however, experientialists can, and indeed must, make a distinction between welfare-enhancing experiences and welfare-diminishing experiences, keeping in mind the fact that the *content* of these experiences can dramatically differ among persons or even among distinct stages of a single person's life. This consequence of experientialism accords well with our common-sense understanding of an individual's welfare. We tend to think that two persons, when confronted with one particular situation, can be influenced quite differently and have their well-being differently modified. Upon hearing of Kennedy's assassination, some people became depressed and so were harmed by the news, while others were not affected "on the inside" at all, and so their well-being was left unchanged. More perverted individuals may have actually had their well-being enhanced.

Nor should experientialism be saddled with the rather implausible claim that there is a single introspectively discernible feeling that pervades all welfare-enhancing experiences and another that runs through all welfare-diminishing ones.[8] There is little point to introducing, or pretending to find, a particular "feel" that we experience when we quench a thirst, read a novel, or reflect on our children's successes. It would be equally foolish to invent a phenomenological identity among the experiences of stepping on a thumbtack, remembering the Nazi atrocities, or recalling some verbal blunder delivered to a business associate. There are, at best, families of welfare-enhancing and welfare-diminishing phenomenologies. In fact, one needs to exercise some care in understanding the notions of phenomenologies or feels. Experientialism need not be encumbered by a reductionism that makes these welfare-modifying experiences atomistic feels or sensations. The enjoyment we receive from reading a novel is typically far more diffuse than the enjoyment we receive from biting into a juicy peach, and an individual is far more likely to describe the latter sort of welfare-enhancement in terms of sensations that he undergoes. Stretching the meaning of the term "sensation" would likely add confusion to the use of a term that already has more than its fair share of ambiguity.

Although one may use the terms "pain" and "pleasure" as abbreviations for what the experientialist deems as welfare-diminishing and welfare-enhancing occurrences, respectively (and I will, at times, avail myself of this shorthand), some caveats should be made explicit. To use "pain" and "pleasure" elliptically, we must understand pains and pleasures as being phenomenologically bad and good. An experientialist need not have any particular independent view of the nature of pleasant and painful sensations. She need not own, for example, opinions as to whether painful sensations are necessarily painful or whether the experience of a painful sensation is itself something that diminishes how one is doing from the inside. The commitment of the experientialist is simply that if and only if the pain diminishes the individual's subjective welfare is the pain bad for its possessor. In common parlance, "pain" is frequently used as a term that automatically carries the connotation of a diminished subjective state; we feel worse when we are in pain. If understood in this fashion, experientialism tells us that pains do, in fact, diminish our welfare.

Let us consider one plausible, but hardly inevitable, line of thought that accommodates this idea. Kripke believes that we "fix the referent" of "pain" by the way it feels to us.[9] I take this as implying that in every possible world in which pain exists, it hurts; it is necessarily true that pain hurts. If hurting is understood as some form of feeling bad from the inside, as something that is *suffered* through, then the experientialist is committed to the notion that pains, in and of themselves, diminish an individual's welfare. The general populace would hardly find this shocking.

Obviously, this analysis is not sacrosanct. Functionalists, for example, do not think of the phenomenology of pain as essential to its existence. These philosophers conceive of pain as a function that mediates between certain inputs and outputs. So, for example, pain is identified as that state which, given certain input (say, being hit with great force on the hand with a hammer), is apt to produce certain behavior (say, moving your hand away from further blows of the hammer). Whatever plays this functional role is a pain, and since the way pains feel in this world would not appear to be logically required for them to play their causally assigned role, pain and its phenomenology are only contingently related. Nor does one who disavows a necessary connection between pain and feeling need be a functionalist. We frequently hear the story about a gung-ho soldier being shot several times during his attempt to capture some enemy territory. We are urged to see this as a case in which the soldier is enduring pain (after all, he has just been shot) and yet is not conscious of any painful sensation (this knowledge we acquire either from his behavior at the time, or from his sincere statements after he is led back to safety).

Experientialism does not dispute these accounts of pain. If pains are items that can exist without an individual being aware or conscious of certain feelings, then pains can occur without an individual's well-being being affected. If, on the other hand, pains can only exist when experienced, as being part of the modified consciousness of individuals, then they must contribute to the welfare of an individual. Experientialism remains neutral as to which understanding of the nature of pains should be adopted. This is the way it should be; a theory of welfare should not have commitments about the ontology of the mind. The fact that experientialism does not require a theory of mind allows it to have greater appeal.

Experientialism's neutrality regarding the essential nature of pain may be illustrated by the fanciful case of Phyllis and Susan. Originally, both women are suffering through great pain. Some would claim that it is possible to provide Phyllis with a drug that eliminates her pain but not her suffering. Upon ingestion of the drug, she reports no pain, local or general, but still sincerely expresses not feeling well. Her conscious experiential state is still displeasurable in exactly the same manner as it was when she truthfully acknowledged her pain. Others would claim that this description is conceptually muddled; to feel precisely as one feels when one is in pain is just being in pain. The prior description attempts the impossible task of driving a wedge between one self-same state of affairs. No matter to the experientialist. Insofar as both parties agree that Phyllis continues to feel poorly from the inside after the ingestion of the drug, her well-being is being diminished. Susan, on the other hand, is administered a drug that putatively has the effect of eliminating her discomfort without eliminating her pain. That is, before and after the administration of the drug, Susan sincerely acknowledges that she is feeling the same sensation and she identifies the sensation as one of pain. We know Susan to be a normal adult human who is not prone to mock seriousness; she knows what pain is, and, especially in the surroundings in which she finds herself, is not likely to act deceptively. The drug is not an analgesic; it does not relieve the painful feeling that one experiences. Rather, it results in the individual's no longer being bothered or displeased by the painful sensation. In this scenario, experientialism sees Susan as prudentially unaffected. Again, some would find this case incoherent. If Susan is not feeling poorly in the same way as she was when she was feeling pain, then, protestations to the contrary, she is no longer in pain. On the other hand, if she is still actually in pain, then since pain is conceptually conjoined with a poor phenomenology, Susan is still faring poorly from the inside. The experientialist, as before, may remain neutral. If and only if Susan's present conscious mental state is not one in which she is (subjectively) suffering is her well-being not being diminished.

If pain is always (perhaps necessarily) welfare-diminishing or harmful to an individual, then, in accordance with experientialism, any individual with the capacity to suffer pain is a moral patient and is therefore deserving of moral consideration. In fact, we would have an explanation of why it is wrong to gratuitously inflict pain; it is wrong because it makes the individual worse off. (Of course, this would not be "ultimately satisfying" to one who questioned why making someone worse off, all else being equal, is doing something wrong.) If pains are sometimes not harms—if, more perspicuously, pains sometimes have no effect on the individual's welfare—then the capacity to suffer pain would not imply his moral patienthood. Moreover, we would not have our typical, general explanation of why the infliction of pain, all things considered, is wrong. If pains are never harms—if, more generally, they never (or perhaps necessarily never) modify the well-being of an individual—then, too, the capacity to suffer pain would not guarantee moral patienthood. Moreover, we would lack an obvious explanation of why we should even consider the infliction of pain upon a subject as the commission of a wrong act toward the subject.

(VII)

If we conceive of pain as something that is suffered through, and if we similarly conceive of pleasure as something that is enjoyed—if, that is, pleasures and pains are conceived as phenomenological modifications— what would motivate someone to deny what appears to be the mundane truth that pains harm and pleasures benefit? At least some impetus for disenchantment with experientialism can be quickly dispatched. Some believe, quite correctly, that some pains produce good; if a criminal is placed in prison, this might be better for him, not worse. The experientialist is free to agree but would justifiably claim that this goes no way toward showing that his suffering in prison was not a harm to him. Experientialists do not claim that good cannot come from bad, or even that, all things considered, it is better for the subject to have harm inflicted upon her at a particular time than not. There is nothing mysterious about this. We implicitly assume this idea when we voluntarily go to the dentist. Some claim that there are some pains so faint that they cannot reasonably be thought of as harms. This seems to be verbal haggling; to the extent that the person agrees that he is conscious of being made unpleasant by a certain feeling, he is being made worse off. The experientialist would agree that if the pain is negligible, so is the negative effect on the individual's well-being, but would find this no reason to think that he is illicitly using the term "harm."

There are cases of what might be called "aberrant pains" and "aberrant pleasures." As an example of the latter, consider the enjoyment that Hitler presumably received when he heard that the gas chambers in Auschwitz were working at peak efficiency, thus expediting the slaughter of millions of Jews. Does it not seem perverse to think, as apparently experientialists are committed to thinking, that Hitler's life was enhanced by this very conscious enjoyment? I think not. In fact, our attitudes indicate that, odious as it seems, Hitler was benefited by his improved subjectivity. We believe that Hitler did not *deserve* his enjoyment, did not merit this subjective benefit, and we are angered by the prospect of someone's being made better off when he clearly did not deserve to be. If we did not think of Hitler's enjoyment as being beneficial for him, there would be no reason for our anger; our sense of justice, cosmic or quotidian, would not be offended. Our outrage is predicated on, and is a testament to, our belief that Hitler's enjoyment benefited him.

Another recent suggestion is that for pain to be bad, in and of itself, there must be some feature of it that makes it worthy of avoidance.[10] It is granted that we hate the way that pain feels and try to avoid it, but it is contended that this aversion to pain does not make pain a bad thing. In effect, the suggestion is that the conditions experientialism places upon what accounts for an individual's being harmed do not suffice for her being made worse off. Regardless of how poorly one is faring from the inside, there is no guarantee that this phenomenology, in and of itself, diminishes an individual's well-being. It is claimed that without some feature that makes the pain worthy of avoidance, it cannot be considered as intrinsically bad for the sufferer. But I see no reason why we should restrict ourselves in this way. We frequently describe persons as being harmed by events that we believe ought not to have bothered them. Our writing style is demeaned by a co-worker who not only has no writing ability of his own but is also unrelentingly mean-spirited. His opinion should not be taken as an accurate reflection on our writing abilities, and we ought not to be bothered by his comments; nevertheless, we are. At times, we have only ourselves to blame for being bothered. If only we were more reflective or less self-absorbed, for example, what brought about our feeling poorly would not have had this effect. Consider a colleague who makes some demeaning comment about the color coordination of our shirt and tie. Being narcissistic, we are hurt; had we a better grasp of what is really important, such a comment would have had no deleterious consequence at all. But, regardless of the merit of the source of these pains, the pains still present their subjects with harms, harms that may be as detrimental to an individual as the most deserved pain. It may well be that we ought to be somewhat less sympathetic to an individual who experiences pain in virtue of some character defect, but this does not show that the pain is any less harmful to him than a pain suffered despite his having a good character. To hold that one cannot be harmed by pains unless they are worthy of being avoided seems to be an exercise in pure stipulation.

Perhaps the motivation behind identifying what is bad or harmful for an individual with what is worthy of being disliked is the thought that without the use of some normative explication, the experientialist would have no means to claim that harms ought to be avoided. And perhaps what grounds this belief is a commitment to some Moorean or Humean argument that forbids traveling from an "is" to an "ought." But the experientialist is not committed to the view that harms ought to be avoided except in the trivial sense that in order to enhance one's well-being one (prudentially) ought to avoid events that diminish one's well-being. In the more robust sense that the objection presumably uses—in the sense, that is, that an individual (morally) ought to avoid harms—the experientialist may remain uncommitted.

(VIII)

Experientialism, like all theories of welfare, does not attempt to give a stipulative or definitional account. It would be the height of absurdity if the dispute among different theories of well-being were nothing more than a disagreement about what is, or should be, the synonyms for "having an enhanced welfare," "having a diminished welfare," and the like. No theories of well-being should be viewed either as reports about what is "really meant" by certain linguistic expressions, or even as suggestions about how various linguistic expressions should be used. We begin, and in fact must begin, by accepting the fact that we have some prereflective beliefs about welfare. To put the point semantically, we begin by accepting the fact that the term "welfare" is not a technical one, but rather one that has a common and fairly well-entrenched meaning. It is not a debate, therefore, about whether improving one's well-being makes one better off; rather, it is a debate about what constitutes enhancing or diminishing an individual's welfare and so is, in effect, a debate concerning the appropriate domain of the (prudentially) welfared.

A helpful comparison may be made with the contemporary epistemic debate concerning the "analysis of knowledge." If viewed as a dispute about meanings, the debate is justifiably caricatured. If the discussion is to have any substance, we must begin by agreeing that "knowledge" is not a term of art, and that most of us have the same pretheoretical idea of when this term is to be applied. If we do have some worries about the meaning of the term, resolution takes the form of consulting our dictionaries. The question is not, then, what "knowledge" means, but rather what are the conditions under which an individual knows? In much the same way, theories of welfare try to tell us the conditions under which individuals are made better and worse off and so delimit which types of individuals have so much as the capacity to possess a well-being. Experientialism theorizes that individuals are better off under the condition of being subjectively better off. Having an enhanced phenomenology is what constitutes being benefited, while having a diminished phenomenology constitutes being harmed. If an individual is doing well from the inside, if one is in an enjoyable mental state, then that individual's life is going well; if, from the inside, the individual is suffering, then the individual's life is not going well. The domain of those with a welfare is exclusively and exhaustively constituted by those with phenomenologies.

Experientialism, like all theories of welfare, is meant to provide a *fundamental* account of what makes individuals better and worse off. Thus, for all theories, certain types of "why" questions are necessarily unanswerable. If we were to ask an experientialist why (that is, in virtue of what) does what occurs from the inside constitute an individual's welfare, no answer could be forthcoming, for the experientialist is committed to there being no deeper phenomena than these subjective experiences that account for well-being. If it were admitted that there are nonexperiential items that account for personal well-being that are even more basic than one's experiential life, then such a person has abrogated his claim to experientialism. As this basicness is a necessary feature of all accounts of welfare that purport to tell us what constitutes individual well-being, it can be neither an advantage nor a disadvantage for any theory.

This notion of being fundamental is intimately connected with the idea that "welfare" is not a term of art. Suppose someone were to propose a theory of welfare that made an individual better or worse off relative to the number of lamps within her field of vision; the more lamps she could see, the better off she would be. The advocate of such a theory maintains, just like any other welfare theorist, that his account is basic, and so he cannot reasonably be asked to explain *why* such a state of affairs accounts for well-being. Perhaps, at bottom, there is not much we can say to such a devil's advocate other than to iterate that such an account has no connection with what we mean (or, redundantly, "ordinarily mean") by "welfare," and so the lamp-welfarist is stipulating a sense for a term that shares only homonymy with the term in which we are interested. One might mistakenly believe that we can do more, that we can show that on his theory, we encounter utterly unacceptable results. For example, on his theory one would be better off perceiving a thousand lamps and undergoing inordinate pain and suffering than feeling great pleasure but being in the proximity of no lamps. But such putative problems will only be understood as real problems if one shares with the objector a sense of "welfare" that, apparently, the lamp-theorist finds foreign. This reinforces the point that theory construction must begin with *some* commonality assumed.

Any satisfactory account of well-being must take into account the facts that welfares of individuals can improve and degenerate and that intrapersonal, as well as interpersonal, comparisons of welfares are possible. It is sometimes thought that the purely subjective nature of experientialism makes fulfillment of this criterion difficult, if not impossible. But the evident fact is that we make subjective comparisons all the time, many of which have nothing to do with personal welfare. We say that the journey to New York seemed much shorter on this occasion than on the prior one, and that the second reading of the *Critique* was less of a chore than the first. We make intrasubjective welfare comparisons when we judge our enjoyment of seeing two movies or when we assess our pain on one occasion as being far more severe than on another. At times, we make cross-comparisons, as when we claim that we had more enjoyment seeing *Raging Bull* than we had displeasure on our trip to Tierra del Fuego. Admittedly, intersubjective comparisons are frequently proffered more tentatively. We claim that our enjoyment at viewing *Raging Bull* was greater than our friend's at seeing *The Sound of Music*. We can respond with justification for this assessment. Although history has proven us equally frugal, ex post facto, my friend would have spent only $5.00 to see her movie, while I would have spent $20.00 to see mine. Our faith that we are making sense when these claims are made is not shaken by the concession that these comparisons, perhaps particularly in interpersonal cases, are extremely difficult to quantify. I may not be able to discern whether I am doing half again as well as I was yesterday, let alone that I am 25 percent better off than you now are, but I am fairly certain that my well-being has improved over the past day, and we can both agree that my life is presently going somewhat better than yours. None of this is meant to imply incorrigibility. We both may be wrong. Still, the claims are sensible. Be it in interior monologue or external dialogue, discussion about the truth of these claims occurs, discussion that frequently, though not inevitably, leads to resolution. We should not find subjectivity the obstacle that some take it to be, especially since experientialism provides us with standards for comparison. Phenomenologies are compared along two major vectors, intensity and duration. We compare how much we enjoyed viewing last night's movie with yesterday's baseball game and even, albeit with more trepidation and less precision, my enjoyment at the game with your reading of the novel. Duration has an obvious role; all else being equal, the longer the enjoyment and the shorter the suffering, the better off the individual is.

There are other concerns seemingly particular to experiential comparability. All else being equal, it is commonplace to judge an individual born sightless as having a welfare inferior to that of a normally sighted individual. Despite the fact that the blind individual does not miss his sight—he never had it to begin with—the individual is judged worse off than his sighted counterpart. Experientialism can deal with this sort of case rather routinely. In assessing the blind person as worse off, we are making the reasonable assumption that the individual would have had better experiences, would have been better off from the inside, had he been born with sight. So, in some judgments involving an improvement or diminution of welfare, we compare actual with counterfactual experiences. These kinds of judgments are hardly uncommon. When we talk about the fact that we would have been better off staying home rather than going to the movie, we employ just this type of comparison. Perhaps there are some deep philosophical problems of analysis lurking behind our use of counterfactuals.[11] Nonetheless, we have a fairly clear idea what we mean when we make comments like these, and these problems, whatever their exact nature, are certainly independent of experientialism.

A related but more interesting case is presented if we are asked to consider the welfares of a normally sighted person and an individual who, in addition to normal sight, also possesses X-ray vision. The point here is that we normally do not think of the average human being as having a diminished welfare in virtue of his lacking X-ray vision (or, say, the ability to fly unaided). But, the objection may continue, experientialism should, all else being equal, judge as before; we normal humans should assess ourselves as being worse off. But, at least when described in this way, the objection has the seeds of its own answer. We typically do not think of ourselves as *suffering* from normal vision because we tend to normalize what is typical. That is, at least in terms of sensual capacities, that which is typical is thought of as a standard of what is good or right regarding a particular ability. The practice of imbuing the statistically average with normative significance is manifested dramatically in the acceptable ranges of many blood tests. It is only relatively recently that I became aware that the acceptable range of many of these tests is determined strictly by screening the actual blood work of many patients. The acceptable range is simply that range in which 95 percent of the patients fit; "within normal limits," a phrase that is meant to suggest goodness or rightness, is derived solely from this statistical analysis of samples. This concomitance, however, can be severed. Although a cholesterol reading of 120 is not within normal limits, we now know that this is indicative of a level of blood lipids that is better for the patient than one within the normal range. Somewhat analogously, we are not bound to see our statistically normal vision as criterial of being what is best for us. When we compare it to an even more discriminating vision, we can be seen to suffer by comparison. Such a result comports quite well with experientialism. We suffer with our statistically normal vision to the extent that our experiential life would not be as pleasurable as one that incorporated more powerful sight.

Experientialism can allow that an individual is made better or worse off without knowledge that she is so affected, at least where this type of knowledge is taken to imply a rather sophisticated and complex attitude toward one's own conscious mental life. There are philosophers, like Descartes, who are transparentists. These epistemologists believe that if an individual is in a particular mental state, he knows that he is in that mental state. Thus, necessarily, if one is depressed, angry, lustful, and so forth, one knows that he is depressed, angry, and lustful. There is a somewhat extended sense of "knowledge" with which experientialists can be transparentists with Descartes. An individual's relationship to his experiences is unlike his relationship to the external world in that the external world can be other than how it appears to the individual. In the case of one's experiences, this distinction is conflated; the very essence or identity of the experience is constituted by how it seems to the individual. There is a sense, then, in which the capacity to have experiences requires the capacity to recognize experiences, and if, with rapprochement in mind, we take this recognition to be a type of knowledge, experientialists may concur with Cartesians on this point. Yet it needs to be emphasized just how attenuated this sense of "knowledge" must be to secure conciliation. Transparentists are not now free to argue from an individual's inability to possess knowledge to his inability to undergo experiences, where this may be based, for example, on some analysis of knowledge as justified true belief. This use of *modus tollens* is illicit because it equivocates on "knowledge." Transparentists cannot agree to a very weak notion of knowledge when trying to convince experientialists to support their platform and then use a far more robust account (one, were it initially used, that would have carried no conviction) to try to severely narrow the ranks of the morally considerable. Using "knowledge" in its ordinary sense, the onus is surely the transparentists' since the possibility of an individual being made better and worse off without his knowledge comports with common sense.

With this rather technical caveat, however, experientialism is unabashedly Cartesian. The picture is that one's welfare can be determined by isolated introspection; one can look into one's own mind without the need to view the external world and, in most circumstances, be able to discern just how well one is doing. Experientialism may disavow the essential epistemic privilege that one has to his own well-being. There is no commitment in experientialism that necessarily makes the possessor of a welfare the best judge of how she is faring. Still, the idea that the agent is *typically* in the best position to adjudicate her own well-being is one that the experientialist, rather than shunning, should gladly embrace. After all, it is a common belief about welfare that, all else being equal, the agent is in the best position to assess how well she is doing. Experientialism would seem to align with this perfectly. In most circumstances, who is better justified in claiming how things appear from the inside than the individual whose welfare is being investigated?

I earlier alluded to the fact that experientialism is naturally viewed as a theory that accounts for personal welfare in terms of intrinsic properties. It should come as no surprise that we can employ a Cartesian idea to fortify this notion. Recall that Descartes's skeptical use of his Dream Argument rested on the assumption that all wakeful sensory experiences were, in principle, reproducible in dreams. Thus the observation of any sensory experience was insufficient to ensure that one was presently awake. Another moral that can be drawn from this scenario is that modifications in the relational or extrinsic characteristics of an individual do not dictate changes in the (conscious) mental states of that individual. One may have precisely the same interior life (again, so the Cartesian scenario seems to imply) with all of one's relational properties changed. After all, if a person is dreaming, then she is not actually the second person in queue speaking to a grocery clerk but is, instead, lying down peacefully at home. Still, from the inside, the wakeful and dream lives are indistinguishable, and this interior perspective, to the experientialist, is all that matters. From the fact that no relational properties need have an impact on the experiential content of an individual, we reach the conclusion that should strike few of us as epiphanous; experiences are intrinsic properties of mindful individuals.

At the end of this discussion, it seems fair to say that, minimally, experientialism is a viable theory of welfare from which we derive a plausible theory of moral patienthood. Individuals are morally considerable only if they can have a prudential welfare, and it at least seems reasonable to claim that only one's subjective experiences can ultimately affect how well or how poorly one is doing. Thus, an individual has moral standing if and only if he has phenomenological or sentient capacity. The view is captured in many of our adages and conforms to our (prereflective) commonsense and common practices. We talk of happiness being all "in the head," and "what you don't know can't hurt you" (with the implication that what you do know, can). These expressions, although obviously coarse, are indicative of a more sophisticated notion of what makes persons better and worse off; a *theory* of welfare, if you like. Moreover, our commonsense moral categorizations of individuals fits well with experientialism. Consider the items in the world that we deem worthy of moral consideration. We think of ourselves—normal adult human beings—as paradigms of moral patienthood, and surely it is uncontentious, if anything is, that we have the capacity for sentient experience. Similar reasoning applies to many nonhuman animals. We take monkeys, dogs, cats, and so forth as capable of similar experiencing, and so, religious prejudices to the side, deserving of moral consideration.[12] Descartes, though opposing the attribution of patienthood to nonhuman animals, based his rejection on his belief that animals were mindless automatons, incapable of having experiences of the robust sort that experientialism requires. So Descartes should not be viewed as disavowing experientialism in his denial of considerability to dogs, cats, and other nonhuman animals. On the contrary, he is best seen as implicitly accepting this criterion for patienthood, although rejecting the contemporary commonplace that these creatures have phenomenologies.[13] Finally, experientialism is confirmed by our judgments of what is not worthy of consideration; we think of rocks and pieces of chalk as lacking patienthood and also lacking the capacity for sentience.

Experientialism is a bona fide contender.

2

The Desire Theory

(I)

We have proffered a theory of personal welfare, and so a theory of moral patienthood, that accords well with our pretheoretical ideas concerning both well-being and the constitution of our moral domain. It will come as no great surprise, this being a philosophical enterprise, that misgivings are not difficult to unearth. Unfortunately for the experientialist, allusions to the nature of dream experiences that were used to forward the contention that (conscious) experiences are quintessentially intrinsic properties can also be manipulated to suggest problems for the theory. If we grant the Cartesian point that dream and waking experiences may be indistinguishable to the agent, and since, to the experientialist, all that matters to the welfare of an individual is how life is "from the inside," it would appear that the well-being of an individual should be left unaffected by the *source* of his experiences. At first hearing, at least, this consequence seems innocuous. To see this, let us make the helpful but unnecessary supposition of materialism. It does seem difficult to understand how two individuals who are molecule-for-molecule identical (even numerically identical if we allow one of the two individuals to reside counterfactually) can differ in regard to how well their respective lives are going. The powerful intuition is that regardless of the history that led up to their respective states, the welfare of the individual is purely a matter of the state she is now in. We can put the point somewhat picturesquely. Assume that God exists and that He has accounted for every momentary state of your life. If the states of your life had been precisely identical but ultimately caused by the Big Bang, there seems no possible reason for distinguishing this counterfactual life as being better or worse off than the actual one.

And yet the source or genealogy of one's experiential life does seem to matter. To dramatize the point, consider Jane and Jack. From an interior perspective Jane's life is somewhat superior to Jack's; Jane is having more pleasurable and more intensely pleasurable experiences than is Jack. Assume, however, that Jane's experiences are (virtually) all dream experiences, while the great majority of Jack's experiences are of the usual waking sort. Experientialism would need to judge Jane's life as being better off than Jack's, for the only significant factor in the assessment of personal welfare is how one's interior life is going. This, however, strikes many of us as unacceptable. We share the lament of the Everly Brothers that in dreaming our lives away, regardless of the quality of the subjective experiences, our welfare is greatly reduced. The same point, appropriately enough, can be made by envisaging a genius who manipulates the brain of an unwary agent, resulting in the agent's having (subjectively) wonderful, albeit nonveridical, experiences. The fact, if indeed it is one, that we would characterize this genius as evil rather than either benevolent or morally neutral suggests that well-being is constituted by more than what merely transpires from the inside.

Admittedly this possibility is perhaps only logical. It may be, for all we presently know, physically impossible to have identical molecular structures in states produced, on the one hand, in dreams and by malevolent geniuses and, on the other, in waking states and by the ordinary perception of the external world. Nevertheless, this scarcely minimizes the ironic threat that these Cartesian thought experiments pose for the viability of any theory of well-being, like experientialism, that relies on the intuition that welfare is exclusively a function of how an individual's intrinsic properties are modified.

Although acceptance of these thought experiments suggests changes in experientialism, the effects should not be exaggerated. If we are convinced that Jack's life is better than Jane's and that a person suffers a reduced well-being merely in virtue of his experiences being formulated by a (nefarious) neurosurgeon rather than being produced by the usual interaction between the external world and our sense organs, experientialists are compelled to admit that extraexperiential factors can modify welfare. But we should not overstate the consequences of this concession. There is nothing in this example that coerces us to accept the fact that an individual, capable of sentient experiences only when produced in dreams (or by wicked scientists, or by evil demons), does not have any well-being whatsoever.[1] Indeed, I suggest that our intuitions argue otherwise—that, for example, those bedeviled by a Cartesian malevolent genius do, in fact, have better and worse ways of being. Surely it seems that a subject of these experiences would be far better off if the demon provided pleasures rather than pains, even if the source of these pleasures were not as we were given to believe. To see this point more clearly, consider the limiting case of an individual whose only capacity for sentient experience is dream experience. When placed in an external environment, an environment that is sensually efficacious for typical human beings, this—admittedly bizarre—creature is left completely unaffected. When not dreaming, the individual has the inscape that we all attribute to stones and pencils, which is to say, the individual has no inscape at all. In a dreaming state, however, the individual has a phenomenology; now, from the inside, the individual can enjoy the paintings of a Rembrandt and be saddened by thoughts of the Holocaust. It would appear that the individual is not denied a welfare, although the pervasive cause of his experiences is never of the common sort.

Nor does the case of Jack and Jane demonstrate that, necessarily, an individual with the capacity for veridical experiences is better off than an individual whose capacity is only for illusory experiences. And, once again, I believe our intuitions suggest this; a life of illusory pleasures would seem to be better than a life of real suffering. What the thought experiment does suggest is that there is a *dimension* to well-being beyond that of the capacity for sentient experience. It shows only that, all else being equal, a distinction in welfare can still result where the sentient experiences of two individuals are identical. Were the (pleasant) sentient experiences a product of veridical experience, the individual so affected would be better off. If a sentient individual lacked the capacity for absorbing veridical experience, she would be, in theory, at a disadvantage. There is nothing in these Cartesian thought experiments that requires either that individuals without the capacity to experience obtain moral standing or that an individual requires something in addition to the capacity to experience to be accorded moral status. For all that has been argued, experientialism has been precisely on the mark in delineating which individuals have moral status. Its failing is only that it has unduly limited the ways in which these individuals can be made better or worse off. The caveat suggested by these narratives is that we should not infer, from the fact that all and only individuals with phenomenological capacity are moral patients, that only what transpires from the inside can benefit or harm these individuals. The acceptance of these Cartesian thought experiments requires a modification in experientialism as a theory of welfare; it does not demand a change in the domain of patienthood that experientialism suggests.

On the other hand, although experientialists are not compelled to rescind their ethical demarcation of individuals, acceptance of the putative morals of the story of Jane and Jack does commit them to retracting one of the claims that helped give their theory impetus. If experientialists are now convinced that prudential well-being is not exclusively a matter of what transpires from the inside and that the etiology of the interior states plays a role in the assessment of an individual's welfare, they must reject the initial intuition that only modifications of intrinsic states can enter into the accounting of well-being. Causal relationships are paradigmatically extrinsic; they can, as we have seen, dramatically differ without any concomitant interior modification.

Similar efforts attempting to show that what transpires from the inside cannot exhaust well-being come in the form of thought experiments introduced by Robert Nozick and Robert Kane.[2] Nozick has tried to disabuse us of the idea that only our experiential life matters—that we value only our interior, conscious lives—by creating the figure of an experience machine. We are to imagine a machine constructed with the capability of providing us with any experiences that we desire. If we want the experience of meeting a deceased icon—be it our father, Gandhi, or Babe Ruth—all we need do is program the machine to yield these experiences. The experiences of great dining, sex, and excitement are literally ours for the asking. Although none of these experiences would reflect events in the actual world (there really is no meeting with Gandhi or dining at La Scala), it would seem to you as if everything were real. From the inside, from the subjective point of view, the two situations would be indiscernible. It is probably fair to say that if this machine were offered on a limited basis—if, that is, we could avail ourselves of the machine periodically—most of us would quickly agree to make use of it. The interesting case is the all-or-nothing offer, in which we can make use of the machine only if we agree to stay plugged into it, uninterruptedly, for our entire lives.

Nozick believes that we would reject the offer and presents this rejection as demonstrating that items other than our experiential life matter to us or have value for us. We want, for example, to have not merely the experience of meeting Gandhi, but to have this experience in virtue of actually meeting him. We want the experience of having our novel read, but in virtue of the novel's actually being read. Additionally, in a way that matters deeply to us, the experiences provided by the machine, regardless of how lifelike and desired, are phony; they are not really ours. Remaining attached to the experience machine makes our life a sham, a masquerade. The rejection of this offer shows us that we want our lives to be authentic; we want to earn and be masters of our life experiences and not have them merely handed to us. The unbridled use of this machine is cheating, and the users are the individuals being cheated. Nor will the "experience of authenticity" fill this void. We want not just to feel and believe that we are living authentically (this *would* be a matter of our interior lives), but to really be living authentically. Subjectivity, then, regardless of its content, does not exhaust what we conceive as mattering to our lives. Our lives can be both enhanced and denigrated by factors that are extrinsic to our conscious experiences.

Nozick's conclusion can be supported by reflecting upon our concerns about free will. It is frequently proffered that our worries regarding the freedom of our will and actions are a result of ethical concerns. We tend to believe that freedom is a requirement of legitimate moral accountability, and so, without freedom, ethical assessment is vacuous.[3] If it is true, as many have believed, that determinism precludes freedom, then there can be no morality in a deterministic world. Without wanting to diminish these ethical concerns as a powerful source of our interest in the free will problem, there is an independent and equally powerful metaphysical motivation. If all of our acts, both internal and external, are ultimately determined by forces over which we have no control, then it appears that we are nothing more than relatively complex marionettes with every thought and movement a product of something other than ourselves. Our lives are no more authentic than the "life" of a clock; the "choices" we make and the experiences we undergo are no more a reflection of ourselves than the clock's "decision" to move its minute hand is reflective of its inner self. This is not to say that determinism implies these dire consequences—the battle between compatibilists and incompatibilists has hardly been settled—but it is to suggest, in support of Nozick, the significance we impute to authenticity in our lives. Think of this in two ways. If you were notified at the moment before your death that determinism and incompatibilism were both true accounts of the world (at least up to this very moment), would you not feel cheated and believe that your entire life had been a sham? Or, from the other temporal extreme, were you given a choice at the moment of birth which of two lives you would like to live—one in which you really make the choices and decisions that result in the life you live, and the other as described by determinism—would you not prefer the former even if the quality and quantity of the interior lives were identical?

It is clear that Nozick does not consider authenticity the only non-experiential property that we value. The number of such properties, or even whether there is a determinate number of these properties, is not germane. Be there one or a thousand, the important consequence of Nozick's discussion is that we believe that things of value, items that matter to us, are not exhausted by what transpires from the inside.

Consider a complementary scenario employed by Robert Kane. We are to imagine the rich friend of Alan, a very ill artist, arranging to have Alan's paintings purchased at gaudy prices. Alan, completely unaware of his friend's ploy, believes that his paintings are being recognized for their artistic merit, has the normal desires to have his work appreciated, and consequently garners some enjoyment in his otherwise bleak days. We are now to conceive of two worlds that include Alan. The first is the world just described, in which Alan's spirits are lifted in virtue of his friend's successful deception. The second world is one in which Alan's experiences are the same as those he has in the first world, but his recognition is deserved; Alan's paintings really are wonderful. In both worlds Alan dies a subjectively happy man.

Let us further suppose that, after describing these two possible worlds to Alan, we ask him which one he would prefer, which world he would desire to see actualized. If his answer is that he would prefer to see the second (undeceived) world actualized, this is taken to demonstrate that nonexperiential items matter to Alan, that he values living in an undeceived world even though his (subjective) experiences are identical in both worlds. Kane believes that most of us would have the same desire as Alan; we would choose to actualize the undeceived world. To live undeceived, and not merely believing that you live in an undeceived way, "means something to him as it does to most of us" (Kane, 74).

It is clear that the stories provided by Nozick and Kane are close relatives of the Cartesian scenarios. A difference is that the narratives of both Kane and Nozick make explicit use of the notion of *desire*. As Nozick sees it, authenticity is recognized as a value to most of us by virtue of the fact that most of us want our lives to be authentically lived. Similarly, in Kane's view, we know that living in a nondeceptive world is a benefit because this is, all else being equal, the sort of world that we desire. It might be suggested that the notion of desire was already present in the Cartesian scenarios; without the implicit assumption that we desire veridical as opposed to dream experiences, there would be no basis on which to form the view that we would be better off living in the former world. Similarly, the narrative involving the mad scientist has no implications for personal well-being unless we presuppose that we desire our experiences be formed in the ordinary ways. Indeed, it may be pressed, the Cartesian genius and the Nozickian experience machine are really the same characters in slightly different garb.

This attempt at conflation may be a bit quick. After all, it may be argued that we directly infer from the Cartesian thought experiments to the benefit of having veridical experiences without using the intermediary of desire. Still, there is no reason to press the point. Whether or not one finds the Cartesian narratives persuasive independently of invoking desires, the stories created by Nozick and Kane will prove a fertile avenue to pursue. These latter stories, unlike the Cartesian scenarios, will quite clearly suggest alternative theories of well-being.

(II)

We may begin by paying close attention to how both Nozick and Kane identify which nonexperiential items matter or have value to individuals. It is essential to realize that both use the desires of an individual to determine (in the epistemic sense of discovering) what is valuable for that individual. The person who turns down the offer of the experience machine does so because he desires to live an authentic life, a life that the machine cannot purvey. Similarly, Alan wants, all else being equal, to live in a world in which he is undeceived. It is first worth noting that there is no necessity attached to desires being used as the means to identify or pick out nonexperiential values. One may, for example, employ an intuitionist account, according to which at least some individuals have the capability to intuit which nonexperiential values matter. Or one may suggest that the means of identification is constituted by the feelings or sensations of individuals. On this sort of account, the feelings possessed by an individual are a reliable, even inerrant guide, to what is valuable. So, for example, instead of asking Alan if he would prefer, all else being equal, living in a world in which he was undeceived to living in a world in which he was deceived, we now ask Alan to look inside and determine which world makes him feel happier. In this scenario, there is no mention of what Alan desires. Nor, it should be emphasized, would the use of feelings commit one to the claim that all that matters is experiential. On the contrary, one might argue that there are nonexperiential things that matter, but the use of our experiential life best determines what those items are.

Unfortunately, however, although both Nozick and Kane are clear in imputing desires with identificatory power, they also share a particularly important obscurity. Recall that Kane, and presumably Nozick, believe that living an undeceived life has nonexperiential value for Alan. What is not completely transparent in either account is whether this sort of life has value for Alan in virtue of his desiring it, or whether this sort of life has value for Alan independent of Alan's desires. The first interpretation imputes a constitutive or creative function to our desires; the second assigns a merely identifying or discerning function to personal desires and makes no commitments as to what, if anything, makes these nonexperiential items valuable to Alan. Significant consequences for the nature of value and desire are at stake. Under the first interpretation, it is strongly suggested that value is person-relative; something has value for a particular individual in virtue of the fact that the person desires it. The second interpretation suggests that an item has absolute (nonrelative) value, value that exists whether or not an individual has a desire for it. One might go further and account or explain our desire for that item as a function of that item's being valuable or of our recognition that the item is valuable. If we accept this addition, we can say that the first interpretation explains the source of value of the nonexperiential, while the second interpretation accounts for the foundation of our desires for the nonexperiential. We can articulate this distinction in terms of "direction of fit." The constitutive interpretation has value fitting our desires while the identificatory interpretation has desires fitting what is valuable. Under the first interpretation our desires are infallible indicators of what is valuable in much the same way (at least to J. L. Austin) as an umpire's declaring a batter out is an incorrigible indication of the batter's being out.[4] Whereas the umpire's decision makes it the case that the batter is out, one's desiring a certain state of affairs confers value upon it, at least for the individual who desires it. Under the second interpretation one can, in theory, grant different degrees of concomitance between the desire of the individual and the value of the object of the desire. One may aver that, although the desire does not create value, it is nonetheless an infallible indicator of value, or, one can hold that there may be great distance between an individual's desire for an object and the object's actually being beneficial to the agent. Of primary importance is that an object's value is independent of an agent's desires for it.

One can notice a tension between these two interpretations more clearly in Kane's writings than in Nozick's. Kane does make many comments that seem to relativize the notion of value to Alan. He talks, for example, about the difference that these two worlds make *to* Alan and asserts that there is an important difference in value in the two worlds *for* Alan. This, together with the comment that to understand what "objective worth" means to Alan we would need to know which world he would rather live in (i.e., which world he would prefer to inhabit), suggests something along the lines of the constitutive rendering. What is at least conversationally implied by these comments is that objective worth is created by Alan's desires; had he different desires, other qualities would be objectively worthy to him. But Kane also tells us that we "begin to understand what objective worth is all about when we ask whether it *should* make any difference to Alan which of these worlds he lives in" (Kane, 74, my emphasis). This at least suggests the identificatory rendering of the notion of being deceived. What the talk of "should" implies is an absolute, as opposed to person-relative, conception of items that are objectively worthy. Thus the suggestion here is that regardless of Alan's particular desires, living in the deceived world has negative objective worth and therefore has disvalue for him.

In passing, we may note that the distinction that is obscured in the accounts of both Nozick and Kane applies equally to other accounts claiming that what matters is not exhausted by what goes on "inside the head." Those who argue that intuition is the means by which to discern the valuable face the task of clarifying whether we are to think of intuition as having a constitutive or merely identificatory function. A similar charge awaits the proponent of the experiential technique; do these interior states create what is of value, or are they merely indications of what is independently valuable? The constitutive/identificatory distinction, then, apparently is applicable toward all of these accounts of value. Those who believe that value is a personal matter, an item that tends to vary with different individuals, or even vary throughout time for the same individual, find desires to have just the nature that serves their purposes. After all, it is a commonplace that different persons frequently have different desires, and that a single individual's desires are likely to change over time. The fluidity of desires comports quite well within a constitutive view of value. But this seems also to be true of one's interior life. Just as the content of desires varies greatly over individuals and time, so, too, do the objects of enjoyment and suffering. It is less clear what intuitionists would say about this; there is simply nothing even approaching a monolithic account of intuitions. Still, at least on some accounts, as, for example, with those who identify intuitions with considered beliefs, there is no barrier that would preclude their rampant variability.

Regardless of whether one interprets the Nozick/Kane thought experiments as advocating a constitutive or identificatory role for desires, the implications are great for the experientialist theory of well-being. Under both interpretations, how one fares from the inside is no longer the fundamental metaphysical or epistemic criterion for well-being. Under the constitutive rendering, what confers welfare to an individual is the capacity to have one's desires satisfied and frustrated, and to realize how well or poorly one is doing requires that we recognize the quantity and quality of the desires being fulfilled and thwarted. Let us call the theory of well-being that naturally emanates from the constitutive interpretation of desires the "desire theory of welfare" or, more simply, the "desire theory." Under the identificatory rendering, what bestows welfare upon an individual is the capacity to possess certain properties, properties that, although valuable independently of any individual's desires, are epistemically accessible to individuals by way of desires. Let us call the theory of welfare that naturally emanates from this identificatory interpretation the "perfectionist theory of welfare" or simply "perfectionism." We first turn our attention to the desire theory.

(III)

The desire theory tells us that an individual has his welfare modified insofar as his desires are satisfied and frustrated. The associated theory of patienthood claims that one is a moral patient just in case that individual has the capacity for satisfiable and frustratable desires. Since the notion of a desire being either satisfiable or frustratable is pleonastic, we can simply express the conjunction of the two points as the claim that all and only individuals with the capacity to possess desires have a welfare and thus are moral patients. Insofar as a desire is fulfilled, the owner is benefited; insofar as a desire is thwarted, the agent is harmed. The realm of the morally enfranchised for the desire theorist *may* be congruent with the realm selected by the experientialist. We will return to this in somewhat more detail, but one should recognize that a desire theorist may hold that all and only those with the capacity to possess desires are those with the capacity for sentient experience. It is a material point, one not settled merely by definition, whether a desire theorist sees the class of moral patients as a proper subset of those so deemed by experientialism. This would occur if the desire theorist believed that the capacity for desire formation entailed the capacity for sentient experience, but not conversely. Or, perhaps atypically, the desire theorist may hold that the class purported to have moral standing by experientialist lights constitutes a proper subset of those whom he so considers. Here the capacity for sentient experience would entail the capacity for desire formation, but not conversely. Last, and for the sake of completeness, the desire theorist may see no overlap whatsoever in whom he believes deserves moral patienthood and what experientialism dictates. In this case, there would be a mutual lack of entailment between the two capacities.

Of prime importance—what is not a matter of choice to the desire theorist—is that well-being is no longer a matter of what transpires from the inside. What imbues an individual with a welfare, what is responsible for an individual possessing a well-being, is the fact that she has the capacity for possessing desires. To the desire theorist, what makes the nondeceptive experiences beneficial to their possessors is not any phenomenology that may be distinctively associated with these experiences, but rather the fact that these nondeceptive experiences are desired. It is this "objective" fact, the fact that our desires are satisfied, and not any fact about how life seems from the inside that accounts for the value of these nondeceptive experiences. Since the relationship of satisfaction is purely extrinsic, the desire theorist is required to denigrate the significance of the intuition that modifications in personal well-being must involve the intrinsic properties of an agent. To denigrate is not to annihilate, but there should be no uncertainty about the desire theorist's insistence that we must rescind the claim that welfare modification requires change in the agent's intrinsic properties. Although Descartes's Dream Argument (and the variants of this argument in the guises of Nozick's experience machine and Kane's scenario about Alan) casts grave doubt on the idea that there is any distinctive feel to nondeceptive experiences, experientialism would not be resurrected if, *mirabile dictu*, deceptive and nondeceptive experiences were phenomenologically distinguishable. The fact would still remain that an individual is better off in virtue of fulfilling her desires and not in virtue of experiencing any particular conscious mental state. We should not, however, confuse this theory of value, this theory of benefits and harms for individuals, with a causal explanation of why we come to have the desires we have. There is no inconsistency with advocating the view of value that emanates from a constitutive rendering of desire with a causal account of desire that hypothesizes that we desire a certain state of affairs because we believe that the existence of that state of affairs will bring us pleasure. The point here is not to endorse this causal account of desire, but only to highlight the fact that one *can* adopt a constitutive rendering of desire and still find an important place for experiences in a general theory of value.

Personal phenomenologies may also play an important role in the desire theory in the obvious respect that we ordinarily desire pleasant interior lives and shun unpleasant or painful ones. Nonetheless, even in this quite circumscribed arena, the desire theory and experientialism should not be conflated. Whereas experientialism would claim the individual is benefited (harmed) insofar as, and in virtue of the fact that, she is feeling good (bad) from the inside, the desire theory tells us that our benefit resides in the fact that our desire for feeling good has been satisfied and our harm is constituted by a frustration of such a desire. Where experientialism held conscious mental states as having *inherent* value to their owner (i.e., value to the agent in and of themselves),[5] the desire theory takes such mental states to be only instrumentally useful in the production of welfare. In respect of their influence on individual well-being, how well one is doing from the inside has no privileged position relative to any other state of affairs that the individual desires. The content of the desires never has primary place. What has priority regarding one's welfare is the fulfillment and thwarting of the individual's desires. It may turn out that particular individuals have more powerful and constant desires for interior well-being than other objects, and so the satisfaction of these desires may have greater influence on the individual's welfare than other preferences. Still, the conscious mental states, in and of themselves, are not what make an individual better or worse off.

We will return soon to the very special circumstance wherein the content of an individual's desires are hedonic states, but it would be well to articulate the major moral to be drawn from the narratives of Nozick and Kane—that we value nonexperiential items—in a slightly different way. When we read these narratives from the perspective of a constitutive interpretation of desires, we arrive at a theory of welfare that tells us that these nonexperiential items can both benefit and harm us in virtue of their being desired. While this theory of welfare—the desire theory of welfare—is always relational, it also is an extrinsic theory when the contents of desires are not interior mental states. To say that it is relational is to say that an individual is made better and worse off in terms of the relation (satisfaction or frustration) that a certain state of affairs has to a desire. Even in the case where, for example, we desire to feel pleasure, the desire theory holds that we are made better off because this hedonic state of affairs satisfies our desire. The only difference between this circumstance's benefiting us and any other satisfied desire's enhancing our welfare is that, in the former case, one of the *relata* is a subjective mental state. To say that when the *relata* of the desire are not phenomenological states the theory is extrinsic, is to say that neither the satisfaction nor frustration of the desires necessitates any modifications in the intrinsic properties of the agent. This is tantamount to claiming that individuals can be made better and worse off without any robust change in the constitution of the agent. In particular, individuals can have their welfare modified without any cognitive or affective appreciation of this fact. Not to place too fine a point on it, we may say that the (conscious) mind of the agent need not be modified in order for her welfare to be affected. It is this last consequence of the desire theory that grates against one of our guiding intuitions of well-being, and it is examination and exploitation of this consequence that I set as my immediate task.

(IV)

Consider John's desire that the Yankees win the 1999 World Series. Shortly before the start of the series, John leaves the country on business, loses touch with the baseball happenings back home, and never discovers whether the Yankees won—never, that is, finds out whether his desire was satisfied or frustrated. Obviously, in such a case no subjective or intrinsic change in John occurs. Yet, according to the desire theory, John is benefited if the Yankees win the series and harmed if they lose. The objects of desires not being subjective mental states, the fulfillment and satisfaction of desires is a matter of how the external world fits with a particular desire. This match is "objective"; no subjective modifications enter into the conditions that either enable a match to occur or fail to take place. It is when the contents of the desire are nonphenomenological, as in the case of John and the Yankees, that the external world, in constituting the satisfaction conditions of the desire, plays an ineliminable role in the welfare of the individual.

Is it really credible that John is made worse off, even to the smallest degree, by the unrecognized frustration of his desire for the Yankee pennant, or that his welfare has been enhanced were the Yankees, unbeknownst to him, eventually to win the series? If we agree that these judgments are not credible, it seems difficult to imagine a more plausible explanation of the incredibility than attributing it to the fact that John, in virtue of never becoming aware of the Yankees fortunes, is, from the inside, left unaffected by the eventual state of affairs. In a robust sense, in the sense that something that is really about John (i.e., in a sense that his intrinsic properties are called into play), nothing happens. From this perspective, the win or loss by the Yankees is irrelevant. If this explanation of our dissatisfaction of the verdict of the desire theory is correct, experientialism fills the lacuna perfectly, for experientialism mandates that benefits and harms are a function of the modification of how one is faring from the inside. Being neither an extrinsic nor a relational theory, it makes it impossible that a modification of well-being can occur to an agent without a robust change in the constitution of that agent.

Does such a criticism already presume that experientialism, or a theory very much like it, is correct? I think not. We begin with some prephilosophical, pretheoretical beliefs about personal well-being, for this is the inevitable beginning of any exercise approaching conceptual analysis. These are points of departure, but ones that may be modified or totally rescinded in the course of discussion. I take it that we prephilosophically believe that John, as described, would be neither benefited nor harmed by the Yankees' success or failure. This tells against the desire theory, which mandates otherwise and speaks in favor of experientialism. The truth of this latter theory is not presupposed in the criticism. It is, rather, a natural outgrowth of both our prereflective concern and the explanation of the source of this concern. The problem begins to exploit the fact that the desire theory—when not limiting its applicability to subjective states of mind—is an extrinsic theory of welfare. It permits individuals to be made better and worse off without any concomitant change in their intrinsic or nonrelational properties.

Neither this criticism nor any of the subsequent ones will place any weight upon the refinements that any plausible desire theory needs to explicate. In claiming that items have value for individuals to the extent that they satisfy and frustrate desires, it is incumbent upon the desire theorist to give us some understanding how the notion of an individual becoming better and worse off is susceptible of degrees. The desire theorist cannot plausibly hold either that all fulfilled desires count equally toward the benefit of the individual or that all thwarted desires count equally toward the individual's detriment. Minimally, the desire theorist should talk about the dimensions of duration and intensity. Common sense dictates that, all else being equal, the longer and more intensely an individual desires some state of affairs, the greater the value that state of affairs has for him. Precisely how these two factors work together is a matter of detail and, as such, will remain unscrutinized. Furthermore, because experientialism also needs to deal with the nuances of duration and intensity, albeit of an individual's phenomenology rather than his desires, it would be unfair to hold the desire theory to a higher standard of acceptability.

The strategy against the desire theory continues by recalling that we normally think of ourselves as essentially having a privileged position regarding our own well-being. We need not overstate this point by regarding our special access to our own welfare as incorrigible; we on occasion do admit that we misjudged how well or how poorly we have been progressing. The desire theorist, however, making the welfare of an individual a function of the satisfactions and frustrations of his desires, would need to weaken the epistemic relationship we normally understand to occur between ourselves and our well-being. With the vast number of desires whose content is not mental, with, that is, the vast numbers of desires with an objective nature, there would be no reason why another should not know, as well if not better than ourselves, whether our desires have been satisfied or thwarted. In these cases, we would have no reason to consider ourselves as experts regarding our own well-being. Even in those cases where the content of one's desire is a particular mental state (e.g., the desire to feel pleasure), we typically believe that the individual is the best judge of his welfare not, as the desire theorist would have it—because the individual is in the best position to discover whether his desire for pleasure has been fulfilled—but rather because we take the individual as being in the best position to know if he is experiencing the pleasure.

One is reminded of the philosophical joke about two behaviorists who are passing in the street. One says to the other, "You feel fine. How do I feel?" The humor, of course, is based on a peculiar consequence of (perhaps naïve) behaviorism. If mental states are nothing more than overt physical behaviors, there should be no principled reason to believe that the agent participates in any special epistemic relationship with her own feelings. There is a strong presumption, admittedly defeasible, that a first-person perspective of one's feelings has priority over the judgments of others. Defeaters of this assumption typically are manifested by some psychological malady; one is greatly agitated at the moment and so fails to recognize how well her life is going; another is self-absorbed to the point of inattentiveness to his disintegrating life. Still—and this is intended as a prephilosophical observation and not as a consequence of Cartesianism—distinctive of a mental life belonging to one individual as opposed to another is the fact that, in general, the person who owns the feelings has a privileged access to them.

As with feelings, I am suggesting, so too, by and large, with personal welfare. On the desire theorist's account, the explanation for our asking an individual how well she is faring is that we believe that the individual who is the concern of our inquiry is in the best position to know whether her desires are being satisfied or frustrated. This account, though, seems doubly wrong. On the one hand, there are an enormous number of desires—virtually all that deal with external states of affairs—concerning which the individual, far from being in the best epistemic position for determining whether they are fulfilled, may actually be in a relatively poor one. John manifests this in being abroad, removed from any access to the baseball news back home. It is true, of course, that I am in the best position, normally, to know what my desires are, but this is just to say that my special relationship to my desires concerns its non-relational or intrinsic dimension. The problem enters when the desire theory invokes relational or objective elements as necessary determinants of value. To know what my desires are is one thing; to know whether these desires are satisfied or frustrated quite another. Even assuming that the individual in question has privileged access to his own welfare, the method seems too indirect. When accessing one's own welfare, it does not seem sensible to suggest that one needs to, or even does, investigate whether one's desires have been satisfied or thwarted. Although there may be rare circumstances where something like this method is employed, usually access to this information is direct and immediate, reminiscent, in fact, of the automatic way in which persons realize that they are experiencing either pleasure or pain. Experientialism would be paradigmatic of a theory that accounts for the privileged position that we normally assign to an agent. After all, who is in better position than myself to know how well I am doing if "doing well" is a function of my interior life.

It might be objected that, although I pay lip service to the idea that there are occasions on which individuals do not recognize the true state of their well-being, I severely underestimate just how frequently this circumstance occurs. As a result, the relative merits that experientialism and the desire theory have in accommodating this knowledge are inverted. Insofar as others really are better judges than ourselves in evaluating our welfare, the fact that the desire theory has an extrinsic component while experientialism lacks one actually speaks in the former's favor.

Such a response garners support from ordinary language. We certainly use expressions such as "She really has no idea how well-off she is" and "If she only had more sense, she'd realize how well he's doing," indicating that others with a more objective perspective are in a better position to assess the agent's welfare than the individual himself. Furthermore, the analogy between self-evaluation of welfare and self-knowledge of enjoyment and suffering may be challenged. First, the maladies that affect accurate self-evaluation of welfare—ranging from inattentiveness to serious mental and physical disease—would tend to leave self-knowledge of suffering and enjoyment unaffected. Excruciating pain is just the sort of thing that will jolt one out of an inattentive state; the two are mutually exclusive. Second, youngsters and adolescents are frequently thought of as clueless concerning their well-being although, presumably, they all are as adept as the more mature in recognizing their own enjoyment and suffering.

It is difficult to see how the desire theory is helped by acknowledging these suggestions. We may grant the empirical fact that the aforementioned expressions are sometimes used as a sign that an individual is not always in a privileged position regarding her own welfare, but there is no suggestion in these expressions that the person would have been in a better position for self-assessment had she known whether her desires had been fulfilled or frustrated. When it is urged that she "really has no idea how well off she is," the conversational implication is that the subject is ignorant of the relative status of her well-being. It is not charged that the individual's internal mechanisms have broken down to the point where he can no longer recognize his well-being. A similar response is appropriate to the comment about adolescents. In some cases, they may well be so self-absorbed that they fail to recognize the relative ranking of their well-being. But this condition would hardly be alleviated if they, or anyone else for that matter, had a more exhaustive knowledge of the status of their desires. Claims that the agent normally has a privileged position regarding her own welfare are intended only in a limited sense. It would be unfair in the extreme to burden this privileged perspective not only with knowledge of whether one is being made better or worse off relative to an earlier stage of herself, but also whether she is, at the same time, being benefited or harmed relative to others. Still, there should be no illusions that experientialism garners any advantage here. The task of determining *comparative* well-being appropriately seems beyond the grasp of any viable candidate for a theory of welfare.

Although the desire theory does grate with our intuitions concerning an individual's epistemic access to her welfare, most of the difficulties with the theory are metaphysical in character. Reflect on how much worse off we believe children would be were their desires always satisfied. The desires for eating high calorie foods, playing in dangerous areas, and forming unsavory relationships are just a few desires that, if fulfilled, would seemingly harm the child. To some degree, we assess parents as loving and caring insofar as they ensure that these desires are *thwarted*. In such instances, we see the parents as acting altruistically, acting for the good of the child, and so we view their success in frustrating these desires as enhancing the child's welfare. The desire theorist may be inclined to characterize these cases as peripheral annoyances. She may believe that only minor tinkering is required to allow that there are times at which the satisfaction of desires of an individual other than the agent is what makes the agent better off. In this case, for example, mature and loving parental desires are surrogates for the juvenile desires of their children. Were the children more mature and relatively normal psychologically, their desires for themselves would be tolerably like the desires that their parents have for them. Still, she may insist that her main thesis is secure. It is the satisfaction of a desire (admittedly, now, not always the agent's) that imputes value to the state of affairs in question.

But this concession introduces a dangerously slippery slope. Just as the satisfaction of a child's desire may result in harm for the child, there is no guarantee that the satisfaction of a parent's desire will result in benefit for the child. Obstacles can appear almost anywhere. Some parents, unfortunately, are simply not well intentioned, and others, though well-meaning, in virtue of cognitve or affective lapses or just plain bad luck have their desires mistargeted. Obviously, the same sort of frailties can affect any human desire, regardless of how loving and altruistic the person happens to be. This seems to lead to talk of an *ideal* representative for the child, or at least an individual who possesses ideal desires for the child's welfare. This godlike benefactor is just a picturesque means of ruling out of court any suggestions that the fulfilled desires can lead to anything but benefit for the child. But when the desires that count are this far removed from the desires of the individual whose welfare is being considered, a problem, which was implicit from the start, comes into greater relief. Recall that the desire theorist maintains that it is in virtue of the desire of an individual for a particular state of affairs that the state of affairs becomes valuable for that individual. When the desires and the welfare belong to the same individual, this direction of fit may seem plausible. The attractiveness of this view is greatly undermined when we think of the agent of welfare as being distinct (indeed remote, in the case of an ideal benefactor) from the agent of the desire. What emerges, in effect, is a variant of the problem in the *Euthyphro*. Do we want to claim that the desires of this ideal agent confer value on the state of affairs that he desires, or do we think that the "tracking" runs the other way around? This rhetorical question is intended to indicate that an ideal agent is best viewed as having the desires she has in virtue of recognizing what is independently valuable. But if this is the correct, or at least the better, way of looking at the matter, we have some incentive for turning toward a quite distinct theory of welfare, that is, perfectionism, and turning our back on the desire theory. The case for this switch is bolstered if we simply imagine what is very likely true—that no such ideal agent (or normal agent with these ideal desires) exists, or, even more dramatically, that no relevant desires exists. If this ideally knowledgeable and altruistic creature is a hypothetical entity, it really serves as nothing more than an ad hoc device to save the desire theory. To escape this embarrassment, the desire theorist who maintains this line of defense is committed to the existence of this ideal desirer. Although it may mitigate some concerns to realize that such a being need not herself be ideal— for we could have a less-than-ideal desirer with ideally altruistic desires— the required resurrection of either kind of being would prove a large stumbling block to the theory's acceptability.

Nor is the desire theorist aided by replacing or explicating the notion of ideal desires by "rational" or "well-informed" ones. Presumably, well-informed or rational desires, like ideal desires, would not include those whose objects are unsavory relationships, and so the desire theorist no longer is saddled with the problem of the rambunctious youths. The idea, however, is meretricious, not because of some quibble about the precise ways one is to understand the terms that describe these empowered desires, but rather because these specialized desires do nothing to change the powerful intuition that unsavory relationships are harmful independently of anyone's desires. Complementing this is the notion that what makes a desire well formed or rational is (at best) the fact that it would attach only to those objects that would benefit its possessor. Rationality and well-informedness are, so to speak, mediative properties; by surveying the landscape, they suggest and endorse certain courses of behavior that are apt to produce beneficial results for the individual. What they seem incapable of doing, however, is creating value from whole cloth. They would therefore seem far better suited to a perfectionist view of value wherein rational and well-informed desires are inevitably indicative (but not constitutive) of items that make an agent better off.

Even if we were to set aside the perfectionist rendering of the relationship between satisfied and frustrated desires, on the one hand, and being made better and worse off, on the other, there are powerful forces that speak to the rejection of the tenet that the fulfillment of rational, well-informed desires makes one better off. Reflect on cases that deal with heroism and martyrdom. Consider the oft-told scenario of the soldier who intentionally sacrifices his life for the survival of his compatriots. The brave soldier knows full well that diving onto the grenade will probably result in his death but nevertheless is undeterred. It is implausible, at least in some of these soldier scenarios, to argue that the soldier believes that if he were to choose otherwise—if, that is, he were to choose not to sacrifice himself—his remaining years would be so racked with guilt that he would be worse off alive than dead, and so he is really basing his decision on what he perceives to be his own welfare. That we do not always, or even usually, view cases like these in this way is evidenced by the fact that we supply children with these narratives in an attempt to instill virtuous qualities. Not only do we interpret the soldier's behavior as intelligible and rational, but as admirable as well. It is the type of behavior for which we grant honors and medals. Our sincerity in relaying these stories, and so the effectiveness of them, would be greatly compromised if we really believed that the soldier's actions were a product of his desire to make himself better off. Presumably, the soldier does not believe, nor is it true, that what he did was better for himself, and yet there is no obvious flaw in either the content of his information or in his conceptual abilities. Or consider the real-life case of Gandhi, who, presumably rationally and informedly, chose to allow himself to be mercilessly beaten by British colonialists. Also, in hopes of serving his emancipatory cause, he decided to undertake many hunger strikes. Unless we now are smuggling a technical sense of "well-being," it seems fair to say that Gandhi's satisfied desire does not make him better off.

We should not infer from the narrative about the courageous soldier that there are no cases in which a rational, well-informed person can believe correctly that death is better for him than continued life. Epicurean puzzles to the side, most of us have no trouble understanding how a person, motivated purely by self-interest, may choose to die rather than further absorb inordinate pain and humiliation. Kamikaze pilots frequently believed that a safe retreat to Japan would end in a fate worse than death. If this point needs bringing home, think of being given a choice between continuously suffering from the worst pain that you ever endured and being put to death quickly and painlessly. If we disregard religious factors in the decision—and, again, we are to act only on a self-interested basis—the choice strikes me, at least, as obvious.

(v)

A look at the end of Freud's life provides us with an interesting case study for the desire theory. Suffering severe pain from the ravages of cancer, Freud needed to decide between taking medication for pain relief, which would leave his thinking confused, and maintaining his clarity of thought at the expense of continued physical suffering. Freud, valuing his clarity of thought more than a relatively pain-free existence, chose the latter option. The hope that this case can provide additional illumination of the desire theory resides in the fact that there is no strong pretheoretical consensus about which alternative life makes Freud better off.

I take it that the intelligibility of the Freud scenario would not have been affected had Freud made the decision to opt for the pain-free, but murkier, life. Without losing one whit of rationality or informedness, Freud's choosing differently is perfectly understandable; regardless of which decision Freud makes, we have no inclination to characterize the choice as issuing from anything less than a fully competent, self-interested decider. If Freud had made this alternate choice, the desire theorist would count the fuliginous-thinking-but-pain-free life as the better one for Freud. Since such a life would be diametrically opposed to the one that Freud, in fact, did choose, we receive a poignant reminder of the direction of fit for the desire theory. It is not as though there are better and worse lives for individuals that rational and informed desires happen to pick out. Rather, it is the fact that an individual rationally and informedly desires a particular outcome that makes that outcome better for him than the alternative. In satisfying our desires, we create what is best for us; when our desires are thwarted we become worse off. There are not states of affairs "out there," independent of our desires, that are better and worse for us, from which we, if we are fortunate, pick the good ones and forgo the bad. Rather, in desiring certain states of affairs, we confer personal value to them. From the fact that there is no pre-reflective antagonism toward the acceptance of either alternative action as being the one that is in Freud's interest, we are open to the notion that Freud, in deciding on one alternative, *makes* that alternative the one that benefits him. To this extent, then, the desire theory gains an advantage over perfectionism.

It is easily imaginable that this decision was at least moderately difficult for Freud. He may have wavered in his choice, being uncertain and ambivalent throughout, and perhaps even beyond, his deliberative process. The experientialist has the resources to diagnose his tentativeness; Freud is unsure whether he would feel better from the inside living a relatively pain-free existence or one that is painful but permits clear thought. Roughly, he is involved in a balancing act trying to decide whether pain or disappointment and discouragement supplies the lesser of two interior evils. But the desire theorist loses no ground here, for he, too, has the tools to explain indecisiveness. Freud can be assumed to have the typical desires both not to be in great pain and to think clearly. Although Freud most closely associates with this latter desire, it is a close call, and it is the fact that these two desires have relatively equal strength that make the ultimate choice so difficult.

Nevertheless, Freud does (rationally, informedly) most closely identify with his desire for the clear-thinking but painful existence and, insofar as this desire is satisfied, the desire theorist must assess Freud as benefited. But a problem arises. It surely is possible that some time after making his decision, Freud believes that he had earlier made a terrible mistake. He had thought he was choosing the option that was best for him (the clear-thinking alternative), but he now realizes that he would have been better off opting for the pain-free existence. But the desire theorist's account seems not to allow for such error. If the satisfaction of a rational, well-informed desire makes him better off—and this is precisely what had occurred—then Freud was made better off; he could not be correct in later believing that he had earlier made an error. An attempt at psychological reconfiguration is palpably disingenuous. Freud, in confessing his blunder, is not denying that the earlier desire for clear thought was not the one with which he most closely identified. Moreover, experientialism has a simple explanation; Freud was just mistaken about which state of affairs would bring him the most enjoyment.

(VI)

There is one significant consequence of the desire theory that deserves some close attention. This ramification of the theory has particular significance because, perhaps more obviously and emphatically than any previously mentioned concern, it results from the desire theory of welfare's being an essentially relational theory. Recall that the salient intuition I have tried to mine is that benefits and harms are fundamentally a function of the modifications of an individual's intrinsic or nonrelational properties. It is for this reason, among others, that experientialism entices; there is no theory that has greater right to claim that it is exclusively, let alone primarily, a theory of well-being that accounts for benefits and harms in terms of an individual's intrinsic qualities. The desire theory, on the other hand, is a theory that necessarily incorporates relational elements in its welfare calculus. And, in virtue of the fact that the satisfaction and frustration of desires are virtually always a matter of a match between the mental content of the desire and an external (or "objective") state of affairs, the desire theory maintains a decidedly extrinsic vector.

It is a truism that some of our desires may be satisfied or frustrated without ever being recognized by their agents. We already have exemplified this in the case of John and his desire for the Yankees' success. Indeed, we may immediately forget about a desire, and so from the inside our subsequent life is precisely the same as it would have been had we never had the desire we did. Still, according to the desire theorist, our lives have been enhanced if the desire was fulfilled. In virtue of our desire's being satisfied, we are made better off. That we never come to know about this fulfillment, or even—given that we quickly forget about our antecedent desire—that we never again have the desire pass through our minds, does not undermine the fact that our welfare has been enhanced. What this sort of case most highlights is the fact that the desire theory encompasses relational and (typically) extrinsic elements, and it is this fact that I intend to press to illuminate its most consequential flaws.

What is interesting to note is that the epistemic relationship that an unaware individual has to either the fulfillment or frustration of his desire is precisely the same as that of a dead person to his antemortem desire. From the inside, the relationships between a dead person and his antemortem desire and between a person unaware of whether his desire has been fulfilled and his desire are identical. After all, in this regard, all that the individual's death does (and here I forgo worries about the afterlife and other esoterica) is ensure that the individual never realizes or becomes aware of the satisfaction or frustration of his desire; both the dead individual and his unaware counterpart are equally in the dark. The assurance delivered by death can be incorporated into a scenario with the living individual. We simply stipulate, as we have already exemplified, that he never becomes aware of the status of his desire. The upshot of this is that the desire theorist should have no objection to, indeed should even be an apologist for, the view that individuals can be benefited and harmed posthumously. That is, if an individual can be both benefited and harmed while completely in the dark about the outcome of her desires, the fact that this ignorance is guaranteed should present no additional problem to the desire theorist.

To forestall a possible misunderstanding, I should clarify that I am not imputing to the desire theorist the thoroughly implausible position that dead people have desires. The dead, and I am understanding this in a naturalistic setting, are without any psychological states. They can no more have desires or preferences than they can find a joke humorous. Since dead individuals are nothing more than mixtures of ash, dirt, and bones, and this motley conglomeration of items presumably is incapable of possessing desires, only antemortem persons are capable of being benefited and harmed. To hold that an individual can be both benefited and harmed after death, a position that I attribute to any consistent desire theorist, is to hold that there are certain events which occur after the death of an individual that can satisfy and frustrate desires that the individual had while he was alive. If satisfaction occurs, the individual is benefited, and if frustration occurs, the individual is harmed.

It is true that some panpsychics may take issue with the fact that the dead, even conceived as nothing other than bone, ash, and dust, are incapable of owning desires. This would not commit the panpsychic to holding that such individuals can be made better or worse off; panpsychics may not be desire theorists. Regardless of their position of moral patienthood, panpsychics would find my description of their view as "thoroughly implausible" to be unfairly dismissive. Although I find panpsychism implausible, I have not, nor will I, present any arguments against it. Let me just note that I would not be too upset if any defense of the desire theory rested on a commitment attributing desires to the inanimate.

Since there is no nonarbitrary reason for the desire theorist not to embrace the notion of posthumous benefits and harms, to the extent that the viability of any such account can be compromised, the desire theory suffers. My strategy is to discuss what I consider the best case for the existence of posthumous benefits and harms.[6] Though innovative and sophisticated, I will suggest that it fails and so doubt is cast upon the viability of the desire theory. Obviously, this is hardly constitutes a "knockdown" argument against the desire theory. Were the desire theorist to agree with all that follows, she is within her rights to suggest another account of posthumous benefits and harms that comports with her theory. Nonetheless, it seems fair to say that the acceptance of the subsequent discussion places the onus squarely on the shoulders of the desire theorist.

If we seek a respectable lineage to the idea that benefits and harms can befall the dead, we can do no better than Aristotle. In a somewhat restrained and tentative matter, Aristotle lends his qualified support to this idea:

> Since, then, a man's own misfortunes sometimes have a powerful influence upon his life, and sometimes seem comparatively trivial; and the same applies also to the misfortunes of all his friends alike; although it makes a difference whether a particular misfortune befalls people while they are alive or after they are dead—a far greater difference than it makes in a tragedy whether the crimes and activities are committed beforehand or carried out during the action; then we must take into our reckoning this difference too; or rather, perhaps, the fact that it is questionable whether the departed have any participation in good or its opposite. For the probable inference from what we have been saying is that if any effect of good or evil reaches them at all it must be faint and slight, either in itself or to them—or if not that, at any rate not of such force and quality as to make the unhappy happy or to rob the happy of their felicity. So it appears that the dead are affected to some extent by the good fortunes of those whom they love, and similarly by their misfortunes; but the effects are not of such a kind or so great as to make the happy unhappy or to produce any other such result. (*Nichomachean Ethics*, book 1, chap. xi)

The desire theorist should have no reason to exercise the same caution that is obvious in Aristotle's description. Since the desire theorist situates the entirety of welfare in the satisfaction and frustration of desires, a person should be subject, in principle, to the same quality of benefit and harm he undergoes while alive. As I have emphasized, for our purposes the only relevant difference between living and dead individuals is that the death of an individual guarantees that she will never become aware of either the desire's satisfaction or thwarting, and this is a guarantee of something that, in and of itself, should have no bearing on a person's welfare according to the doctrine of the desire theory. If this is so, then, *pace* Aristotle, posthumous events that constitute the satisfaction and frustration of desires should be able to make an otherwise happy man unhappy or conversely. There is no reason for the desire theorist to attribute less efficacy to desires whose conditions of satisfaction or frustration come into existence subsequent to the formation of the desire.

It might prove useful to have some concrete cases of alleged post-humous harm and benefit before us. First, consider the case of a sculptor, after whose death a false rumor is purveyed to the effect that the highly acclaimed works attributed to her were actually the creations of another woman. These rumors are henceforth accepted as fact, and the sculptor is relegated to a minor historical footnote. Under the assumption that the sculptor had the desire to be remembered as an original and great artist, the desire theory would claim that the sculptor had been harmed. In fact, under the assumption that this desire is one the sculptor fervently and wholeheartedly held, it would seem that the desire theorist should judge the sculptor to be greatly harmed, perhaps to an extent that would turn her otherwise good life into a bad one. As a second example, we can consider the twentieth-century application of Leibniz's calculus to help build an atomic bomb. Because Leibniz was a man of peace who had hoped that all of his discoveries would lead to universal harmony, this undesired implementation of his work is viewed as making Leibniz's life worse off than it otherwise would have been. On the other hand, had his calculus never had this consequence, but had led to only non-violent ramifications, Leibniz would have been posthumously benefited.[7]

It is crucial to emphasize that, to the desire theory, the evaluations of harms and benefits are dependent upon the desires that the subjects actually had. It is not a matter of what either individual actually said, what can be reasonably assumed to be the case with either, or—most important when we contrast the desire theory with perfectionism—what putatively has value independent of the desires of any agents. The correct attribution of harm or benefit to the antemortem individual depends on the "metaphysics" of the case. The match or lack thereof between, on the one hand, the actual desires of the sculptor or Leibniz and, on the other, the states of affairs that come to pass, is all that matters. To make this evident, consider the case in which the sculptor is a rather bizarre artist and actually wants to have his life's works denigrated after his death. He wants nothing more than to have someone else take undeserved credit for his masterpieces. In this aberrant case, the sculptor would have been posthumously benefited by the postmortem misrepresentation and harmed had it, or something like it, not occurred.

To show what is problematic about the notion of posthumous benefit and harm, we consider, in some detail, the case of Bishop Berkeley and his beloved son William, who tragically died at the age of fourteen (Pitcher, 186–87). We are to assume what was actually true: that the elder Berkeley had the typical paternal desires and wishes for his son. Whether or not he explicitly articulated his passions for his son, we are to assume that he deeply wanted his son to lead a full, productive, and happy life. That William lead such a life was in the interests of his father. That William, in fact, did not lead such a life was then clearly opposed to his father's preferences and so was a misfortune or harm to the good bishop. To focus on the question of posthumous harm, let us further assume what was not actually the case, namely that Bishop Berkeley died before his son William, and that moreover, while the bishop was alive he lacked the slightest inkling that his son would die at such an early age. Thus the harm to the elder Berkeley could not be constituted by the knowledge (suspicion, expectation, hunch, etc.) that his son would die young. The harm is firmly situated in the nonintrinsic properties of Bishop Berkeley.

It might be somewhat surprising to realize that the harm suffered by the elder Berkeley could not be constituted by his son's death. Why not? William's death cannot be the event that constitutes the posthumous harm to his father because if it were, the elder Berkeley would not have been harmed until William died. But if the bishop would not have been harmed until William died, then, in the case under discussion, it would have been the postmortem Berkeley to whom the harm would have attached. But the postmortem Berkeley is no more than ash and dust, and these items, we have agreed, can have no interests or welfare. This same point applies to both the sculptor and Leibniz. The sculptor was not harmed at the time that her works were usurped, for by that time, the sculptor was nothing but ash and dust. Leibniz, for precisely the same reason, was not—could not have been—harmed at the time the bomb exploded over Nagasaki.

The harm to the elder Berkeley is constituted by the fact (state of affairs) that William is going to die so young. This harm attaches, as all harms must, to the antemortem individual. It is the living Berkeley whose life is made worse off by the fact that his beloved son will die prematurely. William's death, an event that occurs after the bishop's own, is responsible for the fact that he will die at such a young age. (It should be clear that this relationship is asymmetric; the event is responsible for the fact, but not conversely.) So it is a posthumous event (William's death) that is responsible for the fact that William will die at a tragically young age, which, in turn, constitutes the harm to the antemortem elder Berkeley. Furthermore, this harm to the antemortem Berkeley is best construed as having a fairly lengthy though indefinite duration, beginning when the elder Berkeley first had these fatherly interests for his son (this accounts for the harm's indefinite duration, since there is probably no exact moment when the bishop began to have these desires), and ending with the bishop's death. Also, I would think that the harm, contrary to Aristotle's mandate, would be evaluated as great; one can scarcely imagine more fervent desires than those a mother and father have for their children.

There are two areas that need addressing. The first deals with the question of whether this account of posthumous benefits and harms relies on the phenomenon of backward causation. If it does, this would have to count against the theory's plausibility since the possibility of retrocausation, let alone its viability, is quite contentious. The point at which retrocausation appears to enter the account is when a posthumous event, the death of William, is said to be "responsible" for the harm that attaches to the antemortem elder Berkeley. It surely seems as though this notion of "responsibility," or similar ideas such as "accounts for" or "makes," are to be rendered as causal notions, since were William not to die at the tragically young age, then the bishop would not have suffered this particular harm (and so causation as a necessary condition of an event's occurrence is satisfied), and that William's death, given his father's interests, vouchsafe the bishop's suffering this harm (and so causation as a sufficient condition obtains). Also speaking for a causal interpretation is the difficulty of imagining what else could be right; obviously we are not talking about moral responsibility or accountability here. At the very least, if these notions are not to be understood causally, we need some alternative account to alleviate mystery.

The worry engendered by the possible invocation of retrocausation would be greatly assuaged if cases wherein subsequent events account, or are responsible, for earlier events could be presented where there is no temptation to allude to backward causation. This would be welcome news to the advocate of the desire theory, even in the absence of a detailed analysis of the cases. At least, then, there would be some precedent for this use of the concept of responsibility or accountability, although exactly what that use would amount to may prove difficult to elucidate.

Consider, as a first attempt, the example of the world's being irrevocably destroyed during the administration of the president following Bill Clinton. Such an event would make Clinton, now, the penultimate president of the United States; it is the future destruction of the world that makes Clinton's current presidency the penultimate one. At the time of the world's destruction, there will be no Clinton presidency. Rather, given the timing of this catastrophic event, Clinton, at this very moment and presumably unbeknownst to anyone, is serving as the next-to-last U.S. president. The analogy is clear. As the destruction of the world accounts for the fact that currently Clinton is serving as our penultimate president (i.e., currently it is true that the world will be destroyed during

the term of Clinton's successor), young William's death accounts for the
fact that then, during Bishop Berkeley's life, the bishop is suffering harm
(i.e., during the bishop's life it is true that his son was going to die
tragically young). Since it is proffered as evident that neither backward
causation nor something mysterious need be invoked to understand the
relationship between the subsequent event of the world's destruction and
the antecedent event of Clinton's penultimate presidency, so too, there
should be no special problem in understanding the relationship between
the subsequent event of William's death and the prior event of the
bishop's suffering harm.

A second example involves my wakening at 8:00 A.M. and my eating
breakfast at 11:00 A.M. In virtue of my eating breakfast at 11:00 A.M.,
the event of my wakening occurred three hours prior to my breakfasting.
That my wakening took place three hours earlier did not occur when I
ate breakfast (I had been awake for three hours by that time). Rather, it
occurred when I awoke, although some subsequent state of affairs was
responsible for it's happening three hours prior to my breakfasting. So,
once again, we are putatively offered a mundane example of how a
subsequent event can account for (be responsible for) some antecedent
event.

Let us grant that backward causation is not involved in either case.
We also waive the point that references to commonly used examples
involving contentious concepts does little to aid our understanding of
these concepts. In brief, we accept that although we are not certain
exactly what is taking place in these sorts of examples, retrocausation is
not involved, and whatever is, is not mysterious. Still I want to suggest
that there are significant disanalogies between these cases and the case of
William and his father serious enough to undermine altogether the value
of the analogies.

It is important to note that in both the presidency and the breakfast
cases the description of the antecedent event essentially involves a temporal reference; it is the *penultimacy* of the Clinton presidency that is
accounted for by the world's destruction, and it is the wakening's *being
three hours prior* to the breakfast that is accounted for by my eating breakfast at 11:00 A.M. This seems reasonable despite the fact that we lack a
precise articulation of what "accountability" here amounts to. What does
not seem reasonable, however, indeed what seems impossible without
invoking the notion of backward causation, is how either Clinton's presidency, per se, or my wakening, per se, could be accounted for by some
subsequent event. That is, while it is understandable, at a prephilosophical level at least, how the penultimacy of Clinton's presidency can be a
function of events subsequent to his presidency, it seems impossible,

without employing the concept of retrocausation, that the same could be true of the Clinton presidency itself.

If we call these latter types of facts—the Clinton presidency, the wakening at 8:00 A.M.—"hard facts," we can say that the existence or nonexistence of hard facts cannot be a function of subsequent events; hard facts are "fixed." If we use the label "soft fact" to encompass those facts or states of affairs that have an essential reference, be it explicit or implicit, to future states of affairs, as, for example the fact of Clinton's penultimate presidency, we can say that at least some soft facts are a function of subsequent events, that some soft facts are "unfixed."[8] The problem, then, with defending the charge that the Berkeley case implicitly invokes retrocausation is that harm, unlike penultimacy, would appear to be a hard fact. It seems as though the existence or nonexistence of any harm the bishop suffers can no more be affected by subsequent events than the (non)existence of Clinton's presidency or my waking up one morning. The concept of harm, unlike the notion of penultimacy, does not invoke time.

It is unfair to claim that this begs the question against relational accounts such as the desire theory. The reasoning does employ a pre-philosophical notion of harm as the sort of quality—unlike "penultimacy," for example—whose existence at any particular time is independent of any future course of events. It is not as though this atemporal characterization were a *theoretical* construct, an interpretation that arose from some prior theorizing. If this were the case, the charge of question begging would have some force. The desire theorist is free to argue that our prephilosophical understanding of harms as atemporal events is not propitious, for we have admitted that these points of departure are not immutable. Nevertheless, we should not retreat from our insistence that, in virtue of our ordinary and pervasive use of an atemporal concept of harm, the burden rests squarely on the shoulders of the revisionist.

There is an additional odd consequence of applying the desire theory to posthumous cases. Let us change the Berkeley narrative slightly so that the elder Berkeley dies after, rather than prior to, his son's tragic demise. This change should not affect the harm that the bishop suffered in the previous example, where he dies before his son and suffers the misfortune of his son's being about to die at a tragically young age. But now Bishop Berkeley suffers a distinct and additional misfortune. He now suffers or is harmed by his son's early death. (Recall that this latter misfortune can only be suffered by those who are alive at the time of William's death). But this ramification brings suffering to new depths, for it places individuals like the good bishop in double jeopardy. Not only is an individual harmed by the event that is responsible for one's desire being unfulfilled, but one is antecedently harmed as well by the fact that this event is going to take place. There is enough suffering in the world without recruiting novel efforts to increase it.

Consider finally, as an attempt to revive the desire theory, the following comments, equally applicable whether or not the bishop was alive at the time of his son's tragic death.

> But surely if his friends knew, though Berkeley didn't, that his son was fated to die young, they would have felt very sorry for Berkeley—and not just because there would eventually be the tragedy of his son's early death, but also because then (i.e., before his son's death) there was a grave misfortune in Berkeley's life. What was it? It was the fact that his adored and adoring child, so full of promise, was going to die young. This fact was one that Berkeley passionately did not want to exist, it was totally against his interests (whether or not he knew of its existence). Therefore, it was a very real misfortune for him. (Pitcher, 186)

I suggest a different psychological profile for Berkeley's friends. They would feel sorry for the bishop if they knew that he would live to see the tragic death of his son, but if they knew that he would die before his son, and so not witness his son's premature demise, they might, insofar as this point is concerned, feel happy for the bishop because he would be be spared this horrible experience. We often hear people say things much like this, especially when they are consoling the spouses and friends of the recently deceased (e.g., "At least Frank died before he saw his son succumb").

To sum up: The desire theory has a commitment to an objective component that is most dramatically manifested in the discussion of posthumous benefits and harms. Serious conceptual problems attach to this component in what I take to be the best account of posthumous welfare. To the extent that experientialism as a subjective theory of personal well-being is immune from these criticisms (there are no posthumous experiences under a naturalistic interpretation of death), and to the extent that a position precluding posthumous welfare is at least as pretheoretically plausible as its contrary, we have reason to favor experientialism over the desire theory.

I have tried to argue that serious difficulties confronting the desire theory are consequences of the fact that, in general, the satisfaction or frustration of an individual's desires lack an intimate or necessary relationship with the agent's intrinsic qualities. The motivating intuition has been that unless the nonrelational or intrinsic properties of an individual are somehow affected by some state of affairs, that individual cannot be either benefited or harmed by that state of affairs. The desire theory, which allows, indeed insists, upon an agent's being made better and worse off when no modification of intrinsic properties takes place—as in the cases wherein the individual is simply forever unaware of his desires being either satisfied or frustrated, or, more dramatically, when the individual dies before these conditions for satisfaction or frustration come into existence—runs afoul of this intuition and, as a result, finds itself enmeshed in serious difficulties.

(VII)

As was adumbrated earlier there is one sort of case in which the satisfaction or frustration of a desire does necessarily modify an agent's intrinsic properties. If an individual desires to have the particular mental state of enjoyment (pleasure) and wants to avoid the mental state of suffering (pain), then the respective satisfaction and frustration of these desires are felt by the individual in question. The satisfaction and frustration of these sorts of desires, desires for a certain phenomenological state, necessarily result in a modification of an individual's intrinsic properties. Although we have seen that epistemic advantages still accrue to experientialism regarding the status and means of accessing our own welfare, there appears to be no metaphysical advantage gained by the experientialist in accommodating the motivating intuition that prompted our advocacy of experientialism in the first place.

Perhaps an argument can be made for the superiority of the desire theory when we restrict its scope to personal phenomenologies. Where experientialism, by its very nature, cannot address the question of what it is about pleasurable states that benefit an individual and what it is about painful ones that diminish his well-being, the desire theorist can supply an explanation. Pleasurable states (instrumentally) enhance individual welfare insofar as they form the contents of our desires; painful states (instrumentally) harm us insofar as they frustrate our desires. What is considered basic or fundamental within experientialism is given an explanation within the desire theory, and it is plausible to claim that in this regard the desire theory is to be accorded an advantage. It is true, of course, that the desire theory, in virtue of its nature as a fundamental theory of well-being, cannot supply any reason why it is that the satisfaction of a desire benefits us and the frustration of a desire harms us, but the desire theorist may not see this as anything but a pandemic situation. Justification and explanation must come to an end, but this is no reason not to credit a theory as advantaged if it explains more than its competitors.

The allure of these considerations should be resisted. The experientialist would respond in kind, by claiming the resources for explaining the (instrumental) benefit of a satisfied desire and the (instrumental) harm of a frustrated desire. A satisfied desire makes us better off insofar as the awareness of the satisfaction makes us feel better, and a frustrated desire diminishes our well-being insofar as awareness of this frustration makes us worse off from the inside. So we now have an experientialist explanation of what the desire theory must treat as fundamentally inexplicable. It is true, of course, that the experientialist can go no further. He necessarily lacks the resources to explain why it is that pleasurable feelings benefit and unpleasurable ones harm, but, as the desire theorist was quick to point out, explanations must end somewhere. In sum, then, the two theories, on this point at least, seem to be on a par.

But perhaps the desire theorist can exploit the relationship with personal phenomenologies in other ways. The bulk of the antecedent discussion seems to place an onus on the desire theorist. We have presented considerations that have, effectively, tried to show that satisfied and frustrated desires without an accompanying change in phenomenology, fail to result in, respectively, benefit or harm. The challenge faced by the desire theorist is to present equally persuasive considerations to the effect that, absent the requisite desires, good and bad interior lives fail to make an individual, respectively, better and worse off. Where we can picture the experientialist as being incredulous of the idea that individuals' welfare can be affected when nothing from the inside is transpiring, the desire theorist may be characterized as being mystified by the idea that pleasures and pains can matter to (can influence the welfare of) individuals without being either wanted or not wanted. The argument to this point has concentrated on the extrinsic nature of the desire theory as it is applied to nonphenomenological contents and has tried to suggest some untoward consequences. The symmetric gambit of the desire theorist would be to try to exploit the necessarily nonrelational character of experientialism when the theory is applied to phenomenological contents.

We begin by reflecting upon cases in which an unusual or "conflicting" association occurs between a phenomenological state and a desire. The desire theory tells us that we ought to assess the welfare of the individual as being modified in the direction of the desire; desires trump phenomenology. So, were we to possess a pleasurable state from the inside and yet want to rid ourselves of this state, then—contrary to the dictates of experientialism but in conformity with the mandate of the desire theory—we should view ourselves as being harmed. Similarly, if we are internally faring poorly but desire that mental state, then we ought to view ourselves as being benefited. If such thought experiments are persuasive, then—at least in these restricted contexts wherein the content of the desires are hedonic states—desires, and not phenomenologies, are morally fundamental.

But potentially far more probative than examining these cases is investigation of the point at which the desire theory and experientialism most critically diverge. Just as experientialism tried to take advantage of the relational aspect of desires in emphasizing cases wherein there was no appreciation on the part of the agent that her desire was satisfied or frustrated (epitomized in the discussion of posthumous harms and benefits), the desire theorist may try to take advantage of the nonrelational character of experientialism by examining individuals who, although sentient, are without desires. After all, the basic point of the desire theory of welfare is not the relatively modest one that desires trump phenomenology, but rather that, at bottom, phenomenologies do not count for anything and satisfaction and frustration of desires count for everything. Where the experientialist suggested that the essentially extrinsic nature of the desire theory extended the borders of welfare modification unduly, the ploy of the desire theorist is now to argue that a theory that essentially accounts for welfare in terms of intrinsic properties will allow moral patienthood to run amok.

There are some philosophers, not all of whom are experientialists, who would deny that such a discussion could even get off the ground. They claim that there is a conceptual relationship between the capacity for phenomenology and the capacity to form desires. In effect, then, these philosophers claim that it is a necessary truth that if an individual has the capacity to suffer and enjoy, he has the capacity to form desires.[9] From this, it would follow that there cannot be an individual in the moral domain of the experientialist who is not also in the domain of the desire theorist. If this conceptual thesis is true, there would be no point of critical divergence, since there could be no cases of individuals with feelings and yet without desires toward these feelings. The relationship is typically further specified. It is claimed both that it is necessary that if an individual is feeling badly from the inside, he wants to be rid of that mental state and that it is necessary that if one feels well from the inside, one wants this mental state to be maintained. If we consider the conceptualist's claim with this addendum, it would be logically impossible for an individual either to desire a painful state or not to desire a pleasurable one, let alone have no desires whatsoever when she is experiencing any hedonic state. Accepting this additional conceptualist parameter, we could not test the proposal regarding conflicts between phenomenologies and desires, because it would be held that it is logically required not only that the capacity for desires accompany phenomeno-logical capacity, but that pleasurable feelings be accompanied by desires of subsistence while unpleasurable feelings be accompanied by desires of avoidance. Of course, acceptance of the conceptualist thesis, with or without the addendum, would not establish experientialism (there are conceptualists who are desire theorists), but it would mean that one way that nonconceptualist desire theorists may try to favorably distinguish their theory from experientialism is unavailable.

There are competing pictures that underlie the distinct views of the modal status of the relationship between the capacity for sentient ex-perience and the capacity to form desires. The picture of the concep-tualist is that of an individual experiencing excruciating pain. The rhe-torical question asked is how, under ordinary circumstances, it is possible for such an individual *not* to desire that this pain be eradicated. The qualification "under ordinary circumstances" is not merely decorative. The apologist for the conceptual status may allow that there may be circumstances under which the suffering individual even desires that the pain continue. For example, she may believe that by having the pain continue, perhaps even increase in intensity, she has a better chance of having her penance accepted, and so have a better chance of spending eternity in a more pleasant venue. The apologist can even accept the remote possibility that the individual is indifferent toward whether the suffering continue or not, in the sense that, in a particular circumstance, the weight of his desire to see the excruciating pain cease is precisely offset by his desire to have the pain persist (perhaps, again, for religious reasons). What the underlying picture suggests is impossible is that, all things being equal, or under ordinary circumstances, one would not have the desire to have the pain and suffering desist. What strikes the con-ceptualist as impossible is for one not to desire the annihilation of the pain *qua* pain.

The picture that underlies the contingency status of the relationship between suffering and desire claims that the capacity for desire formation requires more physiological and psychological complexity than the ca-pacity for sentient experience. It is not denied that an individual with the capacity to form desires will not act exactly as the conceptual ad-vocate indicates. The point is that a more sophisticated individual is required for desire formation than is demanded by an individual with merely the capacity for sentient experience. A simple example can be offered. A human infant has the capacity to have sentient experience (on this both parties agree) and yet, at this stage in its human development, is not capable of forming desires. The contingency theorist might gladly agree that *if* the infant had this capacity then, since its infantile state would preclude him from having the relatively complex set of reasons that may act against his natural desire, he surely would desire that the excruciating pain immediately stop. It is just that at this early stage of maturity, he lacks the cognitive capacity to form desires.

I believe that there are some conceptualists who, when presented with this picture suggesting a contingent relationship between feelings and desires, would simply concede that their conceptual thesis was too strongly stated. Instead of claiming that it is a conceptual or necessary truth that a sentient individual has desires, she may now make the weaker necessity claim that if an individual has the capacity to form desires, then if the individual feels pain he cannot but desire to avoid the pain (*qua* pain), and if the individual feels pleasure he cannot help but desire to maintain the pleasure (*qua* pleasure). Although certainly not as tidy as the conceptualist's original assertion, it is far more likely to be met without resistance. Whatever other ramifications it may have, it would allow the thought experiments that are intended to test cases in which the desire theory and experientialism yield radically different results.

Of course, the conceptualist may not be so conciliatory. It is, however, difficult to find any compelling reasons to accept the relationship between desires and phenomenology as conceptual. By understanding suffering or pain as bad ways of internal faring, as negative felt experiences, there is no lexicographic reason for conceptually entwining it with a desire to avoid it. Of course, one *could* do this by fiat: one could stipulate that part of the meaning of "pain" include the fact that persons desire to avoid it or rid themselves of it. But a more hollow victory could hardly be imagined. In effect, what one has done is take an ordinary concept with a well-entrenched meaning and changed it into a term of art. Although I will not pursue the analogy because it is somewhat tangential, I believe that this tactic of redefinition is employed by functionalists when they treat pain as a functional state that mediates between sensory inputs and behavioral outputs. So, for example, pain is that mental state which operates upon tactile sensations to incline the movement of a hand away from the source of those sensations. The details are unimportant. What is significant, however, is that functionalists make the feeling of pain merely contingently related to the pain itself. According to functionalist accounts, an individual can be in pain without feeling anything at all, and this, as dictionaries and common sense abide, eviscerates the mental state of an essential component. Whatever the functionalists are calling "pain," it scarcely refers to that which we intend to invoke by use of the homonymous term. Conceptualist accounts would seem to have the reverse problem; instead of draining the notion of what is particularly essential to it, they imbue its nature with attributes that belong to it only contingently.

Still, there are many who urge that meaning relationships form only a proper subset of conceptual or necessary relationships. Consider Kripke's a posteriori necessities. According to Kripke, for example, gold necessarily has atomic number 79. We became aware of this truth by empirical, scientific inquiry, not by looking up the word "gold" in our dictionaries. Were a dictionary all that is required for this type of knowledge, we would be able to replace Einstein and Newton with a group of lexicographers, and although the latter are experts of a sort, there is no temptation to consider them leading physicists. That "gold has atomic number 79" is a posteriori knowledge is, I think, inarguable. The question of its necessity rests on intuitive, and therefore more likely contentious, considerations. The case rests on reflecting upon thought experiments (e.g., would we call a Venusian substance that looked and behaved just like gold but had the atomic number 80 "gold"?), and it serves little purpose to now survey them. For granting that Kripke has made an interesting discovery about some truths—namely, that some necessary ones are a posteriori—it would appear to be an unlikely model on which to base the putative necessity between suffering and desires. We did not need to perform laboratory work or conduct scientific experiments to realize that individuals want to have their suffering eradicated.

A third conceptualist tactic asks us to consider a (perhaps bastardized) Wittgensteinian suggestion that urges us to look at how we learn the terms "suffering" and "desires to avoid suffering." These two terms presumably are learned together; we see examples of suffering, come to know them as cases of suffering, in virtue of individuals' exhibiting, among other things, avoidance behavior. In normal situations, we are taught, as a seamless whole, that the individual who is suffering wants to avoid that suffering. When we see a person holding his leg after being struck by a car, we have a demonstration of just that sort of confluence of events. We learn what suffering is, in part, when we learn what desiring to avoid suffering is, much as we learn what an itch is when we learn what scratching an itch is. It is urged that there is a sort of natural necessity that occurs in these early learning situations or primitive language games that founds the sort of conceptual intimacy that the conceptualist suggests. In contrast, compare the relationship between suffering and the desire to see it end with watching a baseball game and wanting to see it continue. In the latter pair, unlike the former, we do not learn what a baseball game is by learning about the desire to see it continue. In these cases, there is no temptation, nor should there be, to characterize the relationship as conceptual.

I must admit some hesitancy in commenting upon arguments like these. They are slippery. My one observation, and it is put forward tentatively and provisionally, is that undue significance is placed on the way certain terms or groups of terms are learned. There still seems to be a gap between the way a group of words are learned, perhaps even necessarily learned, and the contingent or conceptual relationship that obtains among these terms. Consider as a coarse analogy that the best way to learn to use a baseball bat may be to "choke up" on the bat. Nevertheless, it may well be that the best use of a bat occurs only when the batter places his hands near the bat's knob. We may later come to realize that the manner in which we learned certain terms needed to travel through falsehoods. This, unlike what the story supplied by the bastardized Wittgensteinian tells us, may be part of our natural inheritance.

If we take a step back, we may reach a perspective from which the chances of success for the conceptualist project do appear dim. Desires typically are characterized as a type of psychological or mental state or disposition. But it would appear that any conceptualist gambit is doomed if it understands the desire to end suffering in this way. After all, how can it be a *conceptual* truth that we are placed in a particular mental state when we find ourselves in a particular experiential state? If this is a truth, it would seem to be a truth of psychology or some other empirical science. The question then invited is how else we can reasonably understand the nature of desires to end our suffering that does not make them elements of our psychology. It is difficult to understand how the conceptualist can meet this challenge without adopting a technical sense of "desire." If this is how the point gets decided, the victory was scarcely worth the battle.

If these anticonceptualist sentiments are persuasive, then there is no a priori reason why an individual cannot either desire a painful mental state (or desire not to sustain a pleasurable one) or have no desires at all toward his hedonic life. Thus, the distinct results yielded by the desire theory and experientialism, born from their treatment of personal psychologies, are legitimate data for theorizing. Yet, it must be admitted that there is great difficulty in providing a plausible example of an individual actively desiring to experience pain as an end itself. Consider the case of St. Francis, which, at least at first blush, seems amenable to the cause of the contingency theorist. The good saint is portrayed as welcoming suffering, indeed even imploring his Lord for greater internal discomfort. It is true, of course, that in being a saint, Francis is rather different from most of us, but it should be kept in mind that he is still human, and so, presumably, no appeals to a divine nature need be invoked to make this case intelligible.

But this case lacks the decisiveness that it may initially appear to have. Apparently St. Francis sincerely believed that by enduring great suffering he would become a better person. Undergoing these unpleasant experiences would allow him to better understand the plight of the less fortunate and therefore to act more beneficently. And he may well have been right. The conceptualist would respond that St. Francis did not desire the pain *in and of itself* but only desired it as an instrument— perhaps even a necessary instrument, given the saint's psychology—of reaching his aim of being a better person. The conceptualist claims that he would find St. Francis's desire for pain, and a fortiori for increased pain, unfathomable, if we assume that he believed that he could become a more sensitive and kind person, toward which end he strived without undergoing any suffering.

What, then, of a case supplied by the realm of fiction? Consider Dostoevsky's Underground Man, who apparently wishes to experience pain for its own sake. At the very least, he seems to desire to experience pain for the same reasons that many of us typically want to experience pleasure. The narrative, although bizarre, seems intelligible. When we read this short novel, it is not as if we throw up our hands, complaining that we are viewing conceptual absurdities. It is true that, even more than St. Francis, the Underground Man is significantly different from all of us. After all, he is fictional. But what prevents one of us from desiring what Dostoevsky's protagonist desires?

Perhaps the conceptualist will respond by pointing out that the Underground Man is clearly irrational—that, paradoxically, the intelligibility of attributing the desire for pain (as well as other desires) depends on the reader's recognizing this fact. It is our knowledge of his fundamental irrationality that allows us to accept the fact that the Underground Man desires pain as an end. In contradistinction, since we work under the justified assumption that St. Francis has all his faculties intact, we do find the claim that he desires pain, in and of itself, incomprehensible. In the case of St. Francis, consistency requires that his desire for the pain must be viewed instrumentally. Since he is of sound mind, his ultimate goal must have been something that he believed pain alone, or most expeditiously, could bring about.

But notice that this response concedes the contingency thesis. The conceptualist no longer maintains that there is logical incoherence in desiring pain or suffering. It is rather suggested that one cannot rationally (and presumably, informedly) desire one's own suffering. But why cannot one do this? The only reasonable principle that presents itself is that one cannot rationally and informedly desire what is not in one's self-interest; one cannot desire that which makes one worse off. But if this is the reasoning that motivates the response, then we have an admission that a particular interior state of affairs can make an individual worse off and yet fulfill a desire. This was exactly the sort of test case for which the contingency theorist was originally aiming. We have a case in which, from the experientialist perspective, the individual is being harmed (since he is undergoing pain), but, from the perspective of the desire theorist, the agent is being benefited (since his desire for this painful state is satisfied). What is interesting is that in the attempted defense of the conceptualist thesis, we eventually receive confirmation of experientialism. It is conceded that the suffering makes the individual worse off, although the agent still desires it. What is demanded in return is that such an individual cannot be acting with informed rationality.

But we need not even acquiesce to this demand. We adumbrated earlier the case of the heroic soldier. If what we have said is right headed, we suffered no conceptual muddle in describing this case as one in which the agent, with informed rationality, acted contrary to his best interests or against his well-being. By finding no compelling reason to adopt the conceptualist thesis, test cases that manifest conflicts between the desire theory and experientialism are legitimate. And they seem to argue in favor of experientialism.

Once we are no longer tethered to the conceptualist thesis, we can examine the even more poignant difference between the desire theory and experientialism when these accounts are applied to personal psychologies. Consider cases in which the individual has the experiential capacity but lacks the capacity to form desires. In such a case, the desire theory must deny moral standing and the experientialist must accord it. These are the points of critical divergence between the two theories. We will discuss this sort of example presently, but is noteworthy that many philosophers, at least implicitly, believe there are individuals with phenomenological capacity but without the capacity to form desires. This belief, in its literal manifestation, would be inconsistent by conceptualists' lights. That this is a belief assumed by many philosophers is demonstrated by the fact that certain questions are discussed at all. To investigate whether an individual with the capacity for sentient experience and yet lacking the capacity to form desires can be benefited and harmed presupposes that the former capacity can be instantiated without the latter. It is just this possibility that the conceptualist disallows. Unless a great number of philosophers are operating under a conceptual delusion (not an impossibility, admittedly), the relationship deemed conceptual by some is actually contingent, and the investigation is intelligible.

(VIII)

We can begin somewhat obliquely by addressing the mirror image of the relationship under investigation. That is, let us consider an individual with the capability of forming desires, although incapable of having any phenomenological life. Under this scenario, the desire for pleasure, to focus on the most significant example, is ineluctably frustrated and the desire not to feel pain is inevitably satisfied. To the desire theorist, then, this sort of creature is morally considerable since benefits and harms can accrue; to the experientialist, in virtue of the individual's (necessarily) lacking the capacity for sentient experience, exclusion from the moral realm results.

It is interesting to note that this possibility is virtually, if not veritably, never considered. Perhaps the reason for this is the presumption that the capacity for forming desires is, in some important way, more sophisticated and developed than the capacity for sentient experience. It seems to be considered a self-evident truth that the capacity for phenomenology is a requirement of the capacity for desire formation. But I see no reason to accept this cavalier verdict. Psychologists assure us that there are individuals with the capacity to desire enjoyable conscious mental states who lack the capacity to have pleasurable experience (e.g., some anhedonics) and who, perhaps, lack the capacity for sentient experience altogether (e.g., some anomics). From the standpoint of the desire theorist, one would be hard pressed to think of a more pitiable plight—creatures who, in virtue of having this sort of desire (one which, presumably, the agent would care very much about) and lacking the capacity to fulfill it, would be forever doomed to making themselves worse off until, and unless, this desire was eradicated. From the standpoint of the experientialist, it would be impossible to entertain a more welfare-neutral circumstance. Roughly, one can view the different outlooks by characterizing the desire theorist as asking, in effect, what could be worse for an individual than wanting pleasure but being unable to attain it and the experientialist responding, in effect, that no harm can result from the desire's being unfulfilled as long as the individual cannot be consciously affected.

The case for the desire theory may appear aided by this sort of case. There is perhaps an initial attraction to the view that such a being really is benefited and harmed by her desires being fulfilled and thwarted, respectively. Nonetheless, I believe that the source of the attraction is illicit. The picture we tend to have is that of an individual desperately wanting to feel good from the inside but continually being repelled and, as a result, feeling frustrated, angry, and despondent. But of course, this interior life is precluded under our working assumption that the individual lacks the capacity for any phenomenology. If we force ourselves to preclude any such interior reaction to the inevitable thwarting of the desires for a good internal life, then the attraction to this picture is greatly undermined. To help facilitate this intuition, imagine the creation of a robot programmed with the desire for pleasurable interior life. Does one really believe that we should judge that this robot would be made better off were his program modified to the extent that his desire for pleasure (a desire which is inevitably frustrated) is replaced by the desire not to feel pain (a desire which is inevitably satisfied)?

Let us now return to our original case, wherein we reflect upon individuals with the capacity for sentient experience, although incapable of forming desires. Frequently, we are told that there are actual examples of such individuals. The usual candidates offered to manifest these dual characteristics are (normal) human infants and (some) nonhuman animals.[10] These examples provide the experientialist with a bonanza. If we do accept the fact that these two groups really contain phenomenological creatures without the capacity to form desires, it is still surely an iconoclastic intuition that would consign them to the ranks of the morally disenfranchisable. Assuming one was convinced of an infant's incapability of forming desires, would a mother be acting irrationally by requesting anesthesia for her daughter during an operation? Surely we are diminishing the welfare of a dog by mercilessly beating it, even if the dog is incapable of desiring that the beating be stopped. The point is that under the assumption that the capacity to form desires is a more sophisticated and later-developing ability than the capacity for sentient experience, the enormously powerful intuition is that the latter, alone, suffices for considerability. If an individual is suffering great pain, but by virtue of some artificial or natural factors cannot form desires about his interior life, it appears perverse not to think of such an individual as having his life being made worse off. What must be kept in mind is that in having the painful subjective experience, the individual is *bothered by* or suffers through the experience, and that being bothered is a state that does not require any desires. Undoubtedly, in most situations, this state of suffering is accompanied by a desire to rid oneself of that state, but this is quite distinct from thinking that the constitution of the state requires a desire (of some sort) concerning it. The inability to form desires about his phenomenological condition does not lessen his agony, nor does it seem to undermine the justification for viewing him as a moral patient.

(IX)

We have found that the essentially relational character of the desire theory can be exploited. Since the sole criterion for welfare modification is a function of the satisfactions and frustrations of an individual's desires, there is, in general, no need for any intrinsic or psychological change in the agent. We have provided thought experiments—perhaps most dramatically in the case of posthumous benefit and harm—that show the serious liabilities of such a theory. There is a special case in which the satisfaction and frustration of desires does lead to intrinsic changes in the agent. This is when the content of the desire is some hedonic state. This special case provides the desire theorist with an intriguing opportunity. No longer encumbered by the generally extrinsic nature of her theory, if the desire theorist could provide persuasive reasons for understanding well-being in these special circumstances as being a function of the satisfaction/frustration of desires, we would, at minimum, have good reasons for restricting the scope of experientialism. Indeed, contingent upon the nature of these reasons, we might ultimately opt for abdicating experientialism and siding with the desire theory.

We devised some thought experiments that were intended to test this suggestion. Immediately, however, we were confronted by the conceptualist, a neutral observer to this debate, who suggested that there is a conceptual or necessary connection between the capacities for sentient experience and forming desires. Since our thought experiments presumed that the relationship between these capacities was contingent—that, more specifically, the capacity for sentience did not require the capacity to form desires—the conceptualist effectively challenged the propriety of our methodology. We argued that the conceptualist does not have sufficiently strong reasons for overcoming the widespread presumption, a presumption implicit in the arguments of many philosophers, that it is not necessary that a phenomenological individual have desires, let alone that she have desires of a certain sort toward, respectively, unpleasant and pleasant phenomenologies. Thus, the thought experiments are viable and, as it works out, hinder the desire theorist's cause. The desire theory, be it in its typical extrinsic mode or its uncommon intrinsic mode, incurs problems not replicated in experientialism.

Let us turn now to the perfectionist theory of well-being.

3

Perfectionism

(I)

Let us return to the Nozick/Kane thought experiments and remind ourselves that they contain the seeds for a theory of welfare distinct not
only from experientialism but from the desire account as well. I have
argued at some length that, although the figure of the experience machine may be successful in showing that nonexperiential items matter to
us or have value for us, the somewhat natural inclination to thereby
adopt a desire theory of welfare, a theory that tells us that the valuable
is made valuable in virtue of our desires, should be resisted. The "perfectionist theory of welfare" or, more simply, "perfectionism," removes
the constitutive power from desires and replaces it with, *at most*, a merely
identificatory efficacy. Although examination of our desires may provide
a good, or perhaps even infallible, indication of what items have value
for us, the desires, themselves, have no efficacy in conferring value. What
makes us better and worse off does not benefit or harm us *because* we
desire those items that do, in fact, affect our well-being. Moreover, the
power to makes us better or worse off does not derive from the fact that
we experience those items in any particular way. As opposed to experientialism, those items that make our lives better do not do so in virtue
of the pleasant phenomenologies associated with them, nor do the items
that harm us owe their detrimental qualities to the fact that they feel bad
"from the inside." This is not to say that a perfectionist view of well-
being precludes experiences from the list of those things that can enhance
or diminish our welfare. Nor does it preclude the contents of our desires
from such a list. What perfectionism denies, and this is what essentially
distinguishes it from experientialism and the desire theory, is that value
is a function of either what we feel from the inside or what we desire.

To this point the characterization of perfectionism has been contrastive and negative. What we need from perfectionism is an answer to the metaphysical question: What makes those items of value that perfectionism claims are valuable, valuable? Alternatively, what plays the role in perfectionism that the satisfaction and frustration of desires and pleasant and unpleasant phenomenologies play, respectively, in the desire theory and experientialism? In answer to this, perfectionism claims that there are certain items, the possession of some of which make their possessors better off and the possession of others of which diminish their recipients' well-being, where this welfare modification occurs in virtue of the nature of the items themselves. There are, then, items which by their very nature are good to possess, and items which by their very nature are bad to possess. The inherently good items are analogous both to the experientialist's feeling good from the inside and the desire theorist's satisfied desire; the inherently bad items are analogous both to the experientialist's feeling bad from the inside and the desire theorist's frustrated desire. Just as the experientialist has no answer to what makes feeling good from the inside welfare-enhancing and the desire theorist has no further explanation as to why a satisfied desire makes its possessor better off, the perfectionist has no answer as to why those properties that make one better off do so.

Perfectionist values are independent of any personal psychology. Thus, for example, if an individual does not desire a particular positive perfectionist value (assuming the specific form of perfectionism allows this discrepancy to exist), the individual is, nonetheless, better off. Similarly, if an individual who was aware of possessing a positive perfectionist value was made to feel poorly from the inside because of this realization, the agent would, again, still be made better off. In fact—and this will be exploited later—there is no necessary connection between being made better and worse off and having any psychological capacities whatsoever. There is nothing in the thesis of perfectionism that prohibits individuals who lack both the capacity to form desires and the capacity for interior life from being made better and worse off. Obviously, what is of key significance here is what properties the particular perfectionist holds as welfare-modifying. If the properties selected do not require any psychological life, then the psychologically deprived can have a well-being and so can have their careers enhanced or diminished; if the properties are of the sort that only the psychologically capable can have, then only the psychologically endowed can be subjects for benefit and harm.

Although the Nozick/Kane thought experiments suggest a desire-based epistemology for a perfectionist theory of well-being, there is nothing in perfectionism per se that compels this commitment. A perfectionist may claim that an individual can tell which items are welfare-enhancing and which are welfare-diminishing by introspection. So, for example, if an individual feels good from the inside when thinking of a particular perfectionist candidate, we may have some degree of confidence that this item really is a perfectionist value. Or a perfectionist may simply hold an intuitive epistemology; he may just claim that the intuition that a particular candidate for value really is a perfectionist value lends a certain degree of confidence that the candidate is of real value. But notice that regardless of the epistemic device used (desires, phenomenology, intuition, etc.), and regardless of how tight the fit between the implementation of the tool and its actual success, two important commitments of perfectionism are not compromised. First, the items that are objectively worthy are objectively worthy for all who possess it, whatever their particular psychologies or intuitions happen to suggest. Second, even if the access to these values is limited to certain individuals—only if, for example, people with the capacity to have desires are capable of discovering which items are perfectionist values—this, by itself, does not mean that only individuals with this psychological capability can be subjects of benefits and harms. A perfectionist can consistently hold that only the psychologically endowed can have access to value without claiming that only the psychologically capable can have welfares. As we mentioned, perfectionists may limit their values so that only those with desires (phenomenology, intuition) can have a well-being, but this restriction would be derived from the nature of the perfectionist value itself and not in virtue of the type of epistemic access privy to a selected group.

The perceived advantages peculiar to using desires as the epistemic link to value reside in their alleged objectivity and tangibility. An individual's desires can be more definitively expressed than a person's feelings or intuitions, and in a like vein have, unlike intuitions and feelings, a stability fitting to an intimate relationship with something as important as values. The use of desires, alone, may be seen as imputing a cognitive and therefore scientifically respectable avenue to knowledge about value. We can debate the rationality of desires, where similar conversations about interior experiences and intuitions seem, at best, to be strained. Although some recent works on the passions or emotions argue otherwise, the traditional view of feelings is that they form the irrational, or at least arational, part of the psyche. If the bond with value were to be established with something antithetical to reason, something that is not subject to reasonable debate and modification, many might believe (perhaps wrongly) that the moral significance of benefiting and harming persons is eviscerated.

In fact, I find all these independent attempts to justify desires rather than other psychological elements as the best indicator of value quite suspicious. A more dependable, though admittedly more plebeian, course is simply to investigate whether persons' desires, more frequently than their intuitions or phenomenologies, actually pick out what the perfectionist identifies as the correct values. On this account, desires are seen as the favored access because they work, and not in virtue of some putative advantage in objectivity and scientific respectability that they own relative to intuitions and phenomenology.

(II)

Perfectionists have not spoken univocally about which items have perfectionist status, but it is fair to suggest that beauty, knowledge, and moral sensitivity are representative of welfare-enhancing properties, while ugliness, ignorance, and moral insensitivity are examples of welfare-diminishing items. (In beauty and its complement, ugliness, we have examples of perfectionist values that do not pertain solely to individuals with inscapes.) Experiential perfectionist candidates deserve a special mention. It is a rare perfectionist who does not believe that (some) enjoyable experiences are welfare-enhancing; that is, feeling some pleasures is a good. Regarding this perfectionist value, the distinction between perfectionism—a completely objective theory of welfare—and experientialism—a completely subjective theory of welfare—collapses. There is no difference in portraying the joyful experiences of an individual as objectively welfare-enhancing and describing this phenomenon as subjective. This is because the objective nature of an enjoyable experience *just is* its subjective feel, at least on the commonsense, nonfunctional account of phenomenology in which the experientialist has been operating. The perfectionist account of enjoyment and suffering is therefore quite different from the desire theorist's account in which the conflation with experientialism did not occur. While the perfectionist and experientialist offer the same answer as to why a pleasurable experience benefits its possessor—it is in the nature of the experience, or, equivalently, it is just a fundamental property of the experience—the desire theorist suggests that the pleasurable experience is beneficial because it is desired. Thus, a perfectionist who believes that the only welfare-enhancing item is enjoyable experience and that the only welfare-diminishing item is unpleasant experience is an experientialist. In effect, then, a limiting case of perfectionism is experientialism. Similarly, a perfectionist, in theory, may believe that the only welfare-enhancing item is the fulfillment of desires and the only welfare-diminishing item is the frustration of desires.

In this form of perfectionism, it merges with the desire theory. Although experientialism and the desire theory can be viewed as limiting cases of perfectionism, and so the moral domains of one (or both) of the former theories can coincide with the latter, it would be a most Pickwickian perfectionist who was found to be reducible to either an experientialist or desire theorist. After all, one of the motivating factors, if not *the* motivating factor, driving perfectionism is the idea that, although satisfying desires and having enjoyable experiences may well be two of the ways in which individuals are made better off, there are many others that are completely independent of both an individual's phenomenology and desires.

(III)

Perfectionists may begin to marshal support for their theory of welfare by illustrating what they see as a common problem of experientialism and the desire theory—what we may call the "problem of aberrance." When applied to experientialism, this problem expresses itself, at times, in the counterintuitiveness of countenancing the experience of certain pleasures as welfare-enhancing and of certain pains as welfare-diminishing when these phenomenologies are products of "perverse" sources. Because experientialism is a purely subjective and intrinsic theory of well-being, no weight is placed on the origin of these experiences. We have already referred to the example of Hitler, who derived great pleasure from the realization that thousands of Jews were murdered in gas chambers at Auschwitz and Buchenwald. Enjoyment garnered through pedophilia provides a second instance of aberrance. The perfectionist intuition is not difficult to comprehend; the idea of the wicked being benefited, as they would be under the auspices of experientialism, seems a result too repulsive to permit. I have earlier tried to explain away this natural reaction, effectively saying that the reaction is an expression of our anger at injustice, which *assumes* that we do think of these sadists as being better off; but, of course, this explanation may not deter the perfectionists. They may, for example, be convinced that Plato succeeded in showing that it is impossible for evildoers to benefit, and so the offense is not merely to our conception of desert but inimical to logic as well.

The problem of aberrance, when applied to the desire theory, takes a similar form. The notion that, in satisfying the perverse desires of a Hitler, a theory of well-being credits these monsters as having their lives enhanced strikes many perfectionists as a *reductio* of the position. In fact, the perfectionist may claim that a theory should yield the diametrically opposed result; anyone who has such desires satisfied or receives pleasure from recognition of such states of affairs should be evaluated as being worse off.[1]

Consider Evelyn, a mother of two who shares in the ordinary desire for her children's successful, happy lives. She has the fervent wish that her children lead healthy and productive existences. As luck would have it, her children live just the sorts of lives that Evelyn hoped they would, but Evelyn never becomes aware of her children's future. Perhaps, due to some strange circumstances, she loses touch with her children and is unable to reestablish contact. Furthermore, we are to assume that this interruption in her contact with her children does not bring her any sorrow, pain, or discomfort; there is no experiential contribution. The desire theorist invites us to consider, as her theory implies, that Evelyn's life, despite the fact that she never becomes aware of her desires being satisfied, has been enhanced.

Compare this scenario with one involving Evelyn's twin sister Eve. Eve is much like Evelyn and, coincidentally, finds herself in a similar family situation. The relevant difference, for our purposes, between Evelyn and Eve is that unlike her sibling, Eve desires that her (Eve's) two children live unhappy and unproductive lives. Undoubtedly a minority preference, yet still one that is not only possible, but is actualized many times in our society. Let us further stipulate that (1) Eve's desire, just like Evelyn's, is satisfied—Eve's children endure rather horrific lives; and (2) Eve, just like Evelyn, continues her life completely unaware that her fervent desire has been fulfilled. The proposed dilemma is obvious. For the same reasons that Evelyn is said to have her welfare advanced, the desire theorist is committed to Eve's welfare having been enhanced by the confluence of her desire and the world's happenings. The perfectionist finds this assessment perversely counterintuitive. If one evaluates the welfare of both Evelyn and Eve as being modified at all, there is a powerful perfectionist intuition that Eve's life was made worse, not better. And if this is so, the only explanation would appear constituted by the fact that the content of Eve's desire, in and of itself, has disvalue.

In fact, there are cases that shade off from aberrant ones that seem to pose problems particular to the desire theory. If Sue were unwittingly hypnotized (apparently, this is possible) and as a result formed the novel desire for chocolate cake, there is great hesitation in thinking that the satisfaction of this desire enhances her well-being. The intuition that grounds this antidesire theory sentiment is that a desire formed in this way is alien to Sue. She is a passive vessel regarding the desire, rather than being, as in normal situations, an active participant. (There is arguably no analogous case in experientialism; pleasures hypnotically induced still seem beneficial, a verdict that is confirmed by our self-interested acceptance of an intermittent use of the experience machine.) It is true that this assessment changes over time. If Sue reflectively endorses this desire, we may eventually come to think that its satisfaction really does benefit her. Nevertheless, at least immediately, and for some indeterminate amount of time after forming the desire, it seems plausible to claim that neither its satisfaction nor frustration have much to do with Sue's welfare, for it has very little to do with Sue.

Or consider the case of Sarah, a desire theorist, who sets out to improve her welfare. She reasons that since the welfare of her life entirely depends upon the quantity and quality of her desires (that is, roughly, the number and depth of her desires), her goal is best accomplished by developing as many satisfiable, deeply held desires as she can muster. So, for example, although previously she has not had the slightest desire to travel overseas, she tries to get herself to deeply desire to travel to Italy and Israel, two countries she is reasonably certain she will be able to visit. In this effort, she reads travel guides, asks for information from the Rome and Tel Aviv chambers of commerce, and takes classes in Italian and Hebrew. To avoid peripheral issues, we make the simplifying assumption that any desires that are frustrated as a result of Sarah's endeavor must be few and weak.

But where precisely is the problem supposed to reside? The desire theorist may point out that it seems as though Sarah is doing to herself just what her loving and caring parents would do to her when Sarah was just a child. We can assume that at an appropriately tender age Sarah had no desire to hear classical music or become acquainted with the works of Rembrandt and Da Vinci. It was not, of course, that she had the desire to foreclose these experiences from her life's repertoire; it was that she had no desires of either sort, these types of desires generally being formulable only at a later, more mature stage of life. Nonetheless, Sarah's parents, believing that forming these desires would make Sarah better off, lovingly attempted to inculcate these desires, desires that her parents justifiably believed were easily satisfiable. If we can make sense of Sarah's parents' attempts as attempts to improve the welfare of their daughter, we should be able to make equally good sense of an older Sarah's trying to do the same thing for herself.

The perfectionist, however, will be quick to point out that the loving parents do not want their daughter to have just any desires—or just any kind of pleasure, for that matter—but rather desires of, or pleasures from, appropriate sources only. The perfectionist will suggest that the parents must already believe that the appreciation of the works of Da Vinci and Rembrandt has value independent of the desires and pleasures that Sarah comes to develop. It is in virtue of the parents' belief that appreciation of certain artwork is, in itself, a welfare-enhancing attribute that they wish to inculcate the desires for such art in their daughter. Having done so, they may have reasonable expectations that Sarah's desires will evolve in similar ways; she will mature into the type of person who wants to view Tintorettos and forsake Bernsteins. If so, the parents will feel quite fortunate. Sarah's desires, shaped at an early age, have aimed at what is good, and their satisfaction will enhance Sarah's life. Sarah and her parents might have thought of themselves as desire theorists, but they were mistaken. Their story abets, rather than hinders, the case for perfectionism.

We may summarize this impetus for a perfectionist theory of welfare in a picture. We are to reflect upon an altruistic deity confronted with a decision concerning the attributes to parcel out among his human subjects. For reasons that need not be examined, the deity has no knowledge of either the desires or the interior life of the creatures. He can supply or neglect to endow these subjects with knowledge, art appreciation, and moral sensitivity. The perfectionist urges that we believe that this deity, acting solely from the motivation to make his subjects as well off as possible, would confer these qualities upon them, thus demonstrating these items are all inherently valuable.

Of course, experientialists and desire theorists may emphasize that, understood as an attempt to persuade, the narrative is a matter of rhetoric and not argument. The desire theorist, for example, will feel no compunction in announcing that he perceives the act of altruism to be misplaced. Without the deity's knowing and taking into account what desires his human subjects may have, there is no reason to believe that endowing them with moral sensitivity, or any other quality for that matter, will make them better off. Similarly, the experientialist will question how the creature's life is enhanced if she receives no pleasure from their adoption. These two theorists suggest a competing picture. A deity who bestows knowledge and aesthetic and moral sensitivity upon those sentient creatures who both desire not to have these attributes and who would feel better from the inside were these qualities never conferred upon them would be characterized as malevolent. To these theorists, an altruistic deity would have consulted his subjects' mental lives prior to any divine dispensation.

I do not mean to suggest that the motivation for perfectionism derives entirely from a response to perceived flaws in both experientialism and the desire theory. As with these other two theories, a strong pretheoretical component for perfectionism exists. Most of us believe that there are certain properties—virtues—and other properties—vices—that are, respectively, good and bad to possess. Common examples of the former group are courage, kindness, compassion, and wisdom; common examples of the latter are cowardice, meanness, insensitivity, and ignorance. Many of us believe that the possession of these virtues/vices makes us better off/worse off regardless of either their effect on our interior mental state or their satisfaction of one of our desires. These properties, then, are conceived as having inherent value, value independent of our affective or conative lives.

Not all proponents of virtues think of them as inherently valuable. Rather, some believe that they do not supply us with an ultimate explanation of why they have the prudential efficacy that they do. So, for example, some argue that a particular property is a virtue (as opposed to a vice or some neutral property) because individuals desire to behave in certain ways. According to this explication of virtue, were individuals desirous of acting meanly rather than kindly, then meanness and not kindness would be a virtue, and being mean as opposed to being kind would make the individual better off. If one articulated an account of the virtues and vices along these lines, as instrumental to an individual's benefit and harm in virtue of their relationships to desires, she would be a desire theorist and not a perfectionist. Other nonperfectionist accounts of virtues and vices are easy to concoct.

Thus, a virtue theorist, one who prescribes behavior or makes normative judgments of behavior in terms of virtues and vices, may or may not be a perfectionist. The modest fact that some advocate a perfectionist understanding of virtues and vices exemplifies the point that the motivation for a perfectionist view of welfare is not exhausted by favorably comparing it to experientialism and the desire theory.

(IV)

A propitious strategy for assessing the viability of perfectionism is to concentrate on those perfectionist values that can pertain to individuals who lack both the capacities to desire and to have a phenomenology. To focus on these perfectionist values, what may be called "nonmental" perfectionist values will, I believe, prove useful in much the same way that concentration on those desires that had no influence on an individual's conscious mental life proved illuminating when we discussed the desire theory of welfare. Recall that when we discussed those desires whose satisfaction or frustration went unnoticed by their agents, we were able to set into relief the extrinsic nature of desires and provide some especially problematic scenarios for the desire theory that culminated in the problems associated with posthumous benefits and harms. In similar fashion, a discussion of nonmental perfectionist values is an excellent arena in which to test the mettle of the perfectionist theory of well-being. Since perfectionism tells us that certain items are inherently valuable and some are inherently disvaluable, that the possession of certain attributes modifies an individual's welfare independently of an individual's desires or phenomenology, then there is no a priori exclusion of the nonmental from the ranks of the morally considerable. And, in fact, as has been mentioned, most perfectionists implicitly confirm this when they count among those valuable properties beauty and organic unity, two properties that certainly apply to the insentient and, in the case of beauty, even to the inanimate. To the extent that the perfectionist persuades us that nonmental subjects can be made better and worse off, that these subjects can be characterized as having welfares, the perfectionist cause is immeasurably helped. After all, if we are convinced that we should view these nonmental individuals as moral patients, then, since these individuals are precluded from patienthood by both experientialists and desire theorists, we have a very strong reason for abdicating both of these latter views. On the other hand, a failure for the perfectionist to make a case for these types of individuals to own welfares would be quite damaging, as it would lead the perfectionist into some ad hoc restrictions on her theory. It would surely be quite coincidental that the only permissible perfectionist values were those that attached to mental subjects unless the mentality of the subjects (presumably in the form of desires and phenomenology) was playing the pivotal role in the theory. And, if this were the case, there is strong reason to believe that the value of the quality is situated, not in its inherent nature as the perfectionist would have us believe, but rather in its relationship to either the individual's desires or in the phenomenology of the agent. We would be led by a preponderance of the evidence to either the desire theory or experientialism. The additional benefit of using the nonmental as test cases for perfectionism is that we need not be concerned about distinguishing whether something is beneficial in virtue of satisfying a desire or independently of it, or distinguishing whether an item is valuable because it provides pleasure or it provides pleasure in virtue of the agent recognizing its value. If we limit our discussion to nonmental subjects, subjects without both the capacities to desire and to feel, all of these complicating issues are circumvented.

The most recent and most popular manifestation of this natural consequence of perfectionism comes in the form of "deep ecology," the thesis that endows some insentient parts of nature, along with nature's sentient occupants, with moral patienthood. We will concentrate on what undoubtedly constitute the best-case subjects for deep ecology by focusing (although not exclusively) on living but insentient parts of nature. Many people find it initially more plausible to attribute welfares to insentient but living trees and plants than, say, to presidential campaigns. If the case against countenancing the living but insentient as members of the morally considerable is powerful, it is highly unlikely that perfectionist arguments for the insentient and inanimate have much chance for success.

Although the precise constitution of the domain of moral patienthood varies among deep ecologists, we will take them, as a matter of definition, to adhere to the view that there are some insentient items in the universe that are moral patients and that their inclusion is warranted not by any instrumentality that they may have relative to experiential beings, but rather by virtue of possessing some objective (i.e., perfectionist) properties. Deep ecology, then, as I am understanding it, is a sort of pure objectivist or perfectionist position. There are certain mind-independent qualities that are possessed by some of the insentient world that suffice for their moral patienthood; there are segments of the insentient world that can be benefited and harmed. Deep ecologists claim that there are certain individuals which, although lacking the capacity to enjoy, suffer, and desire (when these psychological states are understood in their literal manifestations), can be made better and worse off. As a result, since human beings are, in general, capable of enhancing and diminishing the welfare of these items, humans have direct, prima facie obligations to these entities.

Deep ecology should be starkly distinguished from the much less exciting and inaptly named "shallow ecology." Shallow ecologists believe that humans can have "indirect" moral obligations to the insentient world. What this relatively pedestrian view amounts to is that we ought to act toward the insentient in certain ways, not because of anything special about the inherent nature of that part of the world, but rather because such behaviors will have beneficial or harmful effects on humans or other sentient beings. We ought not to chop down the tree, for example, not because in so doing we are causing any harm to the tree, but rather because in so doing, we would bring grief to its owner or those who make use of it. Shallow ecologists, unlike deep ecologists, do not believe that nonsentient individuals literally have welfares, and so, to this extent at least, shallow ecology can be viewed as espousing a position regarding well-being that is compatible with either experientialism or the desire theory.

A poignant example of the mischief that can arise if this distinction is conflated is provided by those who proffer Kant as a great champion for the rights of nonhuman animals.[2] Kant clearly believed that humans have indirect duties (obligations) toward animals, including, for example, the duty not to shoot a dog who is no longer of service to her owner. To violate this obligation is morally wrong, not because the dog is a moral patient, but rather because such behavior inclines us to "harden our hearts" in actions with fellow human beings who *are* moral patients. Kant's concern was that such treatment of the nonhuman might incline us to take human life cavalierly; the dog's value is solely instrumental.[3] One can see that, using the notion of indirect duties employed by the shallow ecologist, virtually anything can have moral value, for a scenario can be invented wherein some human would be either benefited or harmed by some interaction with any part of the insentient world.[4] Deep ecologists are putting forward an idea much more extreme than the rather tepid one proffered by the shallow ecologists.

Deep ecology can be viewed as an idea whose time has come. One might view the history of ethics as, in part, widening the circle of those who merit moral consideration. Aristotle, for all his greatness, saw moral patienthood as attributable in full measure only to Greeks in the city-state. Barbarians, slaves, and women, let alone nonhuman animals and insentient nature, necessarily lacked the requirements for complete moral status. African-Americans, even in the allegedly enlightened United States, have only recently been seen to deserve full-fledged moral status, and this, many would argue, is an ideal that still has only theoretical and not practical existence. The consideration of nonhuman animals as moral patients, although a passing idea in Western civilization for two millennia, has only in the last generation received anything like widespread support. Perhaps, then, many find the notion of deep ecology attractive in part, at least, because they view it as a natural, perhaps even historically inevitable, unfolding of a pregnant ethical past.

Speculating about the genealogy of deep ecology is one thing; examining the arguments for its plausibility is quite another. It would serve us well to begin by considering Paul Taylor's brand of deep ecology, which, paradoxical as it may initially seem, makes heavy use of Aristotelian notions.[5] Taylor believes that all living individuals, being "teleological centers," have their own welfares and so can be benefited and harmed. Individuals such as particular trees and plants are teleological centers in that their "internal functioning as well as their external activities are all goal-oriented, having the constant tendency to maintain the organism's existence through time and enable it successfully to perform those biological operations whereby it reproduces its kind and continually adapts to changing environmental events and conditions" (Taylor, 121–22). It is not a large leap from the notion of organic unity, a quality deemed inherently valuable by philosophers of an earlier age, to Taylor's central concept of being teleologically centered. In both cases it is fair to view the properties as paradigmatically perfectionist in that their possession requires neither a phenomenological nor desirous subject and their possessor automatically becomes morally enfranchised. To act against an individual's realization of its good (i.e., its natural fulfillment of its teleology) is to harm it, and to act in a way that furthers the realization of its good is to benefit that individual. Since harming an individual is, prima facie, morally wrong and benefiting an individual is, prima facie, morally right (or at least morally permissible), we human beings can engage morally with parts of living, although insentient, nature.

Some may begin to have misgivings about Taylor's account when it is applied to paradigmatic teleological centers—normal adult human beings. In Taylor's view, it is natural to suppose that pain would be harmful in virtue of, and to the extent that, its possessor's internal and external functionings were being interfered with. Insofar as the suffering impaired a human's ability to adapt and cope with its environment, the suffering is legitimately viewed as a harm. It is hardly surprising that Taylor, an Aristotelian, views pains as functions and so sees their badness to their possessors in terms of their presence's preventing the normal operations of the agent. But many find a far simpler and more commonsensical explanation of the badness of pain: pains hurt. This, of course, is not to deny that suffering tends to impair the functioning of a human, that it tends to inhibit its teleological sojourn, but it is to suggest that Taylor's teleological account of benefits and harms, at least insofar as this phenomenon is concerned, missituates the badness of pain. If we subtract the malfunctionings typically (but perhaps not always) associated with pain, pain is still a harm to us. We should surely believe that we are worse off suffering excruciating pain even were we guaranteed that our abilities to adapt to our environment would not be adversely affected. Moreover, it seems that it is in virtue of the way that pains feel (and here we can forgo the question of whether the phenomenologies associated with pains are essential) that they interfere with our normal operations.[6] Taylor's account, as is the case for all functionalist accounts, seems better suited for nonphenomenological mental states. It is far more reasonable, for example, to understand the harm of depression (insofar as it is understood *sans* phenomenological component) as a function of its hindering our coping and adaptive behaviors. But if pain were added to the depression without any further diminution of adaptive abilities, we would surely be even more greatly harmed, an increase that is left unaccountable in Taylor's theory. Taylor's suggestion might be helpful in some evolutionary account of why it is that we feel pleasure and pain, in that the recognition of these sensations aids in the reproduction of our species, but to characterize pain's harmfulness without essential reference to how it feels seems to be missing a large and obvious boat.

A second worry revolves around the correct relationship between being alive and being teleologically centered. Taylor tells us that life requires a teleological center, but there is at least a reasonable question whether there actually is this reputed necessary relationship. If there can be life—more pointedly, experiential and desirous life—without such individuals' owning teleological centers, and we still would attribute moral considerability to such individuals, then Taylor has failed to supply us with a necessary condition of moral standing. Obviously, much depends upon definition, and it is fair to say that no definition has met with unanimous approval. Kenneth Sayre, whose account is typical, tells us that "the typifying mark of a living system appears to be its persistent state of low entropy, sustained by metabolic processes for accumulating energy, and maintained in equilibrium with its environment by home-ostatic feed-back processes."[7] As a definition this will not do, since the notion of a metabolic process already incorporates the idea of a living organism or living cells. This failure reinforces the commonplace that "life" is extremely difficult to satisfactorily define. (A perusal of your dictionary will confirm this.) This makes Taylor's claim difficult to assess. Nonetheless, it strikes me as excessive to make teleologies a requirement for all living things. Although I will not press the point, the requirement would appear not to be conceptual. Not only do I apparently possess the notion of an ateleological living individual, but I have no difficulty with imbuing it with capacities for both sentient experience and desires. This individual would be morally enfranchised by our two previous theories. Only those with powerful pretheoretical functionalist intuitions would likely find Taylor's assertion very plausible at the outset.

Must all teleological centers have life? There would seem to be no principled reason why robots will not someday exist with the capability to act in goal-oriented, adaptive ways—even with reproductive abilities. If we assume that these robots need not (perhaps even cannot) have an interior, mental life, then Taylor, in opposition to experientialists and desire theorists, must allow for such beings' literally having welfares, since it is the presence of teleology and not of life that accounts for patient-hood. One might be uneasy with this consequence, and not, I think, essentially because the robotic career is artificially produced. To test this suggestion, let us supply the robot with both a phenomenological and desirous life. Under these circumstances, I believe our resistance to the idea of an artificially created but welfared individual is greatly mitigated. To buttress this idea, consider whether our moral enfranchisement of others would change if we were to discover that what we believed were biologically produced creatures were really artificially created individuals. In assessing what our moral attitudes would be, it is important that our beliefs about these creatures' sentience not be altered; we still are firmly convinced that these individuals can both feel and desire. As an admittedly rough but I think helpful analogy, consider how a lifelong creationist would morally consider humans were she to become convinced that evolutionary theory, a theory that she admits is irreconcilable with her previous theistic beliefs, is the true account of the origin of the species. I doubt very much that she would now believe that none of us (including herself) deserve moral consideration. The point is that the source of the properties that confer moral patienthood upon individuals is not of paramount importance. Be they artificially or naturally created, mechanistically or biologically produced, what is of prime significance is that the individuals actually possess those properties that are believed to be the ones that confer moral patienthood. If we believe that the insentient robot lacks moral standing but acquires it when imbued with a phenomenological and desirous nature, Taylor's teleologically centered version of deep ecology suffers.

I have tried to show that the assertion of identity that Taylor advocates between teleologically centered and living individuals is tenuous. Insofar as we allow there to be members of one type that are not members of the other, moral patienthood appears to track upon the mental (i.e., experiential and desirous) aspects of the individual in question and not the attribute of being teleologically centered. But there are far more ominous considerations, some of which challenge not only Taylor's particular version of deep ecology but all others. Deep ecology is a programme that is plagued by deep problems, problems that suggest that the enterprise should be abandoned rather than paraded as a more inclusive, and therefore more enlightened, theory of the morally considerable.

(v)

To introduce the nature of these pervasive concerns, it is helpful to recall Hume's treatment of causality. For Hume, the sole objective contribution to causation was the existence of constantly conjoined events. That the first event caused (determined, necessitated) the second event was not some objective occurrence, not some event that happened "out there" in the external world, but was rather a consequence of the idiosyncratic way in which our human minds operate. Our minds are constructed such that, after observing an indefinite number of constantly conjoined events, we form the impression, from which we derive the idea, that the subsequent event must occur after the antecedent event. Visiting Martians—intelligent, percipient individuals whose minds worked differently from humans'—would lack no information about the world if they could not fathom the notion of causation. They would, however, have an informational failing if they could not recognize the universal succession of certain pairs of events. This is neither a denial of causation nor a skepticism toward it, but an explication of it; causation, to Hume, is to be understood as a subjective (mind-dependent) facet of the world. Hume's causation was an anthropocentric projection rather than an independent item of the world's inventory awaiting discovery.

The challenge to Taylor is to explain why we should not conceive of the teleologically centered in much the same way, albeit for different reasons, that Hume conceived of causation. Perhaps somewhat more pointedly, the demand of Taylor is to provide us with "objective facts," facts that reside "in the nature of things" that warrant our appellations of "goals" and "adaptations." Although the analogy with Hume's account of causation should be taken in a limited way, the figure of the visiting Martians applies. Just as there is no informational failure regarding causation if these Martians omit anything but the observed constant conjunction of events from their report, there is likewise nothing lacking were the Martians to include the changes that objects undergo following certain antecedent conditions without mention of met and thwarted goals. Although it is natural enough to account for this anthropocentrism in terms of evolutionary forces acting upon our minds, the challenge need not incorporate the psychological inevitability that accompanied Hume's explication of causation. It is enough to indicate that the way we mark certain chapters of the lifetimes of trees and plants, and, as a result, discriminate benefits and harms to the insentient individuals, is not based on discoveries of objective facts in nature. If this rather deflationary account of teleology is accepted, the cause of many deep ecologists, of whom Taylor is a prime representative, is undermined. Rather than conceiving of welfares as being independent from human activities, they are best appreciated as mere dependencies upon the vagaries of human interests.

Consider the life of a tree. Among the objective, nonanthropocentric facts about the tree are that it grows, that it requires water and other nutrients to grow, and that upon receiving the proper food and care it is better able to resist insect infestation. These facts play the analogue to Hume's universally successive events; were the Martians to omit mention of these sorts of things from their report, they would be guilty of failing to supply a complete account about the nature of our trees. But just as Hume understood the *must* that persons incorporate into the notion of causation as representing nothing that has objective, independent existence, the current suggestion is that the teleological ideas of goal-oriented and adaptive behavior are nothing more than anthropocentric projections onto a world that objectively possesses only regularly successive events. The conceptualization of some of these events as goals and others as adaptations is predominantly a function of human conventionality, a matter, in other words, of invention rather than discovery. We may, for various purposes, or even perhaps in virtue of a species-specific trick that our minds play on us, identify certain stages of a tree's career as salient. Nonetheless, there is no justification, as far as the inherent nature of the tree is concerned, to attribute a special significance to any of them. Humean Darwinism supersedes Taylorian Aristotelianism.

It is true that if and only if acorns are properly watered and nourished will they develop into oak trees. Certain events regularly follow earlier events, and that, as far as an objective picture of the world is concerned, is all there is to it. Martians who conceptualize the withered state of a tree as the tree's goal or final end are not blinded to what transpires in the world; the objective states of affairs argue in favor of neither their nor Taylor's position. With the consequence that contrary "teleologies" are equally confirmed, the whole notion of an objective teleology and the significant moral implications that are elicited become suspect.

The irony of the situation should not be lost. One of the major rallying cries of deep ecologists is the claim that their theory of well-being does away with an unwarranted human chauvinism. To view rationality, linguistic ability, and even the capacities to form desires and to have sentient experience as necessary conditions for moral enfranchisement manifests an arrogance concerning our cosmic importance. We—normal adult human beings—or those like us insofar as they share these qualities are not the only individuals who can be benefited and harmed. Deep ecologists see themselves as moral Copernicans, attempting to overthrow the deeply entrenched but nevertheless untenable view that only humans and their kind can be part of the moral sphere. Yet, if the Humean analogy is persuasive, some versions of deep ecology, exemplified by Taylor's account, rely upon an anthropocentrism that vitiates their theories. The suggestion is that conferring moral respectability onto individuals in virtue of their manifestations of goal-oriented and adaptive behavior is akin to endowing certain items with causal respectability under a Humean analysis of causation. Moral standing, like causal standing, should be earned through some properties inherent to the individuals involved and should not be a consequence of some contrived system of categorization.

None of this would prove particularly useful to the experientialist if her account of welfare were to succumb to the same anthropocentrism that plagues deep ecologists. In terms of our figure, experientialists must claim that our visiting Martians would, in fact, be omitting something of the world's inventory if their report neglected to mention the enjoyment and suffering experienced by certain Earthlings. There would be a factual incompleteness in their report mirroring the factual incompleteness of a report that failed to mention the constant conjunction of certain events. The critical issue is how the experientialist would argue for his claim that suffering and enjoyment are not to be construed as anthropocentric projections upon a world and so can satisfy a criterion for patienthood that Taylor's Aristotelian version of deep ecology (among others) fails to meet. And this invites the more general problem of establishing and justifying a criterion by which we can discriminate those qualities or attributes that are projections from our anthropocentric physiology and psychology from those that are objective properties of the world, properties whose existence is independent of any human perceptual or conceptual ability.

This is a daunting project, and let me straightforwardly admit that I have nothing like a complete and satisfying answer to this traditional dilemma. At best, the following tentative remarks may at least point toward something useful. Hume's case against the objectivity of causation presupposed an empiricist conception of knowledge; all we can ever justifiably claim to know must be ultimately derivable from sensory experience. When asked to closely scrutinize what we see when viewing a game of billiards, we can respond that our visual impressions are exhausted by balls moving and hitting other billiard balls, which in turn move. We see, in short, constantly conjoined events. There is no *must*, no necessity or determination, toward which we can point. Since we have no relevant visual impressions, and, more generally, no perceptual impressions whatsoever, causation is relegated to either mythical or fictive status. Choosing the latter, and working within a naturalistic framework, Hume had no choice but to explicate causation as a projective effect of a human mind.

As a second example, consider the debate over the objectivity (some may say "reality") of colors. Projectivists claim that colors are not components of the objective world but are merely the visual effects upon some sentient creatures that result from the interaction of light and sensory apparatus in an objectively colorless world. It just so happens that the way we are constructed makes configurations of colorless atoms and molecules appear green to us in certain circumstances. *Sub species aeternitatis*, colors have as little (objective) reality as Hume's necessity, and so our visiting Martians would be lacking nothing from their chronicle were they to admit, in virtue of owning different sense organs, to having seen no colors.

But not only would our Martian visitors not be demonstrating any informational failure by omitting the experiencing of either causation or colors, they *should* not, according to the projectivists, have anything of this sort in their reports. The world really does not contain causal relations between events and the world truly lacks colors. It is not as though the Martians, in virtue of the way their minds work, are missing something about the world; on the contrary, they are fortunate enough to have minds that permit them to conceive and perceive the world as it really is. Nevertheless, there is a sort of second-order informational failing on their part. Since the structure of their minds prevents them from experiencing causation as Hume claims we do and also prevents them from experiencing colors, they cannot know, in a robust way,[8] what is (objectively) transpiring in us when we experience the anticipation of a subsequent event's being determined to follow an antecedent one or what is going on in us when we perceive green or blue.

Thus there is no reason to believe that subjectivity is not objective. Less cryptically, subjective experiences such as the Humean experience of causation or the perception of green may well be part and parcel of the objective world, just as much as the mass of a rock. Projectivists, I think, would agree. It is not what is "going on from the inside" whose ontic status is in question, but rather it is the content of these subjective states—the causal relations and colors—whose metaphysical status is being debated. In fact, I would go further. It would be difficult to understand the projectivist project if it did not implicitly assume that the subjective states themselves—the experiences of determination and the perception of green—were real, objective, nonprojective properties of individuals. After all, projection is presumably an objective property that individuals participate in, and so it would seem to require that the apparatus necessary for this process to take place—the seat of subjectivity or the mind—would also be an objective segment of the world.

For these reasons, I find it difficult to envision a powerful argument for the claim that suffering, something that occurs from the inside, is best viewed as an anthropocentric projection. While the projectivist renderings of causation and colors seem viable, although perhaps ultimately unconvincing, a similar strategy for suffering, the claim that suffering is objectively nothing other stimulations of c- and d-fibers (where this is intended to suggest that one can understand the nature of suffering without understanding what transpires from the inside), strikes me as a nonstarter. In making notes only of the neural stimulations without reference to the subjectivity, the Martians would be omitting some facet of the real, objective world.

This result conforms with prephilosophical thought. There are few of the vulgar who would suggest that enjoyment and suffering are items of invention rather than discovery. This result becomes even more philosophically palatable once it is recognized that it does not beg any questions against a materialist view of the mind, and indeed is consistent with such a theory. Materialism would identify experiences of suffering with certain neural states. If a Martian objective report were complete, it would include reference to this state of affairs, although it would not need to use the nomenclature of "neural state" any more than it would need to use the language of "suffering." To think otherwise is to confuse language (reference) with what the language is about (referents). Thus, the argument for the objective existence of suffering does not require that a complete inventory use the terminology of suffering in addition to the language of physical objects. If it eventuates that materialism is a correct theory of mind, either vocabulary can be used at the expense of the other without any sacrifice to objective exhaustiveness. In this regard, at least, there is no difference with other theoretical identities. If a streak of lightning is nothing other than a flow of electrons, a complete objective report of the world's inventory can be accomplished within one lexicon.

It must be admitted that this view is less tolerant of some specific versions of materialism. If we take eliminative materialism as the view that, literally, individuals do not suffer or enjoy, that these ways of being are not actual components of the world, but are, at best, illusions created for various causes and reasons, then we must reject eliminative materialism. This consequence, I must admit, does not fill me with great anguish (real or imagined). Some eliminative materialists have made similar nihilistic claims about beliefs, among other putative mental dispositions, and this has always struck me, as well as many other philosophers, as either self-defeating or an exercise in word play.[9]

(VI)

Lawrence Johnson, who subscribes to a view similar to Taylor's, observes that

> some things, particularly living things, do, in an important sense define themselves. John is a human being and can be harmed and benefited as such, however he might be regarded by others. This is not just a matter of how he regards himself. Any living being, whether or not self-conscious, has an identity, an integral identity, which mere objects and artifacts lack. I shall use the

term *self-identity* to indicate that what an entity is and what serves to maintain it is determined by its own nature. Now, if we cease to regard a tractor as a tractor, then it ceases to be so—though of course it remains a particular object with the make-up it happens to have. If it changes, then it changes, but there is no harm that it suffers, no self-identity that it loses. A living thing, on the other hand, does have a self-identity and does have a well-being that can be harmed or benefited, *no matter how we regard that being.*[10]

He goes on to emphasize that he does not regard "kinds" as ultimate moral categories, and that his major point is that by having "optimal states" living things, unlike tractors, "inherently define what is in their interests" (80).

Apparently, living things and only living things are what they are and subsist in the ways they do, in virtue of their own (nonconventional) nature. Tractors, as exemplars of the nonliving, are tractors and subsist as tractors, solely in virtue of the (conventional) use that we make of them. If our human interests change, tractors, having no self-identity, are no longer tractors although they are still, presumably, a configuration of metal and rubber. Although Johnson is mute about why tractors go out of existence while metal and rubber do not, one can speculate that unlike "metal" and "rubber," "tractor" is conceived as a functional term; tractors owe their identity (not to be confused with self-identity, which they necessarily lack) to the use we make of them and the interests we take in them. An object's self-identity determines what its "optimal states" are (nonliving objects such as tractors, having no self-identity, therefore have no optimal states), and these, in turn, determine which states of affairs constitute harms and benefits to this living individual. Implicit in Johnson's account is his agreement with the claim that individuals can properly be said to have welfares only if benefits and harms can be attributed to them on the basis of the modification of nonconventional (intrinsic) properties. Johnson, however, unlike the experientialist, for example, believes that insentient nature can meet this necessary condition and can do so in terms of aids and hindrances to its "optimal states."

But the criticisms of Taylor seem equally appropriate here. These "optimal states," presumably identical to Taylor's teleological goals, are, *pace* Johnson, optimal only in virtue of the ways humans conceive of the tree. I have no particular quarrel with the notion that items evolve "by their own nature," although I iterate my request for reasons to demonstrate why the natural and biological enjoy priority over the merely mechanical and artificial. The significant problem insinuates when this evolution is thought of as some development toward an objective state that is better for the tree, be it called a "teleological goal" or an "optimal state."

Consider our Martian visitors once again, only this time possessing a wealth of botanical knowledge. They study our pecan trees for years, learning everything there is to know about these trees. Humean Darwinism tells us that the Martians omit nothing from their account of pecan trees if they fail to mention the tree's "development" toward an "optimal state." These categorizations are not dictated by the nature of the tree, but rather are a function of a peculiarly human, anthropocentric perspective. What needs to be included in such a report is the evolution (changes) of the tree. Trees simply change. They typically get taller and wider, bloom, wither, and die. No state is any better or worse than any other state for the tree. The notion of a tree being an end in itself or having its "own right" (Johnson, 79) is a fiction.

Let me try to put this point in a slightly different way. Suppose that you were confronted by an individual with extremely long fingernails. There is no reason to think of this condition as either a harm or benefit to its owner without some relevant behavioral manifestations that this condition makes her (or him) either better or worse off. Such behavior may or may not include verbal behavior. If the agent tells you that she wishes that her fingernails were shorter, that their exorbitant length is causing her mental anguish and physical discomfort, we have excellent evidence for thinking this condition is making her worse off. On the other hand, no verbal language is necessary. If we see her continually trying to shorten her fingernails, it would be reasonable to suppose that the condition diminishes her well-being. The "inner" is not the "outer," but intelligible attribution of the inner requires relevant outer behavior. Trees have no natural expressions of being benefited and harmed, no expressions of modifications of welfare. The decrease in fruit production when the fig tree is left unwatered is no more like a reduction in our vitamin D level when we spend fewer hours in the sun (presumably, a harm), than it is like a reduction of our cholesterol level when we abdicate eating flesh (presumably, a benefit). This is a difference in kind from the natural, and truly indicative, expressions of joy and suffering with which we are so familiar.

A temptation is to counter that this account is provincial, that it settles ontological questions by appeals to our contingent, human psychologies. Why cannot it be that other individuals—perhaps extraterrestrials or even future Earthlings—will see the decreased fruit production as suggestive (or even criterial) of a tree's suffering harm like we now see the groaning and wincing of a child as indicative of a diminished well-being? And if this happens, it surely seems wrong to think that the tree, at the time when these new (and more enlightened) ways of understanding the world occur, first gained the capacity to be made better and worse off. A far more plausible and realistic inference is that trees always had welfares, although it is only with the advent of the extraterrestrials or future terrestrials that this quite important aspect of trees' careers is noticed and appreciated. This objection asks us to consider that trees do, in fact, express their modified well-being, but that at the moment, for whatever reasons, we are unable to recognize the tree's behavior for what it really is. Maybe *we* cannot understand tree behavior for what it represents or symbolizes, but only arrogance makes us believe that neither can any others. While we may be cognitively and affectively deficient, others may not be so.

This presentation provides a compelling picture, but one, ultimately, that can and should be rejected. The problem is that if the cognitive and affective lives of the future humans or current extraterrestrials is so profoundly different from our own, there is little reason to think that they are talking of benefits, harms, and welfares when they use, presumably, similar-sounding words. We can put this point into relief if we think of the aliens or even future humans as no longer using the words "benefit," "harm," and so forth. Surely the objector must recognize this possibility. The question, then, is to explain the rationale for translating the newly coined words as the mundane terms we employ when speaking of well-being. What, in other words, justifies the claim that these two different words express the same concept? It would not do to hypothesize that this discrepancy is so localized that we have good reasons for adopting this translation. The idea that the remainder of their lives and language would be congruent with ours, and so this relatively limited difference could be understood as just that, simply miscalculates how basic and pervasive our activities and responses are to enjoyment, suffering, pleasure, and pain. These practices are not fads that come and go with the passing generations; they are, in a quite literal sense, part of our inheritance as human beings.[11]

It is interesting to note in passing that, in a somewhat subtle way, a traditional rendition of the problem of other minds trades on the fact that the application of certain properties to others requires that they are physiognomically similar to us. Skeptics are forever reminding us of the alleged possibility of existence of robots or zombies—individuals who look and behave like us but who lack any personal subjectivities. We never hear stories of blackboards or magnets who, although possible objects of our temptation to believe in the existence of their minds, do not actually have them. The implication is that a necessary condition for the possession of a mind is that the individual appear to be something

like us, for only under this fuzzy but still substantive supposition does
the attribution of mental states and subjectivity have plausibility and ultimately intelligibility. We would be able to share a way of life with
them, so goes the narrative, in just as full a manner as we would were
we dealing with individuals with subjectivities like our own, and so the
problem of other minds, the problem of justifying our individual claims
that others are subjectively like us, cannot be resolved solely by scruti-
nizing our own mental states.

(VII)

A different sort of deep ecology has its contemporary roots in Aldo
Leopold's "land ethic," which has been both supported and enhanced
by some more recent writings of J. B. Callicott.[12] The guiding insight is
that there is an enormously complicated set of interrelationships among
parts of nature and that this fact can be duly recognized only in a "collectivist" or "holistic" ethical approach. This approach is to be contrasted
with an "atomistic" or "individualistic" ethic, epitomized most clearly
by Taylor, where the locus of patienthood is found in the individual
member of the biotic community. To Leopold the biotic community
("the land"), understood as a collective of human and nonhuman animals, plants, soil, rivers, landscapes, and so forth, serves as the ultimate
object of moral consideration.

Disciples of Leopold differ both in their interpretation of him and
in their own accounts concerning some details of their own proffered
land ethics. We have differences of opinion whether the "nodes" (individuals) in this "biotic web of intrinsically related parts" are themselves
worthy of consideration, and if they are, whether they receive this moral
status either in virtue of their own characteristics (and so there is a part-
nership of collectivism and individualism), or only derivatively, from
being part of the biotic community. There is also lack of consensus
whether items like ecosystems and species are morally considerable and
whether these items are best considered as abstract objects or as spatio-
temporal living things in their own right. For our purposes, we can
bypass these internecine disputes and instead focus on Leopold's holistic
mantra: A thing is right when it tends to preserve the integrity, stability,
and beauty of the biotic community; it is wrong when it tends to do
otherwise.

Instead of speaking of "optimal states" of individuals, Leopold speaks
of the "health" of a biotic community, where a healthy biotic community is one that has the biological capacity for self-renewal; its ill-
health is its degeneration or loss of this capacity. Unsurprisingly, then,

problems that arose with Taylor's and Johnson's accounts will also plague this collectivist view of deep ecology. It is an indubitable nonanthropocentric fact that biotic communities change. Lush tropical forests turn into arid deserts, and conversely, where this gradual evolution encompasses many intervening stages. But there is nothing intrinsic to this series of phases mandating that any one or group of them represents the "healthy" stage of development of this community. There is no fact of the matter whether a glacial movement is disrupting or destroying the healthy state of some biotic community or, instead, is initiating a new, healthy one. It is not as though nature comes to us with labels announcing which phases of the evolutionary process belong to which biotic communities, and whether the activities during these phases are contributing to the health or illness of the land's development. Healthy biotic communities, like teleological goals and optimal states, are simply anthropocentric projections.

Similar comments apply to the specific properties expressed in the collectivist dictum. Stability and integrity are human inventions, not discoveries, properties placed upon a world by humans to serve our needs, desires, or psychological requirements. Appropriating some ideas from Goodman and the later Wittgenstein may prove helpful. Goodman's "grue" paradox can be seen as a demonstration that order and disorder are not intrinsic properties of an external world, but are rather anthropocentrically discharged attributes.[13] There are no external constraints circumscribing which predicates are "projectible"; that is, the choice of predicates that we use for induction is not compelled by objective facts about the external world. The notion of a series of events or states of affairs being ordered or chaotic is an idea that has respectability only if it is recognized as manifesting our specialized human interests. Consider Goodman's own solution to his "new riddle of induction," the enigma of finding what legitimizes our induction upon blue things but not grue ones. The solution is Humean in spirit. Instead of suggesting a justification for our inductive practices, he proposes a psychohistorical explanation of why we behave as we do in terms of the "entrenchment" of certain predicates. The details are of no moment; the point to be gleaned is that order and disorder—and so, by extrapolation, its close cousins stability and integrity—are anthropocentric projections upon a world rather than objective facets of a world awaiting our discovery.

Wittgenstein's contribution to this discussion is most clearly exemplified in his constructivist theory of mathematics, although it also pervades his philosophy of mind. Specifically, what I have in mind are his passages in the *Investigations* concerning "going on in the same way." One moral of these observations is that any series of numbers can be continued in any way whatsoever and yet can be seen as "going on in the same way," as forming a continuation of the series. Thus, if one is provided as part of an infinite series the sequence "2, 4, 6, 8, ——" and is asked to fill in the blank so that the series continues in the same way, any number can be supplied with justification. (The easiest way to see this is to let some arbitrary number—say, 307—fill the blank and continue the series, "2, 4, 6, 8, 307, 2, 4, 5, 8, 307, 2, . . .".) We have a moral identical to Goodman's: Order ("going on in the same way") is not something that the world offers to us awaiting discovery, but rather a projection of ours upon the world. And again, as with order and disorder, so go stability and integrity.

It should come as no surprise that Leopold's emphasis on the interrelationships among individuals in a biotic web reflects a particular conception of ethics. He sees ethics as ensuring cooperative behavior among the members of the biotic community. There is a sense, then, in which humans have a privileged position, for humans, as far as we know, are the only members of the community capable of understanding any formalized code that may be necessary to accomplish such a goal. Leopold presumably would have only normal adult humans as moral agents; it would be a caricature of his position to portray it as assigning blame to glaciers for causing instability to a biotic community. Still, although his conception of ethics allows for the ordinary distinction we make between moral patients and moral agents, it does preclude some areas from moral assessment that are normally thought of as being legitimate within morality's scope. Cooperative behavior is laudable, of course, but it would seem to matter, from a moral perspective, *how* such behavior is ensured; Plato's rationale for the Myth of the Metals and Hitler's Big Lie make this manifest. Leopold's conception of ethics arguably reduces to a prudential conception, but it is just the evident moral questions that we can ask about prudential behavior that makes this conflation a serious mistake.[14]

(VIII)

As serious as the charge of malignant anthropocentrism is, my present suggestion is that this already concedes too much. I want now to argue, by developing some earlier themes, that it simply makes no literal sense at all to attribute the capacity to be benefited and harmed to many of the individuals that are deemed to have welfares by the lights of deep ecology. It is not merely that the Martian report is not incomplete in omitting the anthropocentric "facts" that the tree was better off when it received certain amounts of sunlight and nutrition or that it was worse off in virtue of an insect infestation. Rather, these characterizations are without sense. Deep ecology is a theory of well-being that is in irremediable disrepair.

It is important that the radical nature of this claim should not be minimized or misunderstood. The tree, of course, being a nonexperiential, nonconscious individual, does not *care* what happens to it. It would therefore not care whether it was devoured by insects or successfully repelled their invasion. This would be readily conceded by a justifiably unmoved Taylor, Johnson, or Leopold. Indeed, the desire theorist would also be unmoved, for recall that this theorist believes that individuals can be benefited and harmed in virtue, respectively, of their satisfied and frustrated desires, although no cognitive or affective recognition or response occurs. If the question were understood in this way, it would be viewed (perhaps unfairly) as experientialist question begging. The claim that it is nonsense to impute benefits and harms to trees should not, therefore, be understood as, or reduced to, the claim that the tree cannot care about how it is faring in its environment.[15]

We begin by reflecting upon the aforementioned truism that the concepts of benefit and harm, being better and worse off, and having a welfare are human concepts. They are the concepts they are in virtue of the sorts of beings we are. It is due to the fact and way that we think, perceive, and feel that these concepts (along with all other concepts) have the use and implementation that they do. Part of the use we make of these concepts of well-being is that we ascribe them to others as well as to ourselves. If another is to be credited with a well-being, with the capacities to be benefited and harmed, and these predications are to be understood in their literal and nonstipulative manifestations, then, at the very least, the subjects for these attributes must be enough like us to sustain these attributions. If another is said to be harmed, it must, as a minimal matter of intelligibility, be harmed in ways analogous to the ways in which we humans—the inventors, users, authorities, and paradigms of these concepts—are harmed.

Conceived in the right way, this point should be uncontested. However, confusions have arisen because this point is either unrecognized or misapplied. As an instance of the first source of confusion, consider the oft-heard comment that although there may be life on Mars, it surely will not be "life as we know it." This qualification is nonsense; the only sort of life that there is—and, again, this is a matter of intelligibility and not of biology—is life as we know it. We need not travel beyond the Earth to see the root of the problem. If someone were to suggest that the piece of chalk he now holds in his hand is alive, but not in the way we happen to think of living things, the correct response is to point out that, unless the speaker is using words in an extremely metaphorical or technical sense, he is taking back with one hand what he offers with the other. Presumably the speaker admits that the chalk neither breathes, metabolizes, expends energy, moves on its own, and so forth.[16] The debate is not whether the chalk manifests behavior, albeit in very diminished ways, that mirrors the actions of other uncontentiously living items, like humans, animals, and trees. *This* question would be one best settled by biologists. Rather, the speaker is suggesting that the chalk lives, although not in the "ordinary" manner in which familiar things live. But what could this claim amount to? The chalk, by mutual consent, paradigmatically manifests all the "behavior" of an *inanimate* object. Indeed, the speaker cheerfully admits that the piece of chalk *is* inanimate—inanimate "as we know it." Similar Alice-in-Wonderland tactics are employed for the extraterrestrial form of life whose life as such is unrecognizable to us. What we call "inanimate" is now being labeled "life, but not as we know it," and such verbal legerdemain can lead to only needless perplexity.

The conceptual point that lives just are lives *as we know them* places no a priori limits upon scientific investigation; to think otherwise is to misapply the principle. We might, for all anyone knows, confront living organisms that are not carbon-based. Whether it is a metaphysical fact about the universe that only carbon-based individuals have the capacity for life is certainly not something that can be ascertained in one's private study. If all that is meant by those who claim that we may encounter life on some distant planet but "not as we know it" is that silicon-based life might be forthcoming, then there is no quarrel. Additionally, the conceptual point should not be read as presupposing a sort of behaviorism. The truism does not rest on an assumption that life is reducible to a set of behaviors, let alone that it is reducible to a determinate and restricted set of overt manifestations.

As with life, I suggest, so too with the qualities of welfare, benefit, and harm. For an individual to own a well-being, it must own a well-being *like ours*, where the qualification is nothing more than a pleonasm. To maintain that an individual has a welfare, can be benefited and harmed, but just not in the ways that we recognize as such, is being not merely quixotic but perversely inconsistent. What follows from this is that a necessary condition for another's possessing a welfare is that we be able to "empathetically relate" to what the other is enduring. That is, we—the inventors, users, authorities, and models of our concepts—must be able to understand what it is like for this other to be made better and worse off. This understanding, in turn, minimally requires that the harm or benefit of the other be analogous or comparable to our own harms and benefits. (To this extent, then, there is something com-pelling about the analogical argument for other minds.) This purposively vague requirement is not all-inclusive and so is not vacuous. In order to legitimately attribute benefits and harms to another, we need, minimally, to recognize how *something like* those putative benefits and harms would be benefits and harms to us.

Admittedly this sounds jarring. There is an almost automatic impulse to object that the metaphysical fact about another's being benefited and harmed surely cannot depend on our psychological abilities. At best, so it would seem, these empathetic relationships are required for knowing or appreciating that another is undergoing enjoyment or suffering, but it seems mistaken to believe that these ontic truths about the world depend upon our mental abilities. My point, however, is about the *intelligibility* of these truths, what one means when she attributes welfares to individuals. My claim is that without understanding benefits and harms in a way with which we humans can empathetically identify, the notions of benefits and harms lack sense; all that remain are the homo-nyms of meaningful discourse. It should also be noted, though I will leave the point undeveloped, that this recognition or understanding should not be analyzed in a purely cognitive way. Although cognition probably plays some role in empathetic identification, my speculation is that the affective capacities occupy pride of place. At any rate, the threat of mistaken articulation of this notion is far more likely to be derived from a hypercognitive model than one that places too little emphasis upon the cognitive.

This does not imply that the event that we legitimately attribute to another as a harm need constitute a harm to ourselves. Failure of a math exam may cause Frank great distress and so diminish his welfare, while an equally poor showing by Sally may leave her unaffected. Slapping a cat may bring about substantial pain, while a similarly powerful blow to Mike Tyson's arm would go completely unnoticed. Nonetheless, Sally and Mike, as well as the rest of us, can presumably understand how such events can diminish the well-being of another despite the fact that the acts would not have negative effects on ourselves.[17] The basis for this understanding is hardly enigmatic. Sally realizes that if she failed her government exam she would feel as bad as Frank feels when he fails his math test, and Tyson recognizes that if the blow to his arm were struck with far more force, he, too, would be deleteriously affected. We are able to analogize from events that do not constitute harms to ourselves to like events that do, or would, constitute harms to us. Sally can see how a math grade has significance to Frank by comparing it to the significance that a passing government grade has to her. Tyson recognizes that the degree of the force of the blow is all that separates the cat's pain from his own. And, in these regards, we are all Sallys and Mikes. If we were not—if, that is, we were unable to analogize the events perpetrated upon Frank and the cat as harms *to us*—there would be no justification, indeed no sense, in speaking about those events as harms to Frank and the cat, respectively. And this, in accordance with our previous conceptual point, is just to say that the notion of speaking of them as harms would make no sense.

We can now see that the real problem with attributing benefits and harms to clocks, for example, is not, as Taylor would have it, a matter of clocks lacking a teleological center, natural or artificial, but is rather that there is no (nontechnical, nonstipulative) way to analogize what transpires to a clock as an event that would constitute either a benefit or harm to us. Whereas I can understand how a blow to the cat can be a harm to me by merely intensifying its force, or, what amounts to much the same, I can imagine myself, in the relevant ways, being a cat and so receiving the original punch as a welfare-diminishing experience, I cannot empathetically involve myself with a clock. It makes no sense to entertain thoughts like: If I were a clock, I would be harmed if someone were to destroy one of my springs. The counterfactual, and so the thought, never can get off the ground, not because we lack a sufficiently strong imagination, but because, in the relevant sense, there is nothing for us to imagine. It is not, for example, as though the annihilation of the clock's springs is to the clock like the destruction of one of my legs is to me. Think of how farcical it would strike us to be told that we need to intensify the pain suffered by the clock to get a grasp of the harm that the clock undergoes when its springs are destroyed or that we need to think of our arms (rather than legs) being the parts of our body being destroyed in order to grasp what harm is accruing to the clock when its bolts are ripped asunder.

This idea will not be without its detractors. At first blush, it may seem to make sense to say that if I were a clock, I would be made worse off by someone's pulling apart my springs or that, were I a stove, I would be better off if I were cleaned daily. In grade school, students are sometimes asked what their preferences would be were they a clock or a stove. If my observation is correct, none of these exercises are really intelligible. Yet it seems as though we are imagining *something* when we respond to the teacher's inquiry; it is not as though we throw up our hands and complain that we find her request incomprehensible. We are imagining something. When we accede to the teacher's request, we think of *ourselves* as having Roman numerals surrounding our faces, having thin metal bars for arms, and so forth, but this no more constitutes imagining ourselves as clocks than donning a Halloween costume allows us to imagine ourselves ghosts.

It may be demanded that I provide an explanation why virtually all of us immediately believe that the destruction of a clock's springs constitutes a harm to the clock rather than a benefit and that the cleaning of a stove benefits rather than worsens the career of the stove. The point here is that if it really makes no sense to attribute welfares to clocks and stoves, we seem impotent to explain why we so spontaneously and overwhelmingly think of some events as benefits to their possessors rather than harms, and conversely. It surely defies the laws of probability that these weighted sentiments are merely randomly produced.

I believe that the answer lies in the instrumental value that clocks and stoves have for us. A clock with broken springs cannot serve its function well; it cannot accurately give us the time. Similarly, a dirty stove is retarded in its capacity to cook our meals expeditiously. Some confirmation of this explanation is afforded if we consider a case wherein we ask which of two options is better for a perspectiveless individual, where both options provide us with equal benefit. If we were to ask young children whether it enhances or diminishes the welfare of a piece of chalk to be enclosed in a glass casing or secured in a wooden desk, my guess is that the results would be about evenly split.

The very young are also instructive when they unhesitatingly speak of dolls' being hurt when they fall from tables or cartoon characters being harmed when they fall from cliffs. Surely they attribute modifications of welfare to individuals that lack them because they very much physically resemble the human beings with whom the youngster is associated. Children seem never to be concerned about the well-being of the floor that was impacted by the doll's fall or the welfare of the rock that broke in two as a result of Wily Coyote's misplaced step. Young children see their dolls as they see us, as individuals with faces, arms, and legs. Presumably, most of us learn that our concerns about the welfares of the dolls and cartoon characters were misplaced (which is not to suggest that they did not serve an extremely useful purpose); we learn, again at a comparatively early age, that dolls and cartoon characters are not *enough* like us to sustain the attribution of welfares. Dolls do not cry or wince when they are dropped. Cartoon characters respond to crashes in very unhumanlike ways. Empathetic identification, then, is not sufficient for legitimate attribution of well-being. It is a defeasible criterion that can be subjected to intellectual scrutiny. It remains, however, a sine qua non for the intelligible attribution of welfare to another.

Can we empathetically identify with another knowing that there is no subjectivity lurking behind its behavior? Consider now a robot physically indistinct from other humans. You know that this is a robot, and we may suppose, for the sake of discussion, that this knowledge includes the awareness that this metallic individual has no interior mental life. I submit that our *attitudes* toward this individual would be profoundly different than if we lacked this knowledge. Of course, the figures of zombies and robots are window dressing. The suggestion amounts to the idea, shared by both experientialists and desire theorists, that the possession of subjectivities (points of view, perspectives, "inscapes") are requirements for sustaining welfares. If one finds this thought experiment compelling and recognizes that there would be this dramatic reversal of attitudes after discovering that we are confronting a robot who is "wincing" and "moaning," rather than an individual who is wincing and moaning, then one should be most skeptical about the attribution of welfares to trees and waterfalls. For what does the attitude shift indicate other than that you no longer believe that the individual before you is, for example, ("really") feeling pain ("pain as we know it," to put it redundantly)? If this is a correct characterization of what is transpiring, since the only relevant change is the acquired knowledge that the humanlike individual lacks an interior life, parallel reasoning would suggest that we ought not (and do not) consider trees and waterfalls—entities that we all have agreed lack subjectivities—as having the capacity to be made better and worse off.

(IX)

There is one very different sort of argument that deserves examination in its own right. Deep ecologists, inspired by thought experiments of G. E. Moore, have purveyed powerful intuitive considerations to support the view that even some of insentient nature has a well-being.[18] If my position is essentially right and there is no prospect for the success of any effort that imputes moral standing to those items in the world lacking subjectivity, it is incumbent upon me to address these thought experiments. Let us consider one of these so-called last-man arguments.[19]

Tom is the last conscious, let alone sentient, being in the universe. Tom will die next week, and with his demise, not only will all conscious life disappear from the universe, but no conscious life will ever reappear, as the conditions necessary for such life will be forever absent. Tom knows all these facts, and he also knows that there is a "good ecosystem" nearby (one with the Leopoldian qualities of integrity, stability, and beauty) that has soil, water, plants, etc., but no conscious life. There is a switch that Tom has the power to operate. Tom knows that with insignificant effort he can (1) move the switch upward, in which case the ecosystem will be totally destroyed at the moment of his death and no "good" ecosystem will ever replace it; (2) move the switch downward, in which case the ecosystem will continue to be "good" for an indefinite period of time; or (3) leave the switch alone, in which case the ecosystem's future is completely uncertain in the sense that it will have a 50 percent probability of being totally destroyed as in (1) and a 50 percent chance of indefinite survival as in (2).

This thought experiment is designed to extract the intuition that Tom has an obligation to pull the switch downward. It is suggested that the only plausible ground for Tom's obligation is that the good ecosystem has inherent (positive) value that deserves to be respected. Only by pulling the switch downward and allowing the good ecosystem to continue indefinitely is Tom fulfilling his moral obligation.

I have already argued that the notion of a good (or bad) ecosystem is an anthropocentric projection, and that, at root, the evaluation of nonsentient individuals such as ecosystems as owning welfares is nonsense. But, bracketing all this, it is highly unlikely that the putative goodness of the ecosystem forms the basis for our intuition in this case. For if we replace the good ecosystem with one that lacks beauty, stability, and integrity, I still believe that we would maintain the intuition that Tom ought to act so as to save the ecosystem rather than so as to either ensure its nonexistence or make its nonexistence possible. At this point, it is tempting to ground the intuition that Tom ought not to destroy the ecosystem (of whatever sort) on the belief that, all things being equal, one ought to allow something to exist rather than destroy it. And one may be seduced to infer from this that all that exists, regardless of any of its qualities, has moral standing.

That temptation and its subsequent implication should be avoided, not least because it will involve us in metaphysical muddles. (Are we on the road to compare the patienthood of the existent with that of the nonexistent?) We can account for our belief that Tom ought not to destroy the ecosystem by viewing it as an expression of our negative opinion of persons who wantonly destroy. We almost instantaneously conjure up a picture of Tom as a person with bad character, as an individual who behaves capriciously and insensitively, and my suspicion is that it is this picture, rather than the act itself taken in isolation, that instigates our moral judgment. It may be responded that this analysis unwittingly ensnares me in the very muddle I warned against. After all, if wanton destruction manifests a bad character and it is this untoward character against which we are railing, it would seem that the existent has some moral priority vis-à-vis the nonexistent. If destroying something for no reason indicates a malicious disposition, then it would seem that the mere existence of something, albeit defeasibly, has some moral significance; existence has moral priority over nonexistence.

The way to avoid this quagmire is to realize that, as a matter of psychological fact, individuals with propensities to destroy are most unlikely to limit their actions to those that will have no effect, direct or indirect, upon sentient creatures. We find Tom's behavior deplorable, then, because we think of him as the type of individual who would wreak havoc upon human and nonhuman sentients and not restrict his behavior to rocks, pencils, and ecosystems. If perchance Tom was of that extremely odd sort that limited his destructive tendencies to those without inscape and we were well aware of this, then, I believe, we would not have the intuition that the thought experiment, in the absence of these suppositions, properly elicited. Capricious interactions with rocks are not sins, and insensitive behavior toward rocks is impossible. If this were the extent of Tom's behaviors, he may be eccentric but at least he would not be malevolent.

(x)

Some brief closing statements about perfectionism are in order. Perfectionism, insofar as it is an objectivist theory of well-being, will absorb the problems that pervade any objectivist theory. Thus the problem of first-person epistemic privilege that engaged the desire theory resurfaces. And, of course, privilege is hardly the major epistemic issue. The fact that inanimate objects can be both benefited and harmed means that we have individuals whose welfare is modifiable without their having the capacity to recognize these changes in their well-being. The adoption of perfectionism would require the abdication not merely of first-person privilege but of first-person access as well.

The problem cuts deeper. How are we to know which properties are welfare-enhancing and which are welfare-diminishing? The problems with using intuition as a guide are obvious and well known and certainly do not need to be rehashed. But using desires for identificatory purposes, as the scenarios of Nozick and Kane suggest when interpreted as apologies for perfectionism, proves no more availing. Consider autonomy as a perfectionist value. There are apparently rational persons who would choose the wonderful experiential life at the expense of their autonomy. Perfectionists would need some principled method by which they could separate the trustworthy from untrustworthy desires, desires that pointed to the objectively worthy and those that did not. Unlike the desire theory, which endows desires with the power to create value and so escapes the issue of proper referencing, perfectionism encounters this additional problem in virtue of empowering desires with, at best, an identificatory function. Obviously, we could not rely on anything as ephemeral as a majority vote. Notwithstanding the mundane truth that majority opinions frequently change, we have the more basic issue of explaining why the majority, whatever its constitution, has this amazing power lacking to those who just happen to be members of the minority.

It might be thought that, by relativizing desires, perfectionists can make them inerrant indicators of the objectively worthy. So, if Jane prefers autonomy to inautonomy, then autonomy, for Jane, is objectively worthy. To avoid the appearance of oxymoron, the perfectionist would understand this as describing a particular property, autonomy-in-Jane, as being objectively worthy. The idea is that the possession of this property, regardless of the individual's desires or experiential response, would benefit all those who possess it. Because only Jane could have this relativized property, and because it is supposed that she desires it, we know that it benefits her. If the statistically abnormal Jerry desires a relatively inautonomous life, then inautonomy-in-Jerry is objectively worthy; everyone who has it is benefited, but only Jerry can have it.

Does this work? It should first be noted that the relativization would need to be even more finely discriminating. Individuals change their minds and have different, even conflicting, desires over time. Thus autonomy-in-Jane would need to be modified to, for example, "autonomy-in-Jane-on-Monday-at-5:00-P.M." But this need for ultrarelativization is a comparatively minor problem. A larger one is that although it is true that only Jane could have autonomy-in-Jane, there may be others who desire inautonomy-in-Jane. Thus we cannot allow each person's desires to be inerrant, since this would lead to the intolerable consequence of an individual manifesting contradictory properties. The strategy now, were the perfectionist of a mind to continue on this track, would be to make the desire for the autonomy-in-Jane a desire that Jane could uniquely possess. Perhaps the desire characterized as "the desire for my autonomy" would capture what the perfectionist needs. The idea is that anyone other than Jane who had the desire characterized by "the desire for *my* (in)autonomy" would, necessarily, be owning a desire different than Jane's. The contents of Jane's desire for her autonomy would be different from the content of anyone else's desire for Jane's or their own autonomy or inautonomy, and so consistency of desires would be ensured.

I remain skeptical of the success of this tactic, one that still seems to smack of verbal chicanery. We still, as a matter of fact, are considering the desire of autonomy-in-Jane. Regardless of how one characterizes, describes, or refers to this desire, the desire does not change. Although there is a sense in which certain characterizations of the desire are unavailable to others, others can access this belief just as fully and robustly as Jane can. Admittedly, more may be said, but we need continue this line no further since an even bigger problem faces the perfectionist even were we to grant success on this tactic of using *de se* desires. This larger problem, one that we have previously visited, is the basic supposition that the individual's desires for himself, even when motivated purely by self-interest, are infallible indicators of what is best for him. But surely this is not true. The satisfaction of the desires of both the baby who wants to continue crawling when faced with an impending precipice and of the alcoholic who wants his next shot of whiskey diminish rather than enhance well-being. Jane's desire for her own autonomy may well be of a piece with these.

Expanding the domain of the morally considerable, as perfectionism would, invites difficulties about how claims of welfare are to be verified and evaluated. In both experientialism and the desire theory, claims concerning relative welfares were fairly straightforward. Although interpersonal comparisons might be, in practice, somewhat more difficult to assess than intrapersonal ones, there was no essential mystery about comparing the intensity of joys and sufferings. Similarly, we often seem to accommodate claims about measuring strengths of desires, be they all of a single person or among distinct individuals. (I here forgo issues concerning the "problem of other minds"; this skepticism is of a different magnitude and dimension.) But how are we to evaluate claims about the relative well-being of individuals when we are concerned about beauty? This is difficult enough when we wish to compare the beauty of a Rembrandt with that of a Tintoretto, but how do we even begin to understand the claim that the Rembrandt is more beautiful than the Mozart concerto (and so better off!), or, what seems even more problematic, how do we compare the Rembrandt's beauty to that of the Grand Canyon? Additionally, how are we to distinguish among the alleged harms suffered respectively by a Rembrandt when a small drop of blue paint is accidentally dropped on it and when someone defaces some of the sedimentary rocks of the Grand Canyon?

We have detailed three theories of moral considerability. It is time to examine why this discussion holds far more than mere academic interest.

II

ANIMAL MATTERS

4

Animal Patienthood

(1)

To be considered a moral patient, an individual who has interests, is diametrically opposed to being considered a resource. Resources, or amoral patients, have no inherent value. The only value that they have is instrumental, value in the service of other individuals who themselves have value. In virtue of their nature, resources are not items toward which we can act morally correctly or incorrectly. Precisely unlike moral patients, they are not morally enfranchiseable. Although there may be moral limits regarding our dealings with resources, these boundaries are not prescribed by any inherent properties of the resource itself. Rather, behaviors concerning resources are restricted only by our moral relationships with (other) moral patients. Resources are to be used, and although prudential and ethical questions frequently arise regarding the judicious, wise, or fair use of resources, concerns about the well-being or sake of the resource itself is not, and cannot be, an issue. In addition to different behaviors toward resources and moral patients, we have differing attitudes. We normally care, as we should, how our actions affect the moral patient itself; its well-being is a concern to us. Resources have no well-being and cannot be warranted recipients of such an attitude. Of course, our attitudes and behaviors are intimately connected, and indeed mutually supportive. Undoubtedly, if our attitudes about an individual were other than the way they are, our behaviors would be appropriately modified. Similarly, our repeated behaviors toward an individual tend to reinforce our attitudes. This somewhat less obvious connection is used efficaciously by Christian clerics, who occasionally suggest to parishioners with wavering faith that they continually parrot prayers while fingering rosary beads without, at first, being concerned about the sincerity and heartfeltness of their words. Attitude may be caused by behavior as well as the other way around.

I ask you now to reflect upon a most disconcerting possibility. Suppose that we normal adult human beings have systematically miscategorized the moral status of a particular group of individuals. Suppose, that is, that we have adopted the attitudes and behaviors appropriate to a group of amoral patients toward moral patients. Our reaction to the discovery of our mistake would undoubtedly be affected by the causes of our error. Probably the least psychologically damaging would be to view our previous misjudgment as being completely warranted. Here we would claim that we had good reason for endorsing the attitudes and behaviors we had; given what we could reasonably have been expected to know at the time, we did the best we could. The spectrum of causes would continue through less justified explanations including cases of negligence and inattentiveness. The most reprehensible side of the ledger would comprise explanations of knowing arrogance or indifference.[1] Either the epistemic avenues were readily available and we took neither the time nor effort to utilize them, or we selfishly did not care about the sake of others. But regardless of the reasons for our mistake, upon recognizing the error of our ways we should, I trust, feel sorrow, regret, and remorse. Individuals who had the capacity to be morally considered were not, and although, as a point of logic, this may not entail that they were harmed in the process, as a point of practice this deleterious result is all but assured.

Unfortunately, we need not manufacture fanciful fictions to exemplify this possibility. Throughout the millennia, our attitudes and behaviors toward nonhuman animals has, on literally billions of occasions, instantiated this very possibility. Or at least so it has seemed to many who have seriously thought about the question. In virtue of the contemporary attention, both philosophical and lay, to our treatment of nonhuman animals, various defenses of many of our pervasive practices involving animals have evolved, defenses that, given our prior discussions, can be set in illuminating contexts.

I suggest that we view the defenses of the position that all nonhuman animals are amoral patients or (mere) resources as emanating from an implicit reliance upon one of the theories of well-being that we have discussed. Adherence to the perfectionist theory of welfare suggests that there are certain objective properties attributable uniquely to human beings that endow them with moral patienthood. Advocacy of the desire theory of welfare suggests that the capability to form desires, in particular, is essential to moral personhood and that no nonhuman animals possess this capability. Apologists of experientialism who wish to defend the resource status of animals would claim that animals lack the capacity to have sentient experiences, the capacity that is especially required for moral standing.

If what I have heretofore argued is essentially correct, because experientialism appears to be the most viable theory, those who defend the resource model of animals while advocating experientialism pose the most serious threat to the inclusion of nonhuman animals to the moral domain. Still, those who exclude nonhuman animals from moral patienthood for either desire-theoretic or perfectionist reasons should be confronted anew. There are several reasons for this. One may be unconvinced that my theoretical discussion precludes these latter two theories from serious contention, but yet, by virtue of what follows, be convinced that these theories do not yield the exclusionary results toward nonhuman animals that some of their practitioners claim. The stakes are so large that rejecting these theories for such abstract reasons may leave many unmoved to make some significant life changes that would be required if nonhuman animals cannot be legitimately categorized as amoral patients.[2] Moreover, applications of theories, even deposed theories, tend to elucidate them, and this, I take it, is always salutary. Finally, I hope that some of the issues are worthy of discussion for the illumination they provide on related areas, as well as for being inherently provocative.

Let us, then, begin with the arguments for the disenfranchisement of nonhuman animals based on perfectionism and the desire theory. If they are shown to be less than compelling, we are yet further warranted in the results of the previous chapters. We will then attend to the exclusionary experientialist.

(II)

If one adopts a perfectionist theory of well-being while maintaining that humans are uniquely qualified to be moral patients, one needs to hold that all humans possess certain properties that nonhumans lack. This thesis is available to different interpretations of scope and strength. Presumably, perfectionists, like all other welfare theorists, accept the fact that some human beings—normal adults—are morally considerable individuals. Virtually all extend the sphere of moral standing to other humans. In conformity with some of our most basic ethical beliefs, infants, the (mildly) retarded, and the senile are accorded moral patienthood. Some disparity of opinion may begin to show when we speak of the extremely mentally and psychologically challenged, including, but not restricted to, the heartbreaking cases of anacephalics. The strength of the thesis differs in regard to whether even normal adult humans are de facto moral patients or whether they must be, and, perhaps more interestingly, whether nonhuman animals are precluded from the moral realm as a matter of mutable fact or by some sort of necessity.[3] Notwithstanding these permutations, I will understand a perfectionist-driven defense of unique human moral standing—what we may call, albeit with the hint of some disparagement, "chauvinistic perfectionism"—in what I believe is a most charitable and modest way. According to this account, there are objectively valuable properties such that (1) virtually all human beings, as a matter of fact, have these properties and consequently have moral standing; and (2) no nonhuman terrestrial animals, at least to the best of our knowledge, have these properties and consequently lack moral patienthood.

I have already somewhat explained the qualification "virtually" in (1); it is intended to initially leave the moral status of *severely* marginalized humans an open question. This allows the perfectionist to deny moral status to some humans. (Presumably, the perfectionist would not deny humanity to even the severely marginalized; it surely it is not as if these individuals are of a different animal species, or are a type of vegetable or mineral.) The motivation for this qualification is not merely to allow the perfectionist her best case. I think it needs to be admitted that there is nothing approaching a consensus of considered moral belief regarding these severely marginalized humans. Unlike the inclusion of normal humans in our moral community, which is a sine qua non of any acceptable theory of patienthood, the moral disposition of the extremely marginal is, pretheoretically, tenuous. Thus, as a matter of methodology, no intuitions concerning the moral standing of the severely marginalized, unlike intuitions concerning normal adults, will be used as a touchstone for theoretical acceptability. This is not to suggest that chauvinistic perfectionism will not have implications for the severely marginalized. Once we receive a list of these considerability-conferring properties, we will then be able to determine whether some or all of the marginal possess these properties and so will be able to determine whether these unfortunate humans, by chauvinist perfectionist lights, are or are not moral patients.

The qualifications in (2) are two. The perfectionist allows both that there may be extraterrestrial moral patients and that, contrary to our best current information, there may be terrestrial nonhuman individuals who are morally considerable. Thus, neither the inclusion of human beings nor the exclusion of nonhuman animals from the moral sphere is settled a priori. Obviously, there is one property that is unique to human beings—the quality of being human. But it is difficult to imagine how one might convincingly argue for this quality being essential to patienthood. Why should we automatically exclude from moral consideration individuals who are very much like us but with slightly different DNA structures and with nonhuman parentage? It seems clearly unjustified that Martians or Alpha Centaurians, simply by virtue of being nonhuman, are relegated to the status of mere resources. One might respond that there are objective properties required for personhood and that, as a matter of natural law, only individuals who are human have the capacity to have these properties. One might; but when we see a typical litany of such properties, there will be no reason to suspect that such an argument will be forthcoming. In fact, it is quite difficult to understand why it should prove logically impossible, or even merely physically or biologically impossible, for any of our physical or mental attributes not to be duplicated in creatures who lack two human parents. One should be skeptical that the progress of reproductive science, for example, can be so readily circumscribed. Even if one advocates a nonnaturalist approach and claims that only those individuals with souls can have moral status, it seems arbitrary to restrict the possession of souls only to humans. Western religions permit angels to have souls and, as I understand it, grant God the power to insinuate souls wherever He chooses. At any rate, it would not seem like much of a task for souls to be implanted in extraterrestrials.

Chauvinistic perfectionism also should not be burdened with the claim that no terrestrial nonhuman animals are moral patients. What they are justifiably committed to is the claim that, as best as we can presently tell, only human animals possess the objective attributes that are criterial for patienthood. We should allow them to say that were animals quite different from the way that we currently conceive of them—if, that is, they possessed the qualities they suggest as necessary and sufficient for patienthood—then these animals would be admitted into the moral realm. In fact, were animals as hypothesized, perfectionists must insist upon their moral inclusion. In sum, chauvinistic perfectionism denies nonhuman terrestrial animals moral considerability, if in fact they are so denied, by virtue of the fact that they do not possess certain considerability-conferring properties that are possessed by at least all normal adult humans, and not by the fact that they are not Homo sapiens.

Chauvinistic perfectionists differ as to which qualities morally distinguish human from nonhuman animals. A representative list would include rationality, linguistic ability, moral sensibility, and autonomy. Since I understand autonomy as, roughly, the ability to act in accordance with one's own desires, I will delay discussion of this suggestion to my discussion of how a (chauvinistic) desire theorist may present her case.[4] In fact there is an identity between the chauvinistic perfectionist who argues for her moral apartheid by suggesting that nonhuman animals (empirically) cannot have desires, and a chauvinistic desire theorist who claims that the possession of desires, a purportedly uniquely human phenomenon, accounts for the moral enfranchisement of humans and the exclusion of other animals. They are the same theorist with different appellations.

Nuances aside, we may take as representative of the chauvinist perfectionist the claim that all normal adult humans are rational, linguistically able, and morally sensitive, while all nonhuman animals either lack these qualities entirely or have them to such a minimal extent that they fail to meet the threshold required by moral patienthood. A host of questions immediately present themselves. What constitutes the "normalcy" of a normal adult human? Clearly, it would not do to define "normal" in terms of having the capability for rational action, linguistic behavior, and moral sensitivity. If making the moral grade is fundamentally a matter of degree rather than kind regarding these properties, how is the chauvinist delineating the point of demarcation? We need to be sure that this critical point is not an arbitrary or ad hoc invention used to justify many of our practices toward nonhuman animals. We will, however, not linger over these questions but rather concentrate on the one that has central importance. If the terms "rationality," "linguistic competence," and "moral sensitivity" are used with their ordinary connotations, do their respective attributes have the normative implications that the chauvinist alleges of them?

This last point merits some explication. Let us assume, *arguendo*, that we all concur that there is a property P shared by all and only normal adult human beings. We still need some reason for believing that P has the moral significance that the chauvinists impute to it. If it were discovered that all and only humans, in virtue of their DNA structure, have opposable thumbs, I doubt that anyone would seriously argue that this unique property is what allows humans alone to be morally enfranchised. There must, therefore, be something about P, some effect that P has upon its possessor, that confers moral standing upon only those individuals with P. Thus, even if it is shown that the properties of rationality, linguistic competence, and moral sensitivity are unique to humans, it also needs to be argued why these properties have the reputed moral impact upon their possessors.

My suggestion is that under any ordinary (i.e., nonstipulative) account of these properties, there is no such moral import. For ease of exposition, let us consider the property of rationality instrumentally; an individual is rational to the extent that she uses the most efficient means to accomplish an end or goal. Let us think of linguistic capability as the ability to make syntactical and semantic thoughts or utterances. Let us understand moral sensitivity as the ability to act under the guidance of either moral rules or moral ideals. And, to make the case as favorable as possible for the chauvinist, let us grant what he requires, namely, that all of these attributes are unique to all normal adult human beings. Still, just as surely as chimpanzees, orangutans, and dogs lack these properties (and, here, recall that this has been granted, although I believe a powerful case can be made for its falsity), so, too, do human infants. The chauvinist perfectionist is therefore placed in the unenviable position of excluding human infants from patienthood, a consequence that all but those trapped in a warped philosophical mindset would find unacceptable.[5]

Nor would it help to claim that human infants, unlike the nonhuman animals, have the *potential* to obtain these attributes. In this proposal, the property P now becomes the disjunctive property of either actually possessing rationality, linguistic competence, or moral sensitivity or of having the potential to possess these properties. The quickest response is to simply point out that it is an unfortunate fact that some human infants simply lack even this potential. In virtue of some genetic defects, some young children will not advance to the age at which these attributes would otherwise be part of their physical and mental repertoire. Are we to conceive of such infants as nothing more than mere resources, as items without sakes that deserve moral consideration? More esoteric problems arise. We need to know the limits of potential. It is far from clear that, for many mammals at least, the potential for these attributes is lacking. Does the perfectionist want to claim, for example, that neurosurgical techniques are forever incapable of making some changes in chimpanzees and orangutans (assuming such drastic measures are even necessary) to effect these modifications? Although it is true that this technology does not currently exist, it may in the future. Are we then to claim that, although certain primates and mammals do not presently qualify as moral patients, a certain evolution in science will allow, indeed mandate, their moral inclusion? Suspicions become justifiably aroused when fundamental questions of moral standing are directly answerable to the course of scientific progress.

One might anticipate a response in the form of making a distinction between *natural* and *artificial* potential. The infant, if left to her own devices, would typically evolve into a creature with rationality, linguistic ability, and moral sensitivity, whereas the use of artificial means is necessary to bring about the like changes in a mammal. But then the question to be asked is why this distinction, assuming that its nature can be clarified and made out (is, for example the artificial/natural distinction a difference in kind or degree?), should be imbued with moral significance. Why should individuals with the natural potential to gain the proffered considerability-conferring properties be assigned moral standing, while those with only the artificial potential be relegated to resource status?

There is, however, a more basic difficulty facing any attempt to make distinctions concerning moral status revolve around the notion of potential. Consider an individual with the potential—be it natural, artificial, or both—to attain the special perfectionist properties, who yet, as a matter of fact, never realizes that potential. Compare this individual with one who completely lacks the potential to gain these properties. As a matter of fact, the histories of these two individuals, as far as their relationships to the perfectionist properties are concerned, are identical; neither will be rational, have linguistic competence, or attain moral sensitivity. It seems wrongheaded, to put it mildly, to consider only one of these individuals a moral patient. Reflect upon how odd such a distinction would seem for membership in nonmoral clubs. Suppose a baseball manager were given a choice between choosing a player with no baseball skills and without the potential to gather some, and an equally inept player who does have the potential to gain the requisite skills. But now, let it be guaranteed that the player with potential will never have it actualized; although he *can*, he never will become any better than he is. If the manager knew this additional fact, there is no relevant reason for the manager to pick the player with great, but unactualized, potential rather than the other. The analogy with the "club" of moral enfranchisement is clear, but the moral is far more serious. To be omitted from a baseball team for less than compelling reasons is one thing, to be excluded from those who deserve moral consideration contains consequences that are far more dire.

(III)

Let us now turn to those philosophers, whom we may call chauvinist desire theorists, who adopt a desire theory of welfare and who use this theory as a means to confer patienthood uniquely on human beings. Again, we will allow these theorists the most favorable interpretation, one that characterizes this uniqueness metaphysically de facto and epistemically in accordance with our best available knowledge. We again grant that the group of normal adult human beings can be delineated noncircularly and have the capacity to form desires, and so the theory meets the minimal criterion of morally enfranchising normal adult humans. In disenfranchising nonhuman terrestrial animals, these theorists argue that these creatures lack the capacity to form any desires.

In general, chauvinist desire theorists agree with the commonsense view that some animals have the capacity for sentient experience. Since these desire theorists are *chauvinists* (i.e., since they believe, subtleties aside, that all and only humans have desires), they must view the relationship between "having the capacity to suffer" and "having the capacity to form desires" as contingent, for if they did not, then given their mundane assumption about the sentience of many nonhuman animals, this group would need to be accorded the capacity for desires and so moral standing.[6] Since these chauvinist theorists are *desire* theorists, they believe that the capacity for desires confers moral patienthood. I have already expressed my misgivings with the desire theory. Bracketing these general theoretical problems, I want now to examine the arguments used to support the chauvinism of desires. To the extent that these considerations are found wanting, to the extent that the arguments against animal desires are unconvincing, we—even as desire theorists—have reason to incorporate animals into our moral realm.

(IV)

R. G. Frey believes that nonhuman animals are incapable of having desires because having desires (at least those that are not "instinctive," like the desire for water when one is thirsty) requires either belief or self-consciousness, both of which, in turn, require linguistic ability that animals lack.[7] Why does belief require linguistic ability?

> Now what is it that I believe? I believe that my collection lacks a Gutenberg Bible; that is, I believe that the sentence "My collection lacks a Gutenberg Bible" is true. In expressions of the sort "I believe that . . . ," what follows the "that" is a sentence, and what I believe is that the sentence is true. . . . The essence of this argument is . . . about what is believed. If what is believed is that a certain sentence is true, then no creature which lacks language can have beliefs. . . . I do not see how the cat can be correctly described as believing the laces are tied unless it can, as I do, distinguish between the beliefs that the laces are tied and that the laces are untied and regards one but not the other as true. But what is true or false are not states of affairs which reflect or pertain to these beliefs; states of affairs are not true or false (though sentences describing them are) but either are or are not the case (Frey, 87–90).

We should not find this persuasive. One way to see this is to notice that instead of inferring that an individual believes that P is true from the fact that she believes P, we could, with equal propriety, infer that she believes that P is the case. Now the instantiations are states of affairs and not sentences, and, whatever exactly states of affairs (or events) are, they are clearly not linguistic entities. It is not as though states of affairs need language to exist, although trivially they require language to be described. This criticism, then, can be expressed in two ways. First, that explicating the contents of beliefs as sentences was a biased one, or, if the explication is considered uniquely correct, it illicitly assumes that sentences are the only sorts of things that can be either true or false.

Virtually never, and certainly not in the case presented by Frey, is what is believed (i.e., the content of a belief) a sentence. To avoid unnecessary complications involving indexical expressions (i.e., the use of "my" in Frey's sentence), consider my belief that the sun is bigger than the moon. Presumably, others can have the same belief (or, if this discourages superfluous bickering, "belief-type"), including those who speak Spanish but no English. These exclusively Spanish-speakers, by hypothesis, cannot believe that an English sentence is true. Thus we have a case in which we have identical beliefs corresponding to distinct sentences (either tokens or types), and so the belief cannot be identified with the linguistic entity of a sentence. Problems arise even intralinguistically. Jones can believe that his collection lacks a Gutenberg Bible despite the fact that he lacks knowledge of the word "lacks." When asked if he believes that his collection lacks the Bible, he may be puzzled owing to the fact that his vocabulary is deficient. Nevertheless, by other means, both verbal and behavioral, we may come to be quite certain that "Jones believes that he lacks a Gutenberg Bible from his collection" is true. He may, for example, simply tell us that he believes that he is missing such a book and act accordingly.

Reflection upon our beliefs concerning infants is instructive. Are we mistaken when we claim that a baby believes that his mother is lying in bed with him? It will not do to say that, properly speaking, we can only attribute recognition, but not belief, to the baby, for Frey's argument applies equally well to recognition. Application of Frey's reasoning to the fact that the baby recognizes that her mother is nearby requires that the baby recognize "My mother is near me"; that is, the infant's recognition of her mother requires recognition of an English sentence. Very few infants of two months are equal to this task.

It borders on the truistic to claim that, in order to formulate or state someone's beliefs, one is required to use language. So, if nonhuman animals lack linguistic capability, they will be unable to perform these formulations or statements. And if *this* capability is required for higher-order beliefs, then animals will inevitably succumb to this failure. However, this goes no way in showing what Frey thinks his argument shows, namely, that beliefs require language use. Indeed, the argument seems, if anything, to have inverted the logical priorities between belief capacity and linguistic capacity. Under the supposition that we need the latter prior to the former, it would seem impossible to provide an (empirical) account of language learning. At least in some broad sense of "belief," the infant would need to have some rudimentary and perhaps inchoate beliefs about her parents and the associations they make between words and things.[8] Psychology simply reflects common sense when it tells us that there are preverbal beliefs, a thesis that would necessarily be confused if linguistic ability were a requirement for belief formation. Although inarticulate, the young child believes that his mother is pointing to something when she says "ball." The prelinguistic child comes to expect that (believes that) his mother will comfort and feed him when he cries. Or, at least, so it seems. Philosophers who deny something so basic to the psychology of learning and the experience and descriptions of ordinary parents may not be mistaken, but it should be taken as a caveat that the concept of belief with which they are working appears hypercognitive and quasi-technical. It is a caricature to suggest that we are attributing sophisticated biological beliefs to the infant. Rather, what is implied is that the infant realizes that the woman he approaches has a special (i.e., mothering) relationship with him. The realization is not manifested in any "language of thought," but rather in the medium of action; he approaches her and not others and is manifestly happy when he is with her.

What are we to make of Frey's inability to attribute to his cat the belief that the laces are tied, as opposed to their being untied, if his cat cannot distinguish, being semantically inarticulate, between true and false beliefs? Not very much, I think, without the additional premise that we have already found wanting, namely, that a true (false) belief just is the belief that a particular sentence is true (false). I see nothing wrong with talking about sentences (although perhaps some would prefer talk of propositions) and beliefs as both being the sorts of entities that are true and false, but it scarcely follows that beliefs are just sentences. Even granting Frey his best possible case, in which the truth and falsity are attributed to beliefs and sentences univocally, and furthermore, that beliefs and sentences are the only two sorts of items that can support those attributions, the identity still would not be guaranteed. After all, there may be other properties that beliefs and sentences do not share. It may well be that only items that are either shaped or sized can be colored, but not every item of one category is identical to an item of the other.

Frey's argument for the claim that the self-consciousness required for simple desires—desires such as the desire for food that do not need to be mediated by beliefs—itself requires linguistic ability relies on an (alleged) insight articulated by Strawson in his "ascription principle" (Frey, 105–6).[9] Frey claims that one can only ascribe certain predicates (e.g., "pain") to oneself if one can know that they apply to others. Since Frey accepts a Wittgensteinian, anti-Cartesian view of how such predicates gather meaning, he believes that such terms gain meaning, not in some inward act of ostension and naming, but in virtue of being used in a public arena with public checks upon the correctness of the term's usage. So one can apply these predicates to oneself only if one has mastered, to some degree, a public language. Apparently, then, one cannot desire to rid oneself of pain unless one is self-conscious, and one cannot be self-conscious unless one knows a (public) language.

I have sympathy for a Wittgensteinian picture of language acquisition, but Frey's use of it is illicit. Frey offers no argument, nor do I see any reason to believe, that self-consciousness is to be analyzed or understood in terms of ascribing predicates to oneself. More generally, why should we accept that the phenomenon of self-consciousness is best understood as a linguistic phenomenon? We should not be surprised that Frey takes this approach. He has, after all, provided us with a linguistic view of consciousness when he argues that a requirement for possessing beliefs is the comprehension of sentences. But just as we saw that the fact that "belief that" clauses are followed by sentences does not imply that sentences constitute the content of beliefs, the fact that "I believe that" clauses are also followed by sentences shows no reason to think of self-consciousness as a semantic affair.

But even before this, it is far from evident that the desire to avoid one's own suffering requires self-consciousness of suffering. Consider an individual who cannot conceptualize the pain as his, but nevertheless is fully aware and suffers through the pain. But if, in fact, the suffering that he is aware of is *his* (as, of course, it is), then, as a matter of fact, he is aware of his own suffering and presumably desires to get rid of it. The truth, then, that resides in the claim that the desire to avoid one's own suffering requires the agent's self-consciousness of suffering is that the agent's conceptualization of the content of his desire as his own requires that he think of himself as the one who suffers. When understood this way, it is small wonder that this claim seemed uncontentious; it is nothing more than an innocuous, conceptual truth. But having such a status, it cannot substantively help in the argument. Understood in a substantive way, in its empirical incarnation, we have reason to believe it false.

More fundamentally, it is difficult to discern why self-consciousness should be seen to play an essential role in patienthood unless one already dogmatically subscribes to the desire theory. For the sake of discussion, let us assume that self-consciousness is necessary for desiring that your pain be alleviated. As Frey would agree, self-consciousness of the pain is not required for consciousness of the pain. There is no debate, at this juncture, that the individual is conscious of the pain; he suffers through it. We may concede that the individual cannot conceptualize the pain as *his*, but, without allegiance to the desire theory, it is difficult to see why this privation is morally relevant. Why require the higher-order thought that he knows that he (as opposed to another) is the individual suffering for the agent to be in a state that makes him worse off? It is true, of course, that to Frey, the capacity for higher-level thought is necessary for the capacity for desires, and so, in conformity with the dictates of the desire theory, the individual only now achieves the status of having a well-being. But there seems no grounding for granting the *self*-consciousness of the interior mental state such enormous power. I urge that instead of conferring self-consciousness with the capability of transmuting conscious resources into moral patients, we find additional reason to reject the desire theory. To bolster this intuition, we may look at the situation from the perspective of an individual—a normal adult human being—who is both conscious and self-conscious of his pain. If we subtract the consciousness of her pain from her self-consciousness of it, it would seem as if we are left with no (mental) residue. Minimally, *contra* the implications of Frey's theory, it appears that the agent is still worse off than if she were not in a painful state at all.

(v)

Stephen Stich offers what might be called a deflationary account of animal desires without quite committing himself to the claim that nonhuman animals cannot possess desires.[10] Stich's idea is that we cannot say what animals believe, and, if beliefs are necessary for desires, we cannot say what desires a nonhuman animal has. If this is so, and we accept a belief-desire explanatory model of action, it leaves the explanation of animal behavior mysterious.[11] Where Frey thought that, being languageless, brutes essentially lacked the capacity to form beliefs, Stich's claim is that the content of their beliefs and the reasons for their behavior—if they have any of either—is forever shielded from us.

Stich brings two considerations to bear. First, dogs sometimes get confused when it comes to bones, for example. Sometimes they fail to recognize some bones as bones (e.g., bones of the middle ear), and at times they are fooled by imitation bones. This allegedly shows that dogs lack the concept of a bone. Second, were dogs far better at accurate recognition of bones, they still ought not to be credited with possessing the concept of a bone because they lack the elementary, fundamental facts about bones. They have no idea of their function in a body, what their composition is even roughly like, or what kind of damage may befall them.

Recalling that these are proffered as reasons for believing that we—normal adult human beings—cannot know the content of nonhuman animal beliefs, the argument then must be this: (1) nonhuman animals lack concepts; (2) the possession of concepts by certain individuals is required for us to specify the content of the beliefs of those individuals; so (3) we cannot specify the content of nonhuman animal beliefs. Let me start by suggesting that a poor way to combat this argument is to argue against (1) by claiming that the considerations that Stich adduces for support of (1) only demonstrate the far weaker claim that nonhuman animals lack *human* concepts. The implication is that, for all we know, nonhuman animals may possess a rich conceptual scheme but just not one that is congruent with, or even overlapping, our own. This is not a fruitful tactic for two reasons. Stich may, with warrant, simply change (2) to reflect the modification in (1); that is, he might simply reply that it is the possession of human concepts, and not just the possession of any concepts whatsoever, that is required for us to specify the content of an individual's beliefs. And, as I have argued earlier, the terms "concept" and "human concept" are pleonasms; perhaps somewhat more circumspectly, we can never be justified in attributing any concepts other than human ones to any individuals. If we literally could make no sense of what others were doing, we would have no warrant for describing their behavior as "conceptualizing."

With all this, Stich would agree. But the same considerations that hold for concepts apply to beliefs. Stich seems to agree, at least for the sake of this argument, that nonhumans can have beliefs that are unspecifiable by humans. But if we literally can have no idea what the content of these putative beliefs are, we can have no warrant for claiming that these individuals either have beliefs (understood in the "product" sense) or are capable of believing (understood in the "process" sense). Why, in short, think of "what is produced" or "what is going on" in terms of beliefs at all? Thus, if the conclusion of Stich's argument is accepted, he is unjustified in holding the assumption he uses to produce his argument.

But the assumption of the intelligibility of attributing beliefs to dogs is also utilized in the argument for (1). When Stich speaks about dogs being fooled by imitation bones, this is most naturally understood as claiming that the dog is induced into a false belief about the bone. When he tells us that were the dog's recognition of a bone better than it typically is, it would still not suffice for attributing the concept of a bone to the dog, this naturally suggests, in virtue of what "recognition" connotes, that the dog has some beliefs about the bone. Stich, however, on his own terms, should not have access to there being such beliefs. There is, then, an element of self-defeat incorporated in Stich's reasoning for his first premise.

We can, and do, attribute beliefs to individuals without thinking that the individual thinks about or expresses her belief in the same terms we use in the description of the belief. When we attribute to a child the belief about his mother, we are not tempted to think that the child is operating—or can operate at that time—with (having the concept of) "mother," if what is meant by "having the concept of mother" entails having the language of thought incorporating the term "mother" (or some mental equivalent) passing through his mind. Similar considerations apply to terms such as "physical object" and "other." When psychologists talk about the stage of child development at which one typically grasps the concept of "the other," for example, they are not making any predictions about a change in the brain's neurophysiology that would correspond to the terms "other," "identity," or "self." There is nothing wrong with demanding of an individual with a belief in P that he have the concept of P; this can be understood as a trivial truth. The problem insinuates when, as exemplified in Stich's account, one presupposes a far too restrictive notion about what it is for one to have a concept. Certain infant behaviors entitle us to credit them with the acquisition of certain beliefs and concepts. Similarly, the burying, chewing, and eating behaviors of dogs entitle us to claim that they have the concept of bone and have beliefs about bones. No doubt, the dispositions to acquire these concepts and beliefs (as perhaps are some concepts and beliefs themselves) are innate, produced by millennia of evolutionary pressure. Just as humans would not have survived without acquiring the concept of "other," dogs would not survive without the concepts of "food," "bone," and, for that matter, "other." The deviant dog who tries to eat rainbows rather than bones layered with meat is not likely to last very long; he had better get the relevant concepts, and quickly.

To sum up. Neither Frey nor Stich, two chauvinist desire theorists who advocate a contingency relationship between the capacities for sentient experience and desires, makes a convincing case that nonhuman animals do not own desires. But it is worth emphasizing that any merit that their arguments has seems equally applicable to human infants. Upon reflection, few would disenfranchise nonhuman animals at the expense of also discharging (human) infants from our moral sphere.

(VI)

Let us now turn to the chauvinist desire theorist who holds that there is a conceptual relationship between having the capacity to have sentient experiences and having the capacity to form desires. This type of chauvinism may be argued for in a quite different manner than the sort favored by contingency desire theorists like Frey and Stich. If these desire theorists can demonstrate, contrary to popular opinion, that no nonhuman animals have the capacity for sentient experience, their adherence to conceptualism leads to the exclusionary view of welfare and patienthood that they seek.[12] In advocating the idea that no nonhuman animals can have sentient experiences, the conceptual chauvinist desire theorist is well aware that he is swimming against a powerful tide, and we will detail the arguments for this unpopular position momentarily. However, there is one significant advantage that the conceptual theorist owns over her contingency cohort. She no longer has to concern herself with the powerful intuition that human infants or nonhuman animals, even without the benefit of the capacity to form desires, still seem like proper subjects for moral standing. The concern evaporates because, in the conceptualist's view, it is impossible that a creature without desires could have the capacity to enjoy and suffer. In discussing this theorist, therefore, we need to focus on the independent arguments for the view that nonhuman animals are incapable of sentient experience. We have already discussed the debate between those who uphold a contingency view of the relationship between suffering and desires and those who hold a conceptual interpretation. There is no need to revisit them. What we will do, for the sake of discussion, is accept the conceptualism of this chauvinistic desire theorist and focus our energies on her reasons for rejecting the commonplace that there are some nonhuman animals with the capacity for sentient experience.

A successful argument on the part of the conceptual chauvinist desire theorist would justify a resource account of animals even under an experientialist theory of well-being. That is, the proponent of the argument may just as well be an experientialist—one who makes the capability of sentient experience criterial for moral standing—but may now claim that animals do not make the experiential grade. While it is, as I have suggested, quite plausible to entertain the notion of an individual capable of sentient experience despite the fact that the individual cannot form desires, it is far more unlikely that anyone would hold that some individuals incapable of sentient experience have the capacity to form desires. Yet it is only within this latter scenario that a desire theorist would attribute moral standing to an individual that would lack such standing under an experiential account of well-being. Therefore, the novel considerations brought forth by the conceptual chauvinist desire theorist are tantamount to a defense of "chauvinist experientialism," the view that advances an experientialist view of well-being while claiming that no nonhuman animals have the capacity for sentient experience.

The notion that nonhuman animals lack the capacity to enjoy and suffer is not new. The Cartesian attitude toward nonhuman animals manifests just this position.[13] Descartes believed that all nonhuman animals are nothing more than relatively complex automatons. Since they lack minds, the perceptions of pleasures and pains are essentially divorced from these brutes; even on experientialist grounds, they have no sakes for which any action could be directed. This mindset is epitomized in Descartes's legal defense of his vivisectionist experiments. Neighbors complained about the screams of anguish emanating from the animals being experimented upon at Descartes's home. To these neighbors, the screams indicated the existence of horribly painful experiments practiced on the subjugated animals. In court, Descartes analogized the screams of the animals to the sounds that machines make when there is interference with their internal workings.[14] Just as the grind of pulleys and springs produces unpleasant-sounding noises without any suffering on the part of a machine, the animal sounds, unpleasant though they might be to our human audial sensibilities, were no indication of suffering occurring in the dog or cat. To think otherwise, according to Descartes, was to engage in a sort of category mistake: attributing a quality to an entity, in this case a mind or soul, that God has ordained solely for humans. It is in the guises of the conceptual chauvinist desire theorist or the chauvinist experientialist that this philosophical legacy of Descartes survives.

Peter Carruthers has argued that although nonhuman animals do have experiences, they are not of the requisite sort for moral consideration.[15] To Carruthers, animals are never in conscious mental states, nor do they undergo conscious experiences. Incapable of enjoyment and suffering, they lack the capacity for sentient experience. Even when electric currents are forced through their bodies (as frequently happens in the production of fur attire) or when metal traps are clamped onto their legs (as frequently occurs in trapping), caring, compassion, and sympathy are misplaced attitudes, for in these circumstances, as in all others, the animals are not conscious of any feelings. To the Nagelian question, "What is it like to be a nonhuman animal?" Carruthers delivers a clear and unequivocal response: Nothing, absolutely nothing at all.

When faced with a radically counterintuitive thesis, one immediately suspects a contentious understanding of some key terms. Carruthers tells us that "a conscious experience is a state whose content is available to be consciously thought about (that is; which is available for description in acts of thinking which are themselves made available to further acts of thinking)."[16] What makes my present visual experience of a car a conscious visual experience is that the content of this visually experienced state (the car traveling in front of me) can be described in a conscious mental way. That is, I am disposed to think to myself, "There is a car moving in front of me," where this thinking to myself is itself a conscious act of thinking and so, too, amenable to being the content of further thinkings. Accepting this account of conscious experience leads quickly to the conclusion that brutes are consciousless. Since it is highly implausible to attribute these higher-level thoughts (thinkings about thinkings) to nonhuman animals, we are unwarranted to attribute conscious experiences to them. Animal awareness is a fiction.

What might prompt this account of consciousness? Consider driving your car over a familiar stretch of highway. While driving, you manifest the appropriate behavior; you change lanes at propitious times, use directional lights on relevant occasions, and so forth. Yet during this half-hour journey, your entire (conscious) attention has been exhausted by last night's basketball game. Your mind, as we might naturally put it, has been "someplace else," having spent the last half hour "spaced-out," on "automatic pilot." Less vernacularly, we can describe this as a journey of which you have been completely (consciously) unaware, for neither during the excursion nor after its completion can you supply any details of your relationship to your surroundings. Yet, in some sense, you must have been seen the flow of traffic; the reasonableness of your behavior demands an explanation. Without crediting you with some experience of the environment, the explanation of your appropriate lane changes and signaling would be miraculous and mysterious. This "blindsight" phenomenon is something that almost all of us have experienced.

One can view Carruthers as being motivated by the desire to distinguish these "blindsight" experiences (or, as he calls them, "nonconscious experiences") from our common conscious experiences. Roughly, his answer is that the content of conscious experiences alone can be reflected upon. Nonconscious experiences cannot be made available to later (or even present) reflection, because, from the agent's phenomenological first-person perspective, *nothing* happened; there is nothing upon which to reflect. According to Carruthers, all nonhuman experience is blindsight experience. Brutes can experience sounds, smells, tastes, and even sensations. What they are precluded from doing, in virtue of their inability to have higher-ordered thoughts—an ability that Carruthers believes requires the advent of language—is to consciously experience these things.

But there are good reasons to reject Carruthers's analysis of consciousness. His account seems to generate, for each conscious experience, an infinite number of acts of conscious thinking (n.b. Carruthers's parenthetical comment in his definition of "conscious experience"). Although there might not be anything especially problematic about a normal adult human having the disposition to think to himself about the content of a lower-level (or first-order) experience, it would appear to be beyond the powers of any human to extend his thinkings much further. To gain a sense of the difficulty, manufacture circumstances that are as favorable as possible and attempt to have, say, a tenth-order conscious thought. Carruthers's account yields the intolerable result that there would be no *human* conscious experience. Furthermore, the regress alluded to is vicious. Each higher-level thought seems required prior to the lower-level thought's being conscious. That is, what *makes* any experience a conscious experience is the fact that the individual is disposed to reflect upon it; the disposition to reflect upon the experience does not merely "fall out" from the independent consciousness of the lower-level thought.

Carruthers's account is far too restrictive. Consider a young woman who witnesses the brutal rape and beating of her mother and who, forevermore, cannot even think to herself of what she was so dramatically aware. It is not as though the thought begins to intrude upon her consciousness; on the contrary, her mental defenses make it impossible for her to reflect upon that of which she was so acutely aware. After years of psychotherapy (and this, we may presume, constitutes the most favorable circumstance under which her disposition might be manifested), she still cannot mentally imagine, let alone verbally describe, the earlier horrid experience. In psychotherapists' jargon, the experience has become "inaccessible" or "repressed." Seemingly, we have a paradigmatic conscious experience without the putative necessary availability to reflection.

Carruthers's model is hypercognitive and so succumbs to other, less arcane, sorts of implications. As so often happens in any attempt to disenfranchise nonhuman animals, human infants fail to make the cut as well. Do we really want to be committed, as Carruthers admits he is, to the claim that infants do not consciously feel pain? Would Carruthers, or anyone else, for that matter, withhold anesthesia from their two-month-old child, realizing that their feelings of sympathy for the baby are misplaced? Carruthers might reply that he would not withhold anesthesia, not because the baby would be harmed, but because others who love the baby would suffer great anguish if they knew the baby were operated upon without anesthetic. Thus, the administration of the numbing drug would be done not for the sake of the infant but for the sakes of the infant's loved ones. But if a loved one were himself knowingly given a drug to ensure that he would not feel anguish, Carruthers is committed to claiming that the drug's administration is a waste of time and resources (it would be like anesthetizing a rock before breaking it), and that any reasonable person, in this hypothetical position, would not have the drug administered. This strikes me as immensely counterintuitive. At bottom, the infant's parents want the drug administered not because they want to feel better (although they undoubtedly will), but because they desire that their child not suffer unnecessarily.

I suppose that Carruthers can try to explain our allegedly misleading belief concerning infant suffering by suggesting that most of us are captured by an illusion, born perhaps of our innate psychology, that these infants suffer. To respect these psychologies, to mitigate the pain and suffering of those who, like the parents, greatly care about the well-being of the child, anesthesia should be administered. Perhaps these psychologies are so firmly entrenched that even under the illumination of Carruthers's compelling argument to the contrary, most of us are still unable to dispel our misconceptions. So it is in deference to a psychological malady that is beyond repair by reason (and perhaps even by physiological manipulation) that the anesthetic should be delivered to the young child. This verdict would need to be extended to encompass many autistic, retarded, senile, and other mentally marginalized humans, for these, like the very young children who lack the requisite language skills, would also be without the ability of higher-order thinking. Our belief that these marginal creatures are capable of suffering and enjoyment would then likewise be false but inevitable.

But such a maneuver would cast too broad a net. If this sort of possibility is sufficient for overturning our most deeply held beliefs, virtually everything, including Carruthers's own views, are cast in shadow. Indeed, the ploy is really nothing more, appropriately enough, than a version of Descartes's evil genius. Recall that this devilish individual has the ability to manipulate our minds in ways such that we cannot but believe false statements. To Descartes, the mere possibility of the existence of this creature sufficed for a justified skepticism regarding virtually all that we believe we know.

Finally, Carruthers is faced with the difficult task of reconciling his account of consciousness with a viable theory of language acquisition. I suggested earlier that the possession of some rudimentary beliefs seems required for learning a language.[17] A fortiori, it certainly seems as if a child must be conscious in order to have higher-level thoughts or a language. But if having higher-level thoughts or having a language is required for consciousness, we seem to be viciously encircled. Perhaps by adopting a sort of Platonism one can reject the mutual dependency, but to many of us, especially to an empirically and nominalistically inclined philosopher like Carruthers, such an avenue would be uninviting.

I admit having no analysis of consciousness to supersede Carruthers's. I do not know if one is necessary. One would be hard-pressed to argue that a catastrophic situation has ensued since philosophers have found the "justified true belief" account of knowledge to be wanting. This being conceded, it does seem that Carruthers's account is wrong-headed; whatever consciousness is, it is something episodic or occurrent. When one has a conscious experience, he is experiencing something then and there. Any dispositional account, of which Carruthers's is just one example, fails to capture what seems to be a distinctive and irreducible element of conscious experience. Undoubtedly, conscious as opposed to nonconscious experience inclines or disposes one to behave in certain ways, but consciousness itself seems more basic both in the sense of accounting for our individuality and in the sense of making our personal lives worth living.[18]

(VII)

Another neo-Cartesian, Peter Harrison, believes that the "evidence brought forward to demonstrate that animals feel pain is far from conclusive."[19] Harrison believes that there are three basic types of considerations from which some people have concluded that nonhuman animals feel pain and that none of these considerations should be thought of as persuasive. The first consideration is that animal and human behaviors are similar in the face of similar stimuli. The second argument for the existence of nonhuman animal pain is based on the claim that animals share a similar structure and function of nervous systems with human beings. The third reason for regarding animal pain as real rests on evolutionary theory, a theory that is antagonistic toward the existence of radical shifts in animal evolution, as well as one that utilizes the existence of (felt) pain to explain the adaptation of creatures to their environments.

Before reviewing Harrison's reactions to these considerations, we should notice two points of methodology. Although Harrison correctly pinpoints three considerations that are typically advanced to make the case for the existence of nonhuman animal pain, the considerations are not typically put forth as individually self-sufficient. That is, usually discussions take all three considerations, with perhaps others, as jointly sufficient for a very powerful argument for the existence of animal pain. Thus, even if in isolation none of the three considerations provides strong reasons for the commonsense position that animals feel pain, this by itself is not good reason to reject the view that animal pain does not exist. It is odd that this rather obvious point seems to escape Harrison, since he correctly perceives that discussion about the first consideration quite naturally leads to discussion of the second. Yet, although he acknowledges that the presentation of the argument for the existence of animal pain is hardly likely to concentrate on just one of his three reasons, he seems not to realize that, taken as a whole, the three considerations may mutually support acceptance of the prephilosophical, anti-Cartesian view.

Second, Cartesian arguments against the consciousness of nonhuman animals should not rely on a general skepticism regarding the mentality of humans. Harrison is not, that is, arguing that our skepticism regarding the mentality of animals trivially follows from the fact that the problem of "other minds" has not been solved. This point can be turned on its head; if Harrison suggests an argument against the possibility of ascertaining reliable evidence for the existence of animal consciousness, it had better not be equally applicable against having justified beliefs concerning the mentality of humans.

Harrison finds the behavioral argument far too weak, pointing out that we do not ascribe pain to ants and single-cell organisms that "withdraw from harmful stimuli" (26). Moreover, he suggests that that the nonliving, in the form of advanced robots, can exhibit pain-behavior without possibly feeling pain.

The claim about ants is tendentious. The withholding of pain ascriptions from single-cell animals that withdraw from harmful stimuli (where the characterization of "harmful" presumably is intended to convey that such stimuli are likely to limit the life span of the individual) activates the caveat offered earlier; in the light of other knowledge concerning the lack of neural structure, we have reason to think that this withdrawal behavior is not indicative of felt pain. It also should be noted that this is not so much a manifestation of weakness in the relationship between behavior and phenomenology as it is an example of very skimpy behavioral evidence. Pain behavior comprises far more than withdrawal from the source of the pain, for typically there is grimacing, wincing, screaming, touching of certain bodily parts, and so on. If the behavior were far more complex than that offered by an amoeba or paramecium, then there would be less uncertainty whether pain should be attributed to the individual. Consider what our reaction would be to an extraterrestrial who behaved very much as we do in the presence of painful stimuli, but who had nothing like the neural structure that we now believe is necessary for felt sensations. Some beliefs would need to be abdicated, but I see no a priori way to determine which ones they would be. I have no doubt that robotics will progress to the point that non-feeling machines will have the capacity to manifest overt behavior that mirrors human pain behavior. (This is not to say that it is impossible for artifacts to suffer pain.) But this again just shows what is uncontentious: behavioral data is defeasible. If we know that the individual before us is inanimate, then we (probably) would rescind our judgment that it feels pain. But this does not show that behavioral evidence is weak; it merely makes the indisputable point that it need not be decisive.

Harrison admits that when behavioral considerations are conjoined with ones relating the similar structure and function of the nervous systems of human and nonhuman animals, we have at least the appearance of a stronger argument. Presumably the point here is that our denial of pain to ants, amoebas, and robots can be explained by the fact that none of these entities has a nervous system that is remotely human. The problem with this additional consideration, according to Harrison, is that pain is "intractably mental" (27). This property of pain renders the "nervous system" consideration useless, for it: (1) makes it impossible for mental states to be reduced to physical states; and (2) makes it impossible to project mental states from appropriate anatomical and physiological data.

To put it mildly, we should be suspicious. To accept the "intractable mentality" of pain commits us, a priori, to the rejection of materialism. Harrison's assertion of the intractable mentality of pain is tantamount to saying that our pains reside in immaterial souls. We will proceed to his arguments for this presently, but it should be noted that, although it is far from transparent what the force of "project" is in (2), Harrison's dualism may be even more radical than Descartes's. Although to Descartes, the mind and body were ontologically distinct substances, a mutually causal relationship obtained. It is true that the difficulty in providing a viable account to explain the mechanism of this interaction has proven the bane of Cartesians, but the official view comported with common sense insofar as the mind and body mutually interact. Thus from the grimacing, wincing, and crying of a child, a reliable, albeit defeasible, inference can be made that the individual is in pain. If the "impossibility to project" means that we cannot even make well-founded inferences about a person's mental states from his behavior, the causal relationship of Descartes would seem not to be present in Harrison's account. If the "impossibility to project" is meant to suggest merely that the existence of particular mental states cannot be deductively inferred from anatomical and physiological data, then Harrison's view is compatible with Descartes's. But, in either case, the obvious question is, what reason do we have for accepting the "intractable mentality" of pain from the outset?

Harrison begins his Cartesian defense by telling us that the use of placebos and hypnosis to control pain and the natural differences in pain thresholds all show that the presence of certain brain structures and requisite sensory inputs are insufficient for the prediction of mental states. He also reminds us of the "phantom pain" phenomenon in which an individual claims to have pain in a limb that is no longer part of her body. This shows, to Harrison, that pain can occur without "relevant" physical structure. Further severance between mind and body is suggested by the fact that birds lack a visual cortex, and yet observation of their behavior gives us reason to think that they see. Harrison suggests, as did Carruthers, that perhaps animal experiences are all nonconscious or of the "blindsight" variety. Under this supposition, birds would behave as if they are having conscious visual experiences, although from the inside nothing would be going on. There is precedent for this type of behavior in humans, where some people sincerely claim not to be able to see a particular part of their environment and yet give quite accurate assessments of the shapes and sizes of objects in that segment of the external world. (Recall, in our discussion of Carruthers, the case of the automobile driver on "automatic pilot.") Finally, Harrison interprets Nagel's famous discussion in "What Is It Like to Be a Bat?" as demonstrating that the construction of subjective experiences from brain states is, in principle, impossible.

None of these observations is compelling. The general problem is that Harrison apparently assumes that the existence of deviant cases establishes his general antiphysicalist case. Indeed, the fact that these cases are deviant, are the exception rather than the rule, shows how closely we align physiology with psychology. Unless there is a strong supposition of an intimate connection between these conceptually distinct parts of an individual, the very oddness that Harrison relies upon to substantiate his case would be unavailing. Consider Harrison's reference to the fact that placebos and hypnosis can be used to control pain. What legitimizes

Harrison's description of these techniques as "controlling pain," if we do not assume a very close (admittedly defeasible) relationship between the mind and body? Why believe, as this description suggests, that the individual is experiencing the same degree of pain both with and without hypnosis, but simply can better manage it with the aid of the mental manipulation? Indeed, without the intimate connection assumed, we seem to have no reason at all to believe that the other is experiencing any pain at all. In (2), he describes the impossibility of projecting mental states from *appropriate* physiological and anatomical data. But how is one to make the distinction, which Harrison implicitly employs, between appropriate data on the one hand and inappropriate data on the other? Without some assumed reliability between the physical and the mental, the distinction becomes vacuous. This criticism does not rely on a general skepticism regarding other minds, a general skepticism that, as mentioned earlier, is not to the point. Rather, it is meant to demonstrate how difficult it is to make the separation between mind and body as severe as Harrison would like.

On a more discriminating level, it seems most unlikely, as Harrison implicitly assumes, that one's brain states are in the same configuration with or without either the placebo or hypnosis. Harrison apparently believes that since the brain states are identical in either case, and since the ability to control the pain is different, we cannot infer the individual's behavior from his brain configuration. What I am suggesting is the reasonable hypothesis that the person's brain states are distinct in the situations of being influenced and not being influenced by hypnosis. If this is true, there is no principled reason why advances in neurophysiology will not permit inferences, with great certainty, from the state of one's brain to one's mental state. In fact, this work has already started, and progress seems inevitable.

The example of the visual-cortexless bird to whom we grant sight is also unhelpful to Harrison. The fact that a bird can see without a visual cortex scarcely shows that the possession of a visual cortex is not good evidence for believing that its possessor can see; something can provide excellent reasons for a belief without its being necessary to what is believed. If the fossils of a creature showed it to have had four long legs, a lean body, and little body fat, this would constitute excellent reason for believing that the creature was fast afoot. The fact that there are a few animals who can run quickly without possessing these attributes shows only that the properties are not essential, not that they are not likely concomitants.

Finally, Harrison's use of Nagel's bat is far too sweeping. Granting for the sake of discussion that I cannot know what it is like for a bat to sense objects, in virtue of the fact that the phenomenology attached to sonar detection is lost on me, it cannot be inferred that I do not know what it is like for a seal pup to have her head bashed by some greedy furrier. And, of course, Nagel would agree. Some animals work very much like human beings, much in the same way that human beings act like other human beings. The evidence for this is just the behavioral and physiological evidence that Harrison unjustifiably jettisons. Indeed, if this evidence is as feckless as Harrison would have us believe, his (illicit) appropriation of Nagel should place us all in doubt about what other humans are going through when they fall off bicycles or bang their fingers with hammers.

Harrison takes issue with the argument from evolution claiming that behavior, and not some hypothetical mental state such as pain, adapts the animal: "Those who are insensitive to pain are not disadvantaged by the absence of unpleasant mental states, but by a lack of those behavioral responses which in others are prompted by pain" (32). We know that the behavior can be acquired without the mental state by observation of very simple animals and reflection upon blindsight examples. Moreover, by omitting any reference to mental states, we have a simpler explanation for animals' behavior. Although it is often pragmatically useful to adopt an "intentional stance" toward animals, to view them as if they really had mental states, there are examples in which this stance collapses, and explanation of behavior requires adoption of a "design stance," a viewing of the animal's behavior as the product of natural design.[20] The submitted example is the behavior of the wildebeest, which remains silent when fiercely attacked so that other cospecifics will not be lured to their deaths.

Harrison needs to explain why humans fare differently; why, that is, it is proper to attribute (felt) pains to humans while not to animals. One reason is that only humans have free will and moral responsibility. He tells us that we think of nonhuman animals not as either moral or free agents, but simply as causally determined natural items. But if these brutes are nothing more than causally determined things, then "it makes no sense to speak of pain as an additional causal factor" (36). A second and intimately related reason is that only humans are rational, decision-making creatures. Whereas we can and do make sense of a human's bearing immense pain ("John kept his hand in the fire to show his children the effects of playing with matches"), nonhuman animals, lacking the capability of reason, are precluded from this "language-game"; much of the "logic" of pain necessarily excludes nonhuman animals. The wildebeest has no reason to remain silent, and "if pain never be brought into the sphere of reasons—the mind—then there is no need for it, *qua* unpleasant mental event at all" (37). Without even the possibility of possessing rational or moral considerations that might overrule the natural needs of the body, the attribution of pain is superfluous and entirely without warrant.

Perhaps Harrison fails to think of nonhuman animals as free agents, but I would suggest that he is in a rather small minority. Granting for the moment that they are "merely" causally determined creatures, to assume as he does that this precludes freedom begs the question against two thousand years of Compatibilism. Perhaps Compatibilism is false, but Locke, Schlick, Hume, Hobbes, Ayer, Lewis, and many others cannot have their positions dismissed so cavalierly. Equally problematic is the lack of argument for human behavior's being uncaused. That is, accepting the incompatibilist claim that determinism and freedom are mutually exclusive, what reasons do we have for believing that while nonhuman behavior is causally manufactured, human activity is not? Harrison cannot reply that humans, unlike the brutes, reason, and that reason requires acausality, for in this context, this is mere question begging. At best, Harrison would be entitled to claim that it seems to us that we are free (but why cannot it seem this way to animals?), but we still need to know why this feeling is indicative of truth. There seems nothing inconsistent about a creature's mistakenly believing that she is free, a possibility that is picturesquely illustrated by Spinoza's leaf.[21]

For the sake of discussion, let us grant what seems blatantly false, that humans are free and all nonhuman animals are not. If asked what is it about human beings that accounts for this unique power, Harrison's response is that it is our "intractable mentality." What does this amount to? Something beyond the ken of the causal nexus, something immaterial—in short, although Harrison does not quite come out and say it, our souls make us free. Let us bypass all the usual problems about providing a positive characterization of the seat of our immaterial identity and forgo concerns about the mechanism for its introduction (it seems difficult to see how anything less than divine intervention will do), but direct ourselves only to the specific point at issue, namely our freedom. If, as Harrison says, a causally determined individual essentially is precluded from having freedom, how does the introduction of something that escapes from the clutches of a causally determined world make it possible for us, the possessors of this entity, to be free? This problem has been with us since the inception of Libertarian theories of freedom. We here grant that it is difficult to attribute freedom to an individual who is part of the causal nexus, but it seems at least as difficult to explain how extricating oneself from this network—which, in essence, is what the possession of a soul allows us to do—bestows freedom upon us. We have been down this mysterious road before, invoking transcendental egos (Descartes) and noumena (Kant) in unsuccessful attempts to clarify how the addition of an acausal object solves our dilemma of free will. This is not to say that there are not souls and that their existence alone can explicate individuals' freedom. But it makes manifest just how much Harrison's argument presupposes. Not only does he offhandedly dismiss Compatibilism, he also assumes that Libertarianism has a viable solution to the problem that Compatibilists cannot resolve.

One could also take issue with the claim that nonhumans are not thought of as moral agents. Perhaps my dog Knish does not operate in accordance with some moral principles (neither, very often, do humans), but this need not rule out appropriately attributing morally agential qualities to him.[22] We often, apparently with good reason, think of dogs as loving, courageous, and loyal and talk of dogs' acting from these virtuous dispositions. We have much anecdotal and some scientific evidence for the fact that some animals risk personal injury in acting from these inclinations. I am not suggesting that Knish enters into an internal soliloquy and decides to act out of a sense of moral idealism, but I am claiming that there is no good reason to believe that such "higher-order" thinking is required for beings to act morally. Once again, there is an implicit standard for moral agency that strikes me as hypercognitive. To the extent that one adopts this higher standard and accepts the idea that moral agency requires the individual to act not only in accordance with, but in virtue of, some set of prescriptions, one is likely to exclude much of human morality along with the banishment of animal moral agents. The exclusion of humans will reach far beyond the "marginal" set of infants, retarded, senile, and the like. Its scope will extend to many used-car salesmen, politicians, and university professors.

And why should we accept the claim that animals cannot reason or be incapable of having rational considerations? Anthropological studies have shown that some nonhuman primates use tools and that various mammals and birds implement strategies that are apparently intended to safeguard the future of their families. Many of these behaviors are more than flexible enough not to be considered tropisms by any reasonable account. In a supposition that mirrors his notion that animals essentially lack freedom, Harrison implicitly assumes from the fact that animals, unlike human beings, are "merely" causally determined mechanisms that they cannot reason or have any rational considerations. Again, can we so facilely dismiss the scores of Compatibilists who have tried to reconcile the existence of rationality in causally determined individuals?

And finally, we need, once again, to engage the ubiquitous problem that human infants bring to these conceptual chauvinist experiential accounts. Young infants exhibit behavior that is no more indicative of rationality or respectful of moral considerations than many animals. I see no reason why, therefore, we cannot adopt the "design stance" toward them. Undoubtedly, Harrison would be unwilling to deny moral patienthood to human infants, but it difficult to see, outside of theological dogma, what reasons can be supplied to acknowledge souls in young humans without also granting them to other creatures in the animal kingdom.

(VIII)

Neo-Cartesianism fails, and so we have no good reason to disavow our commonsense belief that many nonhuman animals are capable of conscious, sentient experience. Thus, even if we accept the relationship between the capacities for sentient experience and desire formation as conceptual, we have no good reasons for denying desires to nonhuman animals. Since we may remain comfortable with our commonsense belief that some nonhuman animals have sentient experience, the chauvinist experientialist has nothing tempting to offer us. More generally, excluding the theoretical reasons for rejecting the desire theory, we have not been offered any good reasons—be they from the contingency theorist or the conceptualist—to deny animals the capacity to desire. This failure on the part of those desire theorists who wish to disenfranchise nonhuman animals lends indirect support to experientialism. If we are to incorporate nonhuman animals into our moral domain, experientialism does so in the simplest, most direct and commonsensical way.

We turn now to a popular philosophical theory that, in its typical manifestations, treats animals as resources. To the extent that this theory is acceptable, experientialism—*nonchauvinistic* experientialism—is undermined.

5

Contractualism and Animals

(i)

There is a popular philosophical theory of morality, comprising in part a theory of welfare, that, at least when typically developed, has serious negative implications for experientialism. If this theory is accepted in its usually proffered forms, one is committed to rejecting the capacity for sentient experience as being sufficient for moral patienthood. Such theorists, unlike those who advocate either the desire theory or perfectionism, do not deny that these exempted individuals lack good and bad ways of being, or, equivalently, that they can be both benefited and harmed. Furthermore, unlike the conceptual chauvinist desire theorists or other antiexperientialists, they concede that these individuals can have sentient experiences and that the enjoyment or suffering they experience respectively accounts for their being made better and worse off. What is strenuously denied, however, is that the possession of these qualities alone warrants membership into our moral community. Indeed, without other morally relevant attributes, such individuals cannot *intelligibly* be accorded moral standing.

(ii)

Contractualism—or indifferently, contractarianism or social contract theory—has been unfriendly toward nonhuman animals. At best, contractualists have granted animals "indirect" moral status, effectively implying that the only moral engagements we can have with them are instrumental. We can act morally rightly or wrongly toward animals only in an attenuated sense. Our behaviors regarding them sustain a moral dimension only insofar as they affect moral patients, individuals who, in virtue of their noninstrumental or intrinsic properties, command moral consideration and respect. Kant epitomizes this contractualist perspective on animals when he tells us that a faithful dog who has grown too old for further service deserves to be rewarded and not shot by his master. The desert, however, is not founded on any obligation or duty that we have to the dog per se (for there is none), but rather on the fact that such behavior would help us in our dealings with our fellow humans. If we were to act cruelly toward the dog, we would be inclined to act cruelly toward other humans, and one "would damage in himself that humanity which is his duty to show towards mankind."[1]

The notion that Kant's dog lacks the capacity to be the (direct) object of ethical behavior strikes many contemporary ears as radical. It implies that we do not, for we cannot, abridge the dog's rights were we to torture and kill it. Nor is there friction only when this Kantian consequence confronts the language of rights. We neither act justly toward the dog when we give it water after a long run on a hot day, nor act unjustly toward it when we intentionally withhold the water from it. Although we can act kindly and cruelly toward the dog, we cannot act (morally) rightly or wrongly toward it. When considered solely on the basis of its nonrelational qualities—when considered, that is, on the basis of its intrinsic or inherent properties—the dog cannot be morally enfranchised. He is morally relegated to be a means and not an end.

We need to investigate the reasoning that has led contractarians to this moral assessment of animals. We will find, I believe, that contractarianism has, pace the avowals of some of its adherents, the conceptual resources to welcome animals into the moral realm, and so the ability to distance itself from what is a counterintuitive and, I would hold, repugnant consequence. But the olive branch will be extended only so far; the insistence on excluding all nonhuman animals from the (direct) moral realm and thereby maintaining that those who can enjoy and suffer still do not qualify for moral enfranchisement will lead to an unacceptable theory of moral evaluation.

(III)

Social contract theorists take pains to point out that the attractiveness of their theory cannot be fully appreciated unless it is viewed not merely as a normative ethical theory but as a philosophical moral theory. A normative ethical theory is required merely to tell us which sorts of actions are (morally) right and which are wrong. So, for example, considered only as a normative ethical theory, utilitarianism fulfills its function when it informs us that right actions are those, among all the viable alternatives, that produce the greatest net utility; wrong actions are those that create less. Contractualists demand that philosophical ethical theories do more. In addition to providing normative direction, such theories are typically asked to provide accounts of: (1) how our moral language and concepts come to be employed in the ways they are; (2) the subject matter of morality (or, to put the point semantically, the grounds of moral judgments); (3) the epistemic access we have to evaluate moral judgments; and (4) moral motivation, where this is intended to include explanations of both why moral considerations (justifiably) incline particular actions and why moral considerations are considered stringent and serious. It is in providing a formidable account of an unmysterious means of epistemically accessing moral claims as well as in suggesting a compelling narrative to explain the seriousness and stringency of moral reasons that contractualists generally situate their greatest advantage over rival philosophical theories.

Of course, an opponent of contractualism is not compelled to accept the *desiderata* of philosophical moral theories with which she is provided. She may think that it is not the task of ethical theory, for example, to offer an account of the source of our moral notions. One may submit that such an account is better placed under the auspices of sociology and anthropology. Or one may suggest that our moral concepts are in such a state of disrepair that any inquiry concerning their origins is doomed from the start. An adversary may also argue that formal notions like elegance and simplicity should be appended to the checklist offered by the contractualist. These are fair comments and deserve a hearing. However our immediate purpose is not to argue against contractualism, but rather try to understand why a considerable number of philosophers find it appealing. As long as we have some sensitivity concerning the contractarian aims of an ethical theory, we should recognize the appeal of a theory that putatively achieves those goals.

(IV)

So much for the caveat to understand contractualism as a philosophical ethical theory. To understand the structure of contractualism there is no better contemporary starting point than Rawls's work, notwithstanding his disclaimer that he is presenting merely a contractualist account of justice and not of morality in general.[2] He suggests that morality is best conceived as consisting of the set of principles or rules for establishing social arrangements that would be devised by rational, self-interested parties operating under fair conditions. To help flesh out this conception, we should begin by reflecting on a premoral, presocietal state of mankind. In this Hobbesian state of nature, life is indeed nasty, brutish, and short. Life can and would be better for each if all agreed to a set of principles that would govern a cooperative venture. These societal principles have the primary functions of determining how rights and duties are to be assigned in the basic institutions and providing guidelines for the distribution of benefits and burdens to individuals. We are to think of these principle-formulating individuals (i.e., contractors) as operating under a "veil of ignorance"; no one knows, for example, her own personal social standing, physical and mental abilities, or even personal conception of the good. The veil of ignorance, used as a shield to blind the participants from their individual strengths and weaknesses, has great significance to Rawls; it is what ensures fairness in the contractors' deliberations in this initial situation.

Contractors, rational individuals with their own goals and with a "sense of justice," are moral persons. Rawls conceives of rationality instrumentally; one is rational to the extent that one uses effective means to reach a desired end. There is an even more basic sense in which rationality is demanded of contractors, for these individuals must have the cognitive ability that allows them both to understand the bargaining that is transpiring and to communicate their own desires in the proceedings. In short, they need to have at least a rudimentary understanding of what they have been called to participate in. By "sense of justice," Rawls does not intend to refer to any feeling, but rather to a "normally effective desire to apply and to act upon the principles of justice, at least to a minimum degree" (505). This idea is quintessentially Kantian; where Rawls speaks of a sense of justice, Kant spoke of operating under a moral law. To one no less than the other, this property is essential to moral personhood.

In concluding this brief sketch of Rawlsian contractualism, it needs to be emphasized that regardless of how successful the theory is in answering their self-proclaimed *desiderata* of a philosophical moral theory, the touchstone for its viability still lies in its relationship with our reflective moral beliefs. Rawls himself first alludes to this when he tells us that of all traditional views, contractualism "best approximates our considered judgments of justice" (viii). Subsequently, Rawls explicates this crucial point:

> By going back and forth, sometimes altering the conditions of the contractual circumstances, at others withdrawing our judgments and conforming them to principle, I assume that eventually we shall find a description of the original situation that both expresses reasonable conditions and yields principles which match our considered judgments duly pruned and adjusted. (20)

This process, the process of "reflective equilibrium," has significant implications. To Rawls, neither the circumstances of the original position nor our currently held considered moral beliefs are sacrosanct. Although there are theoretical pressures ("pressures from above," as they may be called) that incline us to change some of our commonsense pretheoretical moral beliefs, there are parallel pressures exercised by our commonsense morality ("pressures from below") that dispose us to modify the conditions of the original contractors. Rawls remains optimistic that ultimately this give-and-take will result in a set of principles derivable from an initial situation that will conform with a modified set of moral beliefs.

Rawls unsurprisingly fails to supply us with any precise criteria for properly conducting this process of reflective equilibrium. Without such ground rules, we seem to be left with a wide spectrum of possibilities. On the one hand, we have those who, being of a conservative nature, would like to maintain the moral status quo. When our commonsense morality conflicts with a contractualist principle, they urge us to modify the original position so that a conforming principle will be adduced. On the other hand, there are the radicals, so enamored with the contractarian theory (perhaps they are overwhelmed by the philosophical theory's success in providing convincing accounts of points 1–4, above), that they urge that conflict resolution should take the form of abdicating that segment of ordinary morality that grates against principles.

Kantians, of which Rawls is proudly one, are on the conservative side of this scale. Kant thought that our ordinary morality was not in need of overhaul, that the ordinary person knew perfectly well which sorts of actions were right and wrong and so needed no guidance from theoretical philosophy regarding his daily behavior. Ethical theory had a justificatory role, serving as a buttress against skeptical attacks. To Kant, and presumably to Rawls, any ethical theory that implies the general permissibility of stealing, lying, and cheating is self-defeating.

Although I see no reason to encumber contractarianism with a Kantian conservativeness, contractualists, like all other moral theorists, must take the role of our considered moral beliefs very seriously. I am not suggesting that there are some considered moral judgments that cannot be relinquished, but I am saying that an extreme radical, one who is willing to sacrifice many of our most deeply held convictions at the altar of philosophical theory, warrants the skepticism and scrutiny that he most assuredly would receive.

(v)

It must be admitted that Rawls has very little to say about the moral status of nonhuman animals, and that what he does say is forwarded with some ambivalence and tentativeness. Once again, his attitude is unmistakably Kantian. Moral persons (contractors) and those with the potential for moral personhood are the individuals who are owed just consideration and treatment. Those with the potential for personhood, those with "moral personality," are (some) human children. While one might think that this concession to confer full moral status upon children is an accommodation to the pressure exerted solely by our considered moral beliefs, Rawls suggests that this is not so. Since the principles that derive from the original position are not to be consequences of "arbitrary contingencies," it is "reasonable to say that those who could take part in the initial agreement, were it not for fortuitous circumstances, are assured equal justice" (509). Pressure to include children as moral patients comes from above as well as below.

Rawls is relatively mute about further articulating this idea. I suggest that the most favorable interpretation to one who believes that contractualism precludes nonhuman animals from obtaining full moral status is to understand Rawls as claiming that since the temporal location of this hypothetical initial situation is purely arbitrary, it is equally arbitrary which stage of a moral person's life intersects the contractual situation. Although an individual may be a human child (or, at least, a human child with the potential of personhood) relative to one time, that individual is a full-fledged moral person at some later date. Since there is no reason to single out one time rather than another for the date of the contractual discussion, it would be baseless to deny children full moral status. If, that is, the contractual date is hypothesized to occur at some later date (and there is absolutely no reason why this hypothesis is not equally reasonable), those who were merely moral personalities under the initial hypothesis are now full-blown moral persons.

Compare this way of including (some) human children into the moral realm with another frequently employed. It is often advanced that children would be included as moral patients as an outcome in the initial deliberations in virtue of the natural sentimental attachments that adult humans have with their young (Rawls, 249–50). This need not violate the stricture imposed by the Rawlsian veil of ignorance, since it can be argued that these sentiments are shared, and knowingly so, by virtually all adult humans and so no knowledge of particular psychologies is being smuggled into consideration. The evident problem is that the idea of "sentimental attachment" is far too generous. There are large segments of the adult human population who feel toward their companion animals much as they feel toward their own children, where this feeling seems to be of the natural rather than acquired sort that is similar to the familial sentiments. One might even argue that similar sentiments attach to the inanimate, as in the case of persons' homes; there are many who go through a grieving process when their home is lost in fire or earthquake that mirrors, to a large extent, what occurs when one loses a child. The significant point here is not that all these sentiments are equally powerful in all; the point, rather, is that the differences are ones of degree and not kind. The concessions that not all adult humans have these attachments and 'that a sizable number feel very close to the nonhuman realm would suggest that this avenue to selectively identify moral patients as only those who are either moral persons or moral personalities is doomed.

Moreover, we need not appeal to the notion of sentimental attachments to account for our favorable considered beliefs about the deceased. We can explain these beliefs, indeed discover the theoretical underpinning for these beliefs, by using the temporal explication of "fortuitous circumstances." Those humans who are dead at some arbitrarily picked time set for the contractual meeting would have been alive if the hypothesized time had been earlier. Once again, since there is no reason to think of one time as being preferential to any other, it would seem completely arbitrary to deny the dead less than full moral privilege. So, for example, if—as contractualists would undoubtedly say—breaking promises to living adult humans is wrong, it is also wrong to break promises that can only be satisfied to postmortem individuals. This does not commit contractualists to the very bizarre idea that the living can make promises to the dead, but only to the notion that if promises made to the antemortem person can be kept only after the promisee is deceased, they ought to be.

Another dividend paid by a temporal elucidation of fortuitous circumstances is that we can include future generations as full-fledged moral beings. Since it is merely arbitrary that we conceive of the contractual situation as occurring prior, rather than subsequent, to our deaths, posterity is conferred patienthood in precisely the same manner as are currently living infants. This is not to imply that some very difficult issues do not remain. While the temporal account can at least suggest how a Rawlsian contractualism might embrace the notion of obligations toward actual future generations, the question of what, if any, obligations we have toward the creation of posterity, is still rather obscure. Still, many of our pervasive beliefs about our descendants can be accounted for by employing the temporal analysis.

Finally, the temporal interpretation of arbitrariness seems to give the desired Rawlsian results regarding nonhuman animals. While we can say of a particular deceased human that had the contractual date had been years earlier he would have been party to the deliberations, and we can say of a particular (normally endowed) infant that she would have been a contractor had the date been a few years hence, we cannot say of a particular dog that he would have been a contractor if only the date of the contractual deliberations had been moved in one direction or another. Rawls, then, has at his disposal a principled explication of "fortuitous circumstances" that accords him just what he wants. If Rawlsian contractualism is to falter from problems of membership, the source of these problems will have to be uncovered elsewhere.

(VI)

Of course, not all children have moral personalities, any more than all adult humans are moral persons. Children, unfortunately, are occasionally born with physical or mental problems that will inhibit typical development. Some of these problems will allow chronological development without the accompanying cognitive or affective development that personhood requires; some will simply die tragically young. Common ailments plague the elderly as well; advanced sufferers of senility, autism, and Alzheimer's disease will be robbed of abilities that they once had, and they now make the position of a moral person, at best, a vague memory. Are these humans to be ethically disenfranchised?

Rawls's treatment of these cases is brief to the point of being dismissive. Since the overwhelming majority of mankind satisfies his criteria of personhood understood as sufficiency conditions, the inquiry into whether these conditions are necessary as well is of peripheral practical importance. He admits that those individuals (i.e., marginal human beings) "permanently deprived of moral personality may present a difficulty" but believes that his account would not be materially affected (510). He hints at the direction his contractualism would take when he claims that even if the capacity for moral personhood were necessary to make an individual a moral patient, "it would be unwise in practice to withhold justice on this ground. The risk to just institutions would be too great" (506).

I submit that the "difficulty" provided by those permanently deprived of moral personality is far more probative of Rawls's contractualism than his abbreviated discussion would have us believe. Far from being tangential to his conception of ethics, it shows, I believe, what many find deeply troubling about it. It should first be noted that, if we consider nonhuman animals as being among those incapable of moral personhood, far from discussing a small minority, we are now speaking about an overwhelming majority. But of far greater importance than the relative number of individuals affected is the manner in which they are affected. Rather than being relegated to a figurative footnote to an ethical theory, these are just the sort of individuals that are frequently used, and appropriately so, to test the mettle of one's moral suggestions. Gandhi saw this clearly when he suggested that the moral progress of a nation is best judged by the way it treats its animals; its treatment, in other words, of those whose capacities fall short of that of the normal human.

The argument here is not that Rawls cannot account for such creatures; I will accept for the sake of discussion that his appeal to the stability of just institutions will accommodate the unfortunate humans (although obviously not their nonhuman counterparts). We need, however, to call attention to the machinations that Rawlsian contractualism must employ to incorporate these marginal humans. They can be enfranchised, but only at the cost of making them instruments of those individuals whose interests really count. This strikes many of us, rightly I think, as fundamentally wrongheaded and antithetical to the moral enterprise. Their disabilities should not diminish what deficient humans justly, and not merely compassionately, deserve.

(VII)

The means by which marginal humans are morally enfranchised provides the impetus to take a step back and see more deeply why Rawls's contractualism is apparently committed to limiting moral patienthood to only those who are either moral persons or potential moral persons. It cannot be in virtue of the contractors' lacking the power to enfranchise nonhuman animals; presumably there is no incoherence in the idea that the contractors simply stipulate that some (or all) animals are to be accorded full moral status. It would appear as if the exclusion of animals is dictated by the conception of morality that informs Rawls's account. That is, there should be some demonstrable inconsistency between, on the one hand, conceiving of morality as principles formed, with limited knowledge, by self-interested rational beings with a sense of justice, and, on the other, nonhuman animals being accorded direct moral status as moral patients.

To even begin the discussion, the contractarian assumption that all nonhuman animals lack the requisite sort of rationality and the sense of justice that constitutes contractorship must be granted. After all, if some nonhuman animals did have these qualities (and some philosophers have at least hinted in this direction),[3] Rawls not only would admit these animals to the realm of the directly moral, he would insist upon it; being contractors, regardless of species, they automatically qualify as moral patients. Granting this, for the sake of argument, the question remains:

What is it about Rawls's conception of morality that precludes the assessment of nonhuman animals as moral patients?

The answer, though never explicit, seems to hinge on the notion of reciprocity that underlies Rawls's notion of contractualism.[4] It is in virtue of this idea that the key impediment to conferring full moral status to nonhuman animals lies not so much in their lack of rationality, but rather in their privation of a sense of justice. For even if we were to concede that some nonhuman animals have life plans that are, for the most part, effectively accomplished within their comparatively restricted means, the fact that animals lack the ability to act in accordance with the developed principles of justice would imply that their inclusion into the moral realm would do us (i.e., rational creatures with a sense of justice) no good. Since the rules that would result from the deliberative process could not, and so would not, be followed by those essentially lacking the desire to morally engage, we would be giving away something for nothing, placing restrictions on ourselves in the form of duties and obligations and receiving nought in return. Anything more antithetical to self-interest would be difficult to imagine.

This analysis answers those who believe the exclusion of animals from the contract is a function of the arbitrary nature of the veil of ignorance. Tom Regan, for example, has suggested that there is no principled reason to allow those under the veil of ignorance knowledge of their species membership.[5] If we darken the veil somewhat, and now make them ignorant of this fact, self-interest would impel them to include nonhuman animals in their contract as full-fledged members of the moral community. The charge, then, is that Rawls has effectively begged the question against the moral status of animals.

But under my account for Rawlsian exclusion, a motivated response is forthcoming. It is not their nonhuman species per se that excludes nonhuman animals from full moral status, but rather the fact that, ex hypothesi, nonhuman animals (essentially?) lack a sense of justice. A condition required for initial deliberation is that the contractors have a sense of justice; thus, under the plausible assumption that animals lack this desire, no nonhuman animals can be parties in the original position. Furthermore, in virtue of this privation, they are incapable of returning benefits bestowed upon them by others, and so, given Rawls's conception of moral principles arising from parties acting self-interestedly, there is no reason to grant nonhumans full status. Indeed, there is all the reason in the world to deprive them of this status.

Still, one might reply that even under the strong assumption that nonhuman animals essentially lack the capability of desiring to act in accordance with the resulting moral principles, there is at least the possibility that the contractors, although all human, may at some later date evolve or develop into nonhuman animals. The claim now becomes that, in the name of self-interest, these normal humans should confer moral patienthood onto nonhuman animals, since we may become them. Indeed, strictly speaking, the modal status of this Kafkaesque scenario is really not at issue, and so arcane inquiries concerning personal identity can be bypassed. More germane is the epistemic question of whether those in the original position believe, at least to the degree that it would rationally command an effect on the deliberations, that this scenario is possible. For if this envisioned story is impossible, but it is rational to believe in its possibility (to a certain meaningful degree), then those in the initial situation would presumably include nonhuman animals as moral patients. On the other hand, if this scenario is in fact possible, but it is rational to believe in its impossibility, then presumably the contractors would exclude animals from patienthood.

But the Rawlsian would reasonably respond that the general knowledge accorded to those in the original position speaks to the inordinately high likelihood that the contractors will not so evolve. After all, they have not noticed any of these bizarre transformations in the past, and so any doubt about the trend's discontinuing would need to be thought of as merely "metaphysical." The contractors may admit it as a logical or even empirical possibility, but not with enough weight for them to incur the duties and obligations that would enjoin the evaluation of animals as moral patients.

But this response is far more prejudicial than it appears. Millions, if not billions, of humans have claimed to have witnessed these putatively bizarre transformations. Although relatively rare in Western culture, it is the norm in the East to believe in reincarnation, where such personal migration need not be limited within a species. The objection then amounts to charging Rawls not with a species bias but with a cultural one. Regan's charge of question begging is ultimately justified, although he misplaced the point of arbitrariness.

It might be suggested that this response is disallowed by the fact that Rawls, presumably representative of all contractualists, precludes any of those in the original position from having any moral beliefs. After all, one of the major motivating forces behind contractarian analyses is that a natural derivation of morality is possible; that is, moral principles can be given an empirical basis. This empirical basis goes a long way toward providing the advantages of contractualism as a philosophical theory, perhaps most saliently in eschewing intuition or some other mysterious form of epistemic access as the means for garnering ethical truths. But this gambit has force only insofar as one categorizes the belief in reincarnation as moral. Although there can be little dispute that this belief has moral implications, the content of the belief itself is nonmoral. The claim that personal identity can be maintained throughout different bodies at different times relies on no moral beliefs. Admittedly, it is not always clear whether its adherents want to consider it as a scientific hypothesis, a metaphysical principle, or something else altogether; nonetheless, the contractualist stricture prohibiting the original contractors from having moral opinions is not violated.

Another response, one seemingly more in line with Rawls's more recent writings, is simply to admit to a degree of cultural relativity and give convention its due within a contractualist philosophical moral theory. The ramifications of this concession loom large, for we can now see that the notion of a single conception of the mutual advantage of rational, well-intentioned contractors, unsullied by idiosyncrasy, is simply a myth. Alternatively put, the conjunction of rationality, sense of justice, and general knowledge still underdetermines what counts as advantageous for an individual. The worry worsens when we contemplate the extent of this fragmentation. Once we begin, can we, in a principled way, stop the slide from culture to community to individual? One of our guiding aspirations in formulating a moral theory is to account for its universal nature. To be told now that Rawlsian contractualism is inconsistent with this Kantian demand is disconcerting, dispiriting, and especially ironic.

Obviously the dialectic could continue. I hope that I have at least demonstrated the stresses that afflict Rawls's brand of contractualism and the theoretical motivations that give rise to these pressures. Perhaps, in the end, Rawls's view can consistently grant human infants full moral status and nonarbitrarily exclude nonhuman animals from the realm of moral patients. Our considered moral beliefs, I would think, classify the former as a valued result, but not the latter. Can contractualism do better?

(VIII)

Rawls is clear that there is nothing sacrosanct about the conditions he sets upon the members of the original position. The version of contractualism offered by Tom Scanlon can be seen as an acceptance of this implicit invitation to make modifications.[6] We begin by instilling in the contractors the desire to justify their actions to others on grounds that they could reasonably accept. The content of morality, then, is the outcome of deliberations among these contractors. Rather than a set of precepts that guide our behavior in the hope of securing mutual advantage, we obtain a set of principles that no one could reasonably reject. As an attempt at clarification, consider Scanlon's contractualist characterization of moral wrongness: "An act is wrong if its performance under the circumstances would be disallowed by any system of rules for the general regulation of behavior which no one could reasonably reject as a basis for informed, unforced general agreement" (110).

One is given great latitude to disagree, for the "only relevant pressure for agreement comes from the desire to find and agree on principles which no one who had this desire could reasonably reject" (111). This is not to deny a place for self-interest in Scanlon's account; one can reasonably reject a principle that would have deleterious effects upon his life plans. Nonetheless, there is a significant difference between Scanlon's conception of ethics and those, like Rawls's, that identify the content of morality with principles that hold the promise of mutual benefit.[7] Scanlon views concerns about personal advantage as instrumental to, rather the subject matter of, morality.

This different conception of morality has a significant impact upon the reasoning concerning moral patients. Roughly, Rawlsian contractualism gives primary place to the idea of reciprocity; one is invited to the moral realm as long as there is a reasonable expectation that the contractor will be compensated. Individuals, in virtue of lacking either rationality or the desire to act in accordance with the formulated principles, cannot return contractualists' bestowals and so will be banished from the moral realm. Scanlonian contractualism, on the other hand, giving primary place to the notion of reasonable agreement, implies that "morality applies to a being if the notion of justification to a being of that kind makes sense" (113). In its broadest interpretation, what this seems to suggest is that an individual is granted moral patienthood if it is intelligible to speak of that individual as a subject for whom there are reasons or arguments for the acceptance or rejection of a proposed principle. What this in turn implies—most important for our purposes—is that the individual needs to have good and bad ways of being; the individual requires a welfare. What it does not imply—again most important for the present purposes—is that the individual needs the cognitive abilities to understand and react to the principles under consideration. If experientialism provides the best account of well-being, as I have been suggesting, contractualism can and should, without the Rawlsian gymnastics, confer moral standing upon nonhuman animals and human infants.[8] Although not championed by Scanlon as such, we have before us a contractualism that complies with the sufficiency condition of experientialism: an individual who, despite lacking the capacity to reciprocate helpful behaviors, becomes robustly morally enfranchised in virtue of the fact that she owns an experiential well-being.

Peter Carruthers, though, has argued that no form of contractualism can countenance nonhuman animals as moral patients.[9] His specific argument against Scanlonian contractualism's having this inclusiveness begins by reminding us that Scanlon's conception of moral rules interprets these principles as ones that no one could reasonably reject as a basis for informed, unforced general agreement by those who desire to find and agree upon such principles. It is then inquired whether Scanlon—who, unlike Rawls, deals with real and not hypothetical individuals, individuals whose desires, temperaments, and the like are known to themselves and others—might allow that some of these individuals have very strong desires to have animals treated well and so might reasonably reject rules that accorded nonhuman animals anything less than full moral status. The question, then, is whether one can reasonably reject such a pro-animal rule. This, obviously, can only be decided on the basis of what is to count as reasonable rejection.

Carruthers correctly points out that it cannot be reasonable to reject a rule on a basis that could, in turn, be used to reject any proposed rule. The one and only pressure exerted on the contractors derives from their shared desire to find some set of rules to found agreement, and so a nihilistic basis for rejection would conflict with this assumption of Scanlon's contractarianism. From this, Carruthers infers that it cannot be reasonable to reject a rule solely on the basis that it conflicts with one of the interests of a particular contractor. Since any substantive rule will conflict with someone's interests, allowing conflict with a personal interest to count as reasonable would result in the rejectability of all rules, and thus the goals and desires of all the contractors could be stymied. If we were to allow the rejection of a principle that accorded no weight to animals' interests as reasonable, we would be committed to permitting the reasonable rejection of precepts concerning dress codes, sexual activities, and ways of worshipping. The Scanlonian enterprise would never get off the ground.

To assuage worries that this may lead to too lenient a basis for nonrejectability, Carruthers assures us that "rules that accord no weight to my interests in general, or rules that allow my privacy to be invaded, or my projects to be interfered with, at the whim of other people" are reasonably rejectable (104). Since others will have similar reasons for rejecting rules that permit me to interfere with their lives, and I want rules to be derived that will govern the conduct of all, I will release any claim to interfere with the lives of others as long as they will release their similar claims on me.

However, it would seem that Carruthers's reasoning concerning rejectability can be used to support pro-animal rules. Consider the rule

(R1) Accord no weight to the interests of animals.

Carruthers implies that we cannot reasonably reject this rule merely because (R1) conflicts with some personal interest, for were this basis permitted as grounds for reasonable rejection, then any nontrivial proposed rule could be reasonably rejected. And this, of course, thwarts the very purpose of the contractual meeting. Yet

(R2) Accord no weight to Bernstein's privacy interests

can be reasonably rejected since, although only Bernstein may have an interest in seeing (R2) rejected, other individuals have respective interests in seeing rejected the rules that refer to their personal privacy interests. What turns an unreasonable rejection into a reasonable rejection of a proposed rule is the fact that all contractors have the same basis for rejecting a similar proposal, one that is individually tailored to express their various self-interests. But then, one who sees animals as deserving of full moral status might suggest that similar reasoning makes

(RA) Accord no weight to Hallie's most significant preference

rejectable, for surely other contractors would have reasons similar to Hallie's for rejecting their personalized versions of (RA). And since there are contractors for whom the moral status of animals is of paramount importance, we would appear to be able to reconcile Scanlonian contractualism with moral standing for animals, even within a Carruthersian framework. Of course, Hallie may have the perverted desire to cause as much suffering as possible to as many animals as possible, but this only brings into relief how formal Scanlon's version of contractualism is.

Carruthers might respond by claiming that the contractors cannot make any reasonable decision about the acceptance or rejection of (RA) until Hallie discloses what constitutes the content of his most significant preference. Furthermore, while this demand may be unfair if requested within the context of Rawlsian contractualism, since the contractors are denied knowledge of their personal conceptions of the good, it appears quite reasonable in the context of Scanlonian contractualism, where the contractors are permitted this personal knowledge. Without this attainable additional specificity, we have no way of knowing whether Hallie's major preference is, for example, to invade the privacy of others, and this, as Carruthers has made clear, would be evidently rejectable by the contractors.

The problem is that this response causes friction with Carruthers's earlier claim that "rules that accord no weight to my interests *in general*" (my emphasis) are clearly rejectable; in fact, (RA) and Carruthers's announcement seem to amount to very much the same thing. We can express this point in the form of a challenge. Carruthers believes that one's interests in general are protected within Scanlonian contractualism. Ultimately, there can be only one justification for this belief, namely, were rules that accorded no weight to an individual's interests reasonably rejectable, agreement of principles for the general regulation of behavior by those who shared the desire to reach such agreement would be impossible. In short, a reasonable rejection of rules of this sort would (conceptually) thwart the Scanlonian enterprise. The challenge is to produce an a priori argument for this conclusion that does not, *mutatis mutandis*, apply to (RA). My suggestion is that no such argument will be forthcoming in virtue of the fact that the rational desire for autonomy (that is, the desire to live in accordance with one's interests or desires) is tantamount to the desire to have one's most important desires fulfilled.

More tellingly, there are grave doubts about the success of an argument purporting to show why, for example, acceptance of a rule allowing violations of privacy necessarily dooms Scanlon's contractualism. Since the point is putatively conceptual, Carruthers is disallowed to invoke any empirical theories of human nature, theories that, in any case, have dubious value. Yet, on the face of it, this is precisely what Carruthers seems to do when he claims that rules like (R2) can be reasonably rejected "since I know that others will similarly have reason to reject a rule that allows me to interfere in their lives" (104). There is no question that the desires for autonomy and privacy are extremely important in most persons' lives. However, to exalt them to some sanctified status is a mistake; there are some perfectly rational people who would gladly exchange their privacy and autonomy for a widespread recognition of nonhuman animals as moral patients.

(IX)

There can be no better proof that contractualism is compatible with according full moral standing to nonhuman animals than providing such an account. In this regard, let us consider a view I dub "altruistic contractualism."

Here we consider an original position consisting of Rawlsianlike contractors insofar as the members are rational and possess a sense of justice. The key difference resides in the fact that those in the initial situation are motivated not by self-interest but by the interests of others. This theory has no problems with pressures from below. Not only is there no reason to believe that our considered moral beliefs invalidate this altruistic point of departure, there is excellent reason to believe that rules prohibiting stealing, lying, cheating, and the like would be consequences of altruistic deliberations just as surely as they would be the outcome of self-interested parties. After all, if I have another's interests at heart, I would reject any rules that would either permit his possessions to be stolen or allow him to be lied to. Though the robber and liar might be temporarily benefited, without rules that prohibit stealing and lying their interests will be served only a very short time. Better for everyone, therefore, that a general prohibition be enacted.

This scenario can be given various twists. A Rawlsian version would have us identify morality with those principles that are derived from a setting of fairness to serve our altruistic motivations. An apologist of Scanlon would identify morality with those principles that would be reasonably agreed upon where a large pressure on the constitution of reasonableness derives from our desires to act in the interests of others. Although these versions result in different conceptions of morality—of what morality, at bottom, is really about—the practical differences would prove negligible. After all, the same data, the same basic moral beliefs, form the touchstone for these two versions of altruistic contractualism, as well as for any other philosophical moral theory. Presumably, although the Rawlsian, Scanlonian, and other contractual variants have different theoretical commitments, all would classify lying, stealing, cheating, and the like as wrong behaviors.

One might argue that a Rawlsian interpretation of even altruistic contractualism yields an exclusionist policy toward animals. Just as a self-interested contractualism leads to the scope of morality extending only to those individuals who could act reciprocally toward us, it might be suggested that an altruistic contractualism leads to a view of morality that includes only those who can act to serve the interests of others. Since nonhuman animals presumably essentially lack the cognitive and conative capabilities required to systematically further the interests of others, application to the moral realm on their behalf should be denied.

But this response mistakes the nature of altruism by conflating it with a disguised egoism. The conception of altruistic contractualism grants membership to all those who have interests that can be either positively or negatively affected by the actions of others. They need not either act altruistically themselves, or even have the capacity for altruistic behavior, to be accorded full moral status. To append this requirement

onto moral membership is effectively to return to the reciprocity demanded of Rawlsian contractualism, the only difference now being that,
instead of requiring reciprocity toward oneself, one now requires reciprocity toward others for fulfilling their obligations. But the major point
of creating an altruistic brand of contractualism was to demonstrate that
this philosophical moral theory can exist without any tit-for-tat.

There is, finally, an objection inspired by Hume. If all those in the
original position are altruists and, let us further stipulate, know both that
all others are altruists and are so by virtue of their "nature," there would
appear to be no motivation for formulating any rules of justice whatsoever. Without the assumption that the contractors have merely "limited generosity," the entire contractual situation appears superfluous. As
Hume put it: "Why should I bind another, by deed or promise, to do
me any good office, when I know that he is already prompted to seek
my happiness?" (*An Enquiry Concerning Human Understanding*, sec. 3, pt.
1). The first point to note is that this objection will only appear forceful
if we assume that the function of the rules of justice is to protect or
secure our interests. Scanlon, as we have already seen, views the content
of morality quite differently. Although concerns about personal security
of interests provide pressure for what will count as a reasonable acceptance or rejection of a proffered rule, the rules themselves function as
legitimate appeals to justify our actions. Thus, under a Scanlonian conception of morality, contractual motivation is not undermined, although
a common but by no means exclusive incentive to accept or reject certain principles is compromised.

Of course, if one adopts the conception of morality that understands
the content of the contracted principles as providing for mutual advantage, this response will carry little weight. The question remains whether
Hume's criticism—in effect a challenge to explain how altruistic contractualism can originate within this latter conception of morality—can
be met.

There is, I think, a straightforward answer to Hume, available to
one who rejects the implicit conception of human nature upon which
the Humean relies. What is apparently presupposed, and what ought to
be rejected, is the idea that all inclinations, dispositions, or character traits
that flow from one's "human nature" are inalterable. If we understand
that these causes for action can change, and in some instances change
without great provocation, we can imagine the altruistic contractors as
being motivated to create principles of morality out of fear that at least
some of those falling under the scope of morality will eventually act self-
interestedly. So, although altruists need not fear that their goods will be
stolen, the specter of these altruists changing stripes may motivate pro-

duction of a contracted morality. The notion that behaviors, although products of human nature, are alterable is hardly radical. There are many social scientists who would urge that man, by his very nature, is violent; few would suggest that it is therefore an exercise in futility to encourage change.

(x)

Contractarians can consistently accord full moral status to nonhuman animals. Furthermore, as I will now try to show, they ought to. To the extent that contractarianism denies moral patienthood to nonhuman animals while conceding that they own the capacity for sentient experience, it is a defective philosophical moral theory. The flaw so fundamentally offends our ordinary conception of morality that, notwithstanding the benefits of contractualism, the philosophical theory should be abdicated.

I submit the following as a true substantive moral principle:

(PS) It is morally wrong to intentionally inflict gratuitous pain and suffering upon another individual.[10]

Understanding (PS) as a defeasible moral principle makes its rejection even more difficult to understand. Still, it is not my purpose to argue for the truth of (PS); it is sufficient for my purposes that one accepts this as a considered moral belief.

As far as I know, all contemporary contractualists subscribe to the force of (PS). Virtually all also accept the commonsense view that there are many nonhuman animals who have the capacity to suffer pain.[11] Thus, with near unanimity, all contractualists concur with the overwhelming majority in claiming that it is wrong to intentionally inflict gratuitous pain and suffering upon dogs, cats, chimpanzees, and so forth. For those contractualists who deny moral patienthood to these creatures—who claim, effectively, that these nonhuman sentient creatures lack the capacity to have any wrong (or right) done to them—the classic maneuver, epitomized by Kant's discussion of a faithful dog, to account for the intuition expressed in (PS) is to interpret the wrongness instrumentally. By harming the dog, we humans run the great risk of harming ourselves. The problem, however, is that (PS) appears just as applicable when we subtract all possible instrumentality from the situation.

Consider that Astrid is accompanied only by her cat on her irreversible journey into space.[12] Surely, it would strike us as horribly wrong if she were to use her cat as a dartboard, firing steel-tipped darts at her for no reason other than whimsy. Moreover, were Astrid to perpetrate such an act, its wrongness would appear to be constituted by the behavior's effect upon the cat; it is precisely the pain and suffering her whimsical act causes that account for the moral wrongness of her behavior. But our contrarian contractarian cannot avail himself of such an explanation, for to him the cat lacks moral patienthood.

One contractualist response to this dilemma has been to suggest a "character-expressive" account of right and wrong actions toward sentient nonhuman animals. According to this account, Astrid's behavior is wrong, not because it brought about pain and suffering, but rather because it manifests the vice of cruelty; her behavior is appropriately classified as "wrong" because it is an expression of a vicious character.

There is no reason for contractualists not to place great importance on qualities of character; presumably generosity, kindness, trustworthiness, and so on would incline individuals to act in ways sought after by contractualists. A Rawlsian contractualist, for example, would welcome trustworthiness in an individual since this would incline the reciprocal behavior he seeks. It would be natural for Rawlsian contractualists to classify dispositions as virtues and vices, respectively, insofar as they would aid or hinder in securing mutual advantage. Moreover, although contractualists deem the virtues as having only instrumental worth, they are not to be justified by utilitarian appeals. Astrid is to be appropriately criticized for her behavior toward her cat not in virtue of any morally wrong behaviors directed toward the cat (for there are none), but rather in virtue of her failure to become the sort of person (i.e., a kind one) who would have been best able to participate in the society envisioned by those in the contractual situation.

Nevertheless, this character-expressive model should be abandoned. Consider a slight variant of the scenario involving Astrid, in which her doppelganger Astrid* is traveling not with a real, sentient cat but with a faux cat made of cardboard. We assume that Astrid* is in precisely the same doxastic state as Astrid. She believes, mistakenly, that the individual before her, the individual that she, just like her twin, uses as a dartboard, is a real, sentient creature. There is no reason to make a distinction between the characters of Astrid and Astrid*; they are both acting equally cruelly. But surely Astrid is perpetrating some moral wrong that Astrid* is not, and Astrid's world contains evil that her twin's world does not. There is only one way to account for this difference and, fortunately, it is the immediately plausible one: Bringing about the cat's pain and suffering is, prima facie, a bad thing to do, a wrong behavior. Alternatively, the cat's suffering makes a world morally worse, and this can only be accounted for if the welfare of the cat morally matters or has direct moral significance.

The force of (PS) extends beyond the applicability of the character-expressive account. At root, this contractualist ploy situates the wrongness of the act in the vicious motivations of the agent. But this, I have tried to show, is a mistake; it conflates wicked people with immoral actions. Evildoers are blameworthy even if their behavior, in virtue of fortuitous circumstances, does not produce immorality. Astrid* is not a better person than Astrid, but fortune has intervened to make her behavior less immoral.

(xi)

Contractualism need not exclude nonhuman animals from full moral status. Once contractualists are made aware that reciprocity is not essential to their philosophical moral theory, they are likely to be more receptive to incorporating experientialism as criterial for moral standing. It is true that some versions, when conjoined with some substantive hypotheses, will result in exclusion of sentients. But in the face of these limited alternatives, the contractualist can remain faithful to his theoretical commitments and still demur. And demur she should, if she wishes to maintain a morality worth having.[13]

Conclusion

Let us briefly review the bidding. I have introduced and articulated three theories of personal welfare, three ways of conceiving how individuals can be made better and worse off. This, effectively, provides us with three conceptions of moral personhood, conceptions that yield the criteria for an individual's having moral standing or being deserving of moral consideration. Experientialism suggests that all personal value is subjective and thereby implies that any individual with the capacity for sentient experience qualifies as a moral patient. The desire theory requires more for moral standing. It is necessary that the individual have the capacity to form desires. She is benefited to the extent that these desires are satisfied, harmed to the extent that the desires are thwarted. Perfectionism tells us that the possession of certain properties—properties that need not be attached to conscious creatures—is determinative of moral standing.

Part I dealt with theoretical concerns and concluded that both the desire theory and perfectionism are hampered by serious internal defects as well as possessing very counterintuitive consequences. Experientialism, with its concomitant view of moral patienthood, does not suffer these failings. The desire theory most seriously suffers from its essentially relational structure. Since it is in this regard that it most significantly differs from experientialism, if the desire theory is found to be flawed, this is the most pertinent sort of flaw to expose. If my argument is correct, tidying around the edges of the desire theory will not do; the problem infects its basic constitution. Perfectionism also has core problems. In fact, I argue the quite strong thesis that perfectionism's natural implications lead to absurdity. We can "save" the theory by substantially restricting what properties it allows as perfections. We are hard-pressed, however, to suggest properties that extend beyond the capacity for sentient experience. Viable perfectionism reduces to experientialism; we save the theory at the expense of its distinctiveness.

Part II may be read as explaining a political ramification of these theories. Nonhuman animals are denied moral standing in virtue of lacking the capacity for desires, lacking certain perfectionist properties (e.g., rationality and moral sensitivity), or, more radically, lacking the capacity for sentient experience. In view of the attacks on the desire theory and perfectionism, the most theoretically viable attack is the most radical one, the one that denies the commonplace that certain nonhuman animals are sentient. I argue that we are proffered no compelling reason to discard our commonsense belief regarding animal sentience. Furthermore, even if, contrary to the conclusions of Part I, either the desire theory or perfectionism should be adopted, nonhuman animals still should be morally enfranchised. There are no convincing arguments showing that animals lack desires, and there are no telling perfectionist considerations that permit the moral exclusion of animals without also making too many individuals into merely ethical debris.

At the end of this journey, Bentham's insight essentially prevails; sentience is what makes an individual morally worthy. I hope this odyssey has enhanced the justification for this belief.

Notes

1. I use the neuter "it" rather than "he/she" in an effort to be as neutral as possible and to not beg any questions against the possibility of inanimate or nongendered animate objects' being moral patients.

CHAPTER 1

1. Here, I equate having the capacity to be made better off with having an interest that can be positively affected, and equate having the capacity to be made worse off with having an interest to be negatively affected. These identifications should not be viewed as begging questions about whether those with the capacities to be made both better and worse off have the capacity to form *desires* concerning these states. This latter question will subsequently play a prominent role. In passing, I should mention that the almost unreflective identification that many philosophers presume between interests and desires is probably not warranted by ordinary usage.

2. See Kagan, "Limits of Well-Being," for a complementary, albeit quite tentatively proposed, assessment. To the best of my knowledge, this is the only other work that conceives, in a very explicit way, of *intrinsicness* being a crucial aspect of welfare.

3. At least so I suggest. I realize that the ontological status of fictional characters is a vexing issue. One might view the proposed characterization and the idea that modifications of well-being involve an individual's intrinsic properties as mutually supporting. For a recent book that deals with the metaphysics of the unreal while clearly discussing a variety of different accounts, see Crittenden, *Unreality*.

4. One might be difficult about this. Isn't Holmes benefited when he solves a case and harmed when he fails to solve one? There are several

ways in which one may respond to this (One bad way, I think, is to try to argue that terms like "benefit" and "harm" are used ambiguously, having one sense in fictional contexts and another in actual situations.) A beginning to an answer is to point out that the welfare verdict about Holmes is intelligible only if the narrative states or suggests it. That is, only if the story explicitly tells us that Holmes was benefited by his discovering the murderer or that earlier commentary about Holmes suggests that he is the sort of character who would be benefited by such a discovery does it make sense to claim that Holmes was so benefited. If there is nothing of this sort in the narrative, the question of his being made better or worse off seems essentially indeterminate in the way that questions about his grandfather's hair color are essentially indeterminate. (Think of how silly it would be to argue about this latter point.) The point is that, at best, metaphysical questions of benefit and harm become transmuted into epistemic ones. This should alert us to the fact that Holmes's being made better and worse off is a very different sort of thing than one of us having our welfares enhanced or diminished.

5. See Kripke, *Naming and Necessity*, for the contemporary *locus classicus* of the idea that there are necessary a posteriori truths and falsehoods.

6. See Nagel, "What Is It Like to Be a Bat?," 165–80.

7. See Hopkins, *Poems and Prose*.

8. See Parfit, *Reasons and Persons*, 493. Parfit's entire discussion regarding personal welfare (493–502) has several points of contact with my own view.

9. See Kripke, *Naming and Necessity*, 152ff.

10. See Kraut, "Desire and the Human Good."

11. Many philosophers have surely thought so. Those interested in this area may start with Quine, who is skeptical of the use of counterfactuals altogether, move on toward Chisholm, Mackie, and Halpin, who discuss a "semantic" interpretation of counterfactuals (the first two as advocates, Halpin as a dissenter) and consult Lewis and Stalnaker, who advocate a "similarity of possible worlds" approach.

12. The truth of this commonsense judgment will occupy us in Chapter 4.

13. This historical dogma has been recently challenged. See Cottingham, "Brute to the Brutes?"; Harrison, "Descartes on Animals"; and Wilson, "Animal Ideas."

CHAPTER 2

1. Malcolm, for example, has argued that "dream experiences" are not a species of experiences any more than a dream knife is a type of knife. As far as we are concerned, this possible debate can be circumvented. At the very least, it seems to the individual *as if* she is having certain experiences. Whether one wishes to characterize this situation as

one in which the agent is *experiencing* (and, frankly, I would have no qualms about so doing), the circumstance, regardless of how characterized, is sufficient to count as something that is transpiring from the inside and so is sufficient for experientialist well-being. See Malcolm, "Dreaming and Skepticism."

2. Nozick, *Anarchy, State, and Utopia*, 42–45, and Kane, *Through the Moral Maze*, 67–101. All subsequent page numbers refer to these two works.

3. The commonplace that moral responsibility requires the freedom to do otherwise has been a hotly contested issue in the last quarter century. See Frankfurt, "Alternate Possibilities," for the origin of this debate, and van Inwagen, Fischer, Zimmerman, and Locke as some prime participants. Fortunately, the resolution of the debate is not required to make my illustrative point.

4. We should not make much about whether this is an accurate characterization of the umpire's call, or whether, in general, "verdictives" behave as the example suggests. After all, it is at least plausible to claim that, although the umpire called the batter out, he was not *really* out (the instant replay clearly demonstrated that the pitch was way outside) or, although the jury found O. J. Simpson not guilty, in fact he was. And, of course, Austin was sensitive to these sorts of comments. Still, I hope that by alluding to this type of speech act—whether or not it can be ultimately maintained—the difference between the constitutive and identificatory functions of desires is further illuminated.

5. Am I suggesting a difference between intrinsic and inherent value? I am using "intrinsic value" to indicate that an item has value in and of itself regardless of whether it is valuable for anything else. I am using "inherent value" to suggest that its possession makes its possessor better off, at least insofar as the individual possesses that item. When we speak of pleasures, for example, as being intrinsically valuable, what is normally meant is that, insofar as the agent is feeling pleased, he is made better off. One who advocates the intrinsic value of pleasures is surely not claiming that there can be agentless pleasures and that these items are valuable in and of themselves. In short, as I use the terms, there is no practical difference in characterizing pleasures as intrinsic or inherent. Both are to be (practically) distinguished from (mere) instrumental values, those values that create value for their possessors only insofar as they ultimately elicit other items that are themselves inherently valuable.

6. See Pitcher, "Misfortunes of the Dead." All page references to Pitcher refer to this article. It should be mentioned that Pitcher does not try to defend a desire theory of well-being. Rather, he uncritically accepts this as a point of departure. This, in itself, is not a criticism of Pitcher, for his goals differ from mine. It is unclear whether he would abdicate his starting point in light of my comments.

7. Bennett, "On Maximizing Happiness," 61–73.

8. The language of "hard" and "soft" facts has its origin with Ockham, who employed the distinction in an attempt to reconcile divine foreknowledge with human freedom. Hard facts, very roughly, are those whose entirety are in the (inviolable) past. Soft facts, very roughly, are those whose constitution necessarily comprised temporal relations. Typically, not all soft facts are thought to be such that humans have the power to bring about their nonoccurrence, so the debate centers not so much on whether there are soft facts as on which soft facts are inviolable. For an introduction to the contemporary debate, see Fischer, "Freedom and Knowledge" and "Ockhamism," and Hoffman and Rosenkrantz, "Hard and Soft Facts."

9. See, for example, Peter Carruthers, who claims that "the very idea of pain seems conceptually tied to the desire for its avoidance" (*The Animals Issue*, 56). The notion that there is a conceptual relationship between feeling pain and desiring that the pain terminate surely expresses a common belief. The anticonceptualist (or contingency theorist) usually replies by pointing out that the capacity for desire formation is far more complex a capability than the capacity for sentience, and so we should expect there to be creatures who possess the latter capacity while lacking the former. These ideas will be further explored in Chapter 4, section (iii).

10. In Chapter 4, sections (iv) and (v), there is a discussion of whether we are justified in attributing desires to animals. At this juncture, I presuppose that this commonsense belief is true. As I soon discuss, using animals as examples of sentient creatures without the capacity for desires is not essential to the point being argued.

CHAPTER 3

1. Some cases of aberrance are quite involved. Consider the inquisitive sadist-in-waiting who hopes to feel repulsed by the upcoming perversely caused sensations but is not. While experientialists and desire theorists will have different judgments about this individual's welfare, a perfectionist *may* hold that the individual is harmed whether or not his hope (desire) is satisfied.

2. See Wynne-Tyson, ed., *The Extended Circle*, 147.

3. I will allude to this Kantian view again in Chapter 5 when I make good on the promissory note to discuss the viability of contractualism.

4. I do not mean to imply that Kant's shallow ecology need be this shallow. He would probably suggest that, as a matter of psychological fact, intrahuman behavior would far more likely be affected by human/nonhuman animal interaction than, say, by human/automobile interaction. So, for example, Kant might not think that the frivolous smashing of car windows is likely to lead to the frivolous bashing of human skulls.

I am not so sanguine. Although, as I shall presently argue, the idea that the smashing of car windows *harms* the car per se is nonsense, the notion that unchecked violence perpetrated against a car may well lead to increased intrahuman violence does not strike me as absurd.

On the other hand, Kant's caveat concerning human treatment of animals garners some empirical confirmation from the fact that virtually, if not veritably, all known serial murderers abused, tortured, or killed nonhuman animals (I owe this last observation to Dr. Nancy Daley).

5. See Taylor, *Respect for Nature*. All parenthetical page reference to Taylor refer to this work. I should note that although my discussion of Taylor is adversarial, I greatly admire his book. It is surely among the best and most influential works in deep ecology in the last quarter century.

6. I would be the first to admit that this is rather quick. For a very recent opposing view, one that argues against the phenomenology of pain being a harm, in and of itself, see Kraut, "Desire and the Human Good." I will soon touch briefly on Kraut's major objection to this commonsense view.

7. Sayre, *Cybernetics*, 91.

8. What does robustness amount to? Perhaps it would be helpful to think of the type of knowledge a blind-from-birth person would have of red as opposed to a normally sighted person. Both the former and latter can know that blood is red, that magenta and scarlet are shades of red, and so on. Still, it seems correct to say that the knowledge of the sighted person is importantly different from the knowledge of the blind individual. In some admittedly imprecise way, his knowledge is deeper or more profound. This is what the idea of robustness is meant to capture. The inability of the Martians to experience the sentiment of necessity parallels the inability of the blind person to experience red. It is this deprivation that makes the knowledge less than robust.

9. See Dennett, Introduction to *Brainstorms*, for perhaps the most straightforward statement of this counterintuitive view.

10. Johnson, *A Morally Deep World*, 78–79. The final emphases are mine. Subsequent references to Johnson refer to this work.

11. See Chapter 1, section (ii), for my introduction of the idea that it is an inevitable and benign fact that our concepts are anthropocentrically configured. I develop this idea in a slightly different way—in section (viii) of this chapter—to suggest a yet more radical charge than the one that deep ecologists are guilty of malignant anthropocentrism.

12. See Leopold's *A Sand County Almanac* and Callicott, ed., *Companion to "A Sand County Almanac."* Other significant articles penned by Callicott appear in the references.

13. Goodman, *Fact, Fiction, and Forecast*, 59–120.

14. In this regard, there is a similarity between Leopoldian and contractualist theories of ethics. Of course, where some may see a conflation

between ethics and prudence, a Leopoldian or contractualist may argue that there is only a justified reduction. Still, in the face of seemingly meaningful questions that require a distinction, the onus is clearly on the side of the reductionists. Much more about contractualism's viability as a philosophical moral theory occurs in Chapter 5.

15. Exactly what is involved in *caring* is a quasi-stipulative matter. Prereflectively, the notion seems to involve components of both the desire theory and experientialism. Although many may find these sorts of hybrid notions fecund areas to explore in hope that the best of both worlds may be fruitfully combined, more often than not, these mixed theories inherit the problems of the other candidates without providing any compensatory illumination. Still, I would be the last person to suggest that investigation in this area will prove useless. Perhaps there is even a criterion of patienthood—we can call it "caring"—that, although not incorporating any of the elements of competing theories, is, metaphorically speaking, between some pair of them.

16. Obviously, I do not put forth these characteristics as definitive of "life."

17. I hope it is evident that I use these examples solely to make the point that empathetic understanding does not require that the agents have similar modifications in welfare when affected by the same event. I am not begging any questions in favor of experientialism since, if for no other reason, I am not here arguing in favor of this theory.

18. See Moore, *Ethics*, esp. 96–108.

19. For a similar scenario, see Wenz, "Ecology and Morality," 499–505.

CHAPTER 4

1. Both Elie Wiesel and George Bernard Shaw have said that indifference is worse than hate. I understand these claims as effectively expressing the idea that there is no worse attitude toward a moral patient than thinking of her as a resource. I find this idea to have great merit. Obviously, Wiesel had the Holocaust in mind when making this statement; I see the systematic and institutionalized attitudes toward nonhuman animals as playing an analogous role, a statement not made lightly, especially given my ethnicity.

2. In this work, these moral obligations are not spelled out. While it is true that countenancing nonhuman animals as moral patients does not, in and of itself, entail vegetarianism, the end of circuses and rodeos, the termination of fur wearing and of cosmetic testing performed upon animals, and so forth, it is certainly a big step in this direction. I would also add that for some of our human practices (I will kindly spare the reader the details of some of the "festivals" held in Spain, for example), the admission of nonhuman animals into the ranks of the morally considerable *does*, for all intents and purposes, mandate change.

3. That is, perfectionists may choose between saying that the uniquely human properties are essential to humans or merely contingent properties of humans and may also choose between claiming that the deprivation of these properties by nonhuman animals is a matter either of necessity or contingency. Decisions here quickly ramify. They suggest, for example, different theories of human and nonhuman nature. Although I do not pause here for reflection on these matters, I think that they are far more interesting and significant than the lack of literature on the subject would make us believe.

4. I give a formal account of this notion presently. The idea is to create the analogue of the chauvinist perfectionist for the desire theorist. Thus, roughly, a chauvinist desire theorist is one who holds that humans uniquely possess desires and that desires are what confer moral standing.

5. This is an instance of the so-called argument from marginal cases. For the classic employment of this argument, see Singer, *Animal Liberation*, 1–26, and *Practical Ethics*, 16–135. It is true that I am using the ethical intuitions concerning infants that I previously allowed myself. Am I being unfair? After all, there have been philosophers like Michael Tooley who hold infants in slightly lower regard. My response is simply to deny that our intuitions concerning human infants share this lack of solidarity. Whether one wishes, in virtue of this, to separate infants from the retarded, Alzheimered, severely brain-damaged, and the like, or to maintain that the rubric "marginal" still applies to human infants, is largely a verbal issue. I ask the reader to consult the results of her own pretheoretical beliefs and see if they are the same as mine.

6. See Chapter 2, section (iii).

7. See Frey, *Interests and Rights*. All page references regarding Frey refer to this work. See also Regan, *Case for Animal Rights*, chap. 2, and Sapontzis, *Morals, Reasons, and Animals*, chap. 7, for complementary argumentation of much (although not all) of what follows.

8. I suppose one may argue that even this admittedly vague claim is too strong. Perhaps the infant is just hardwired to react in certain ways to certain behavioral cues, much in the same way that it is in the nature of a magnet to attract iron filings. If this is the picture under which one operates, then no mind, and so no beliefs of any sort, are required. We would have the preverbal *responses* but no preverbal beliefs. Still, unless one wants to think of the postverbal individual as likewise being without a mind and without beliefs, the introduction of a mind must occur at some time, and it is difficult to see why it is not arbitrary to make the point of demarcation the point at which the infant is transformed from preverbal to postverbal. In fact, I think the assumption that there is a point in time at which this transformation takes place is a fiction. The tags "preverbal" and "postverbal" would best describe stages of an infant's life that merge with no sharp discontinuity between them. Thus—at least if one is not an innatist regarding beliefs—beliefs (and

minds) develop gradually. Believing, like speaking (and reading, for that matter), is not an activity that has a precise initiation point. To argue, then, whether the preverbal infant *really* has beliefs (or has merely pseudo- or quasi-beliefs) seems like an unproductive use of time and effort.

9. See Strawson, *Individuals*.

10. Stich, "Do Animals Have Beliefs?" 17–18. All page references regarding Stich refer to this work. See also Regan, *Case for Animal Rights*, chap. 2, for complementary argumentation.

11. This commonsensical explanatory account, advocated by Aristotle and endorsed recently by Davidson, claims that the explanation of an intentional action consists in giving the agent's pertinent desires and beliefs. So, roughly, I explain my drinking the water by my desire that my thirst be quenched and my belief that drinking water will accomplish that task. By providing my desire and belief I explain *why* I performed that intentional act. Although this model of explanation has come under sustained attack, my problems with Stich are independent of this squabble.

12. See Frey, *Interests and Rights*, 100, where he clearly identifies the human with the nonhuman animal capacity for feeling pain. They both *suffer* unpleasant sensations.

13. Recently, however, this traditional view has been challenged. See Chapter 1, note 13. I personally side with the traditionalists, who claim that Descartes accorded nonhuman animals no minds and so no moral standing, although I think there is some evidence that, by the end of his life, he softened some of his deflationary claims about the mentality of animals.

14. I have been unable to establish the veracity of this court appearance. Although it may be apocryphal, it seems well suited to Descartes's personality.

15. See Carruthers, "Brute Experience" and *The Animals Issue*.

16. Carruthers, "Brute Experience," 263.

17. See Chapter 3, section (iv).

18. For discussions concerning Carruthers's neo-Cartesianism, see Johnson, "Carruthers on Consciousness"; Pluhar, "Arguing Away Suffering"; Harrison, "Neo-Cartesian Revival" (with an appended commentary by Pluhar); Landman, "Educated Folly"; and Lynch, "Is Animal Pain Conscious?" (with an appended commentary by Duran).

19. Harrison, "Do Animals Feel Pain?" 25. All page references regarding Harrison refer to this work. One may also wish to consult Harrison, "Neo-Cartesian Revival."

20. See Dennett, "Intentional Stances," which introduced this language into the contemporary philosophical lexicon.

21. Spinoza's figure is of a leaf thinking (feeling) that it is free as it slowly goes back and forth on its journey from tree to ground. But each

of its movements are strictly determined by the wind and gravitational forces, and so, to Spinoza, the feeling of freedom is illusory.

22. For a complementary discussion of this, see Sapontzis, *Morals, Reasons, and Animals*, 41–46.

CHAPTER 5

1. Kant, *Lectures on Ethics*, 240. See also Chapter 3, section (iv) of this book, where this idea is introduced.

2. Rawls, *Theory of Justice*, 9. All references to Rawls refer to this work. Here Rawls portrays the principles of justice as a proper subset of a conception of a social ideal. Although the conception of a social ideal may well include principles regarding the virtues of kindness, compassion, generosity, and the like, my discussion makes no use of them.

3. See Sapontzis, *Morals, Reasons, and Animals*, 30–40.

4. At bottom, it is adherence to reciprocity, and not merely to self-interest, that causes friction between Rawlsian contractualism and our considered beliefs concerning our moral engagements with infants, deficients, and posterity.

5. Regan, *The Case for Animal Rights*, chap. 5, sec. 4.

6. Scanlon, "Contractualism and Utilitarianism." All parenthetical page numbers regarding Scanlon's work refer to this text.

7. It is not clear that Scanlon himself sees this as a difference that applies to him and Rawls. When Scanlon speaks of advocates of the view that morality is a device for "mutual protection," he mentions Warnock (*Object of Morality*) and Mackie (*Ethics*); Rawls is conspicuous by his absence. I do not know whether this omission is intentional or not; perhaps Scanlon is employing a subtle distinction between "mutual protection" and "mutual benefit."

8. Scanlon seems to require, more than does my "broadest interpretation" for what must be the case, that the notion of justification to an individual to be intelligible. In addition to the individual's having a welfare, Scanlon requires that: (1) benefits and harms that may accrue are comparable in kind to our own; and (2) the individual have a point of view—that is, have a consciousness (114). I would argue that possessing a welfare suffices for both (1) and (2), and so the appearance of Scanlon's view as being more demanding is illusory. In addition, Scanlon is uncertain whether these necessary conditions are jointly sufficient for an individual to be an object of justification. He points out that this is a substantive issue not to be settled by appeal to conceptual analysis. None of this should be viewed as undermining my point, which was not that Scanlon's conception of contractualism implied the inclusiveness of animals, but rather that his conception, as opposed, say, to Warnock's, Mackie's, and Rawls's, is more amenable to the full moral membership of animals (see n. 6 above).

9. Carruthers, *The Animals Issue*. All parenthetical page numbers to Carruthers's work refer to this text.

10. The rebuke can have various sources. One may either argue that (PS) is clearly false or, appearances aside, that it is not pervasively held. Perhaps more interesting would be an argument to the effect that its lack of controversy results from its tautologous nature, and so it is not a substantive principle at all. At one time, I thought that this last consideration may have some merit; I now believe that it lies just this side of analytic, which is where it should lie if it has the foundational role it seems to have in our moral judgments. Obviously, this principle is an extremely close relative to one that has been a leitmotif throughout this essay, namely, the capacity for undergoing pleasant and unpleasant experiences is necessary and sufficient for moral patienthood. Roughly, if living "matters to you," where this is understood affectively and not cognitively, your life *can* and therefore ought to be taken into account or "respected." For years, this has seemed profoundly correct to me and, as such, has driven me to be extremely skeptical of any conception of morality that has its denial as a consequence. This book can be viewed as an attempt to support this intuition.

11. The "virtual," as we have seen in Chapter 4, is not mere ornament. We have already discussed the neo-Cartesians, Carruthers, and Harrison. In his book, in opposition to his article, Carruthers admits some tentativeness in proposing this view and so effectively brackets it from the remainder of his discussion.

12. This example and the subsequent character-expressive account are from Carruthers, *The Animals Issue*, chap. 7.

13. I am very thankful to Michael Almeida and Dan Eckam for their insightful criticisms of this chapter.

References

Austin, J. L. *How to Do Things with Words*. 2d ed. Cambridge, Mass.: Harvard University Press, 1975.

Bennett, Jonathan. "On Maximizing Happiness." In *Obligations to Future Generations*, edited by R. I. Sikora and B. Barry. Philadelphia: Temple University Press, 1978.

Callicott, J. Baird. "Animal Liberation: A Triangular Affair." *Environmental Ethics* 2 (1980): 311–38.

———. "Elements of an Environmental Ethic: Moral Considerability and the Biotic Community." *Environmental Ethics* 2 (1980): 71–81.

———. "Hume's *Is/Ought* Dichotomy and the Relation of Ecology to Leopold's Land Ethic." *Environmental Ethics* 4 (1982): 163–74.

———, ed. *Companion to "A Sand County Almanac": Interpretive and Critical Essays*. Madison: University of Wisconsin Press, 1987.

Carruthers, Peter. *The Animals Issue: Moral Theory in Practice*. Cambridge: Cambridge University Press, 1992.

———. "Brute Experience." *Journal of Philosophy* 86 (1989): 258–69.

Chisholm, Roderick. "The Contrary-to-Fact Conditional." *Mind* 55 (October 1946): 289–307.

Cottingham, John. "A Brute to the Brutes?": Descartes' Treatment of Animals." *Philosophy* 53 (1978): 551–61.

Crittenden, Charles. *Unreality: The Metaphysics of Fictional Objects*. Ithaca, N.Y.: Cornell University Press, 1991.

Davidson, Donald. "Actions, Reasons, and Causes." In *Essays on Actions and Events*, 3–20. Oxford: Oxford University Press, 1980.

Dennett, Daniel. "Intentional Stances." In *Brainstorms: Philosophical Essays on Mind and Psychology*, 3–22. Montgomery, Ala.: Bradford Books, 1978.

———. Introduction to *Brainstorms*, xi–xxii.

Fischer, John. "Freedom and Foreknowledge." *Philosophical Review* 92 (January 1983): 67–79.

———. "Ockhamism." *Philosophical Review* 94 (January 1985): 80–100.

———. "Responsibility and Control." *Journal of Philosophy* 79 (January 1982): 24–40.

Frankfurt, Harry. "Alternate Possibilities and Moral Responsibility." *Journal of Philosophy* 66 (December 1969): 828–39.

Frey, R. G. *Interests and Rights: The Case against Animals.* Oxford: Clarendon Press, 1980.

Goodman, Nelson. *Fact, Fiction, and Forecast.* Cambridge, Mass.: Harvard University Press, 1983.

Halpin, John. "Counterfactual Analysis: Can the Metalinguistic Theory Be Revitalized?" *Synthese* 81 (October 1989): 47–62.

Harrison, Peter. "Descartes on Animals." *Philosophical Quarterly* 42, no. 167 (April 1992): 219–27.

———. "Do Animals Feel Pain?" *Philosophy* 66 (1991): 25–40.

———. "The Neo-Cartesian Revival: A Response." *Between the Species* 9, no. 2 (Spring 1993): 71–83.

Hoffman, J., and G. Rosenkrantz. "Hard and Soft Facts." *Philosophical Review* 93 (July 1984): 414–34.

Hopkins, Gerard Manley. *Poems and Prose of Gerard Manley Hopkins.* Edited by W. H. Gardner. New York: Viking Penguin, 1953.

House, Ian. "Harrison on Pain." *Philosophy* 66 (1991): 376–79.

Johnson, Edward. "Carruthers on Consciousness and Moral Status." *Between the Species* 7, no. 4 (Fall 1991): 190–93.

Johnson, Lawrence. *A Morally Deep World: An Essay on Moral Significance and Environmental Ethics.* Cambridge: Cambridge University Press, 1991.

Kagan, Shelly. "The Limits of Well-Being." In *The Good Life and the Human Good*, edited by E. F. Paul, F. D. Miller, and J. Paul, 169–89. Cambridge: Cambridge University Press, 1992.

Kane, Robert. *Through the Moral Maze: Searching for Absolute Values in a Pluralistic World.* New York: Paragon House, 1994.

Kant, Immanuel. *Lectures on Ethics—Duties towards Animals and Other Spirits.* Translated by Louis Infeld. New York: Harper and Row, 1963.

Kraut, Richard. "Desire and the Human Good." Presidential Address, *APA Proceedings* 68, no. 2 (November 1994): 39–54.

Kripke, Saul. *Naming and Necessity.* Cambridge, Mass.: Harvard University Press, 1980.

Landman, Willem. "Educated Folly about Animal Minds and Animal Suffering." *Between the Species* 9, no. 3 (Summer 1993): 143–55.

Leopold, Aldo. *A Sand County Almanac.* New York: Oxford University Press, 1949.

Lewis, David. *Counterfactuals*. Cambridge, Mass.: Harvard University Press, 1973.

Locke, Don. "Three Concepts of Free Action: I." *Proceedings of the Aristotelian Society*, supp. ser., 49 (1975): 95–112.

Lynch, Joseph. "Is Animal Pain Conscious?" *Between the Species*, 10, nos. 1, 2 (Spring 1994): 1–9.

Mackie, J. L. "Counterfactuals and Causal Laws." In *Analytical Philosophy*, edited by R. T. Butler, 66–80. Blackwell: Oxford University Press, 1962.

———. *Ethics: Inventing Right and Wrong*. Hammondsworth: Penguin Press, 1977.

Malcolm, Norman. "Dreaming and Skepticism." In *Meta-Meditations: Studies in Descartes*, edited by A. Sesonske and N. Fleming, 5–26. Belmont, Calif.: Wadsworth, 1965.

Moore, G. E. *Ethics*. New York: Oxford University Press, 1965.

Nagel, Thomas. "What Is It Like to Be a Bat?" *Philosophical Review* 83 (1974): 435–50.

Nozick, Robert. *Anarchy, State, and Utopia*. New York: Basic Books, 1974.

Parfit, Derek. *Reasons and Persons*. Oxford: Oxford University Press, 1986.

Pitcher, George. "The Misfortunes of the Dead." *American Philosophical Quarterly* 21, no. 2 (April 1984): 183–88.

Pluhar, Evelyn. "Arguing Away Suffering: The Neo-Cartesian Revival." *Between the Species* 9, no. 1 (Winter 1993): 27–44.

Rawls, John. *A Theory of Justice*. Cambridge, Mass.: Harvard University Press, 1971.

Regan, Tom. *The Case for Animal Rights*. Berkeley: University of California Press, 1983.

Sapontzis, S. F. *Morals, Reasons, and Animals*. Philadelphia: Temple University Press, 1987.

Sayre, Kenneth. *Cybernetics and the Philosophy of Mind*. New York: Humanities Press, 1976.

Scanlon, Tom. "Contractualism and Utilitarianism." In *Utilitarianism and Beyond*, edited by Sen and Williams, 103–28. Cambridge: Cambridge University Press, 1982.

Singer, Peter. *Animal Liberation: A New Ethics for Our Treatment of Animals*. New York: Avon, 1975.

———. *Practical Ethics*. 2d ed. Cambridge: Cambridge University Press, 1993.

Stalnaker, Robert. "A Theory of Conditionals." *Theoria* 36 (1970): 23–42.

Stich, Steven. "Do Animals Have Beliefs?" *Australasian Journal of Philosophy* 57, no. 1 (March 1979): 15–28.

Strawson, Peter. *Individuals*. London: Methuen, 1959.

Taylor, Paul. *Respect for Nature*. Princeton, N.J.: Princeton University Press, 1986.

Tooley, Michael. *Abortion and Infanticide*. Oxford: Clarendon Press, 1983.

Van Inwagen, Peter. "Ability and Responsibility." *Philosophical Review* 87 (April 1978): 201–24.

Warnock, G. J. *The Object of Morality*. London: Methuen, 1971.

Wenz, Peter. "Ecology and Morality." In *Social Ethics: Morality and Social Policy*, edited by T. Mappes and J. Zembaty. New York: McGraw-Hill, 1992.

Wilson, Margaret. "Animal Ideas." Presidential Address, *APA Proceedings* 60 (1995): 7–26.

Wynne-Tyson, Jon, ed. *The Extended Circle: A Commonplace Book of Animal Rights*. New York: Paragon House, 1989.

Zimmerman, Michael. "Moral Responsibility, Freedom, and Alternate Possibilities." *Pacific Philosophical Quarterly* 63 (July 1982): 243–54.

Index

animals, 4, 5, 132–33, 161–62;
  altruistic contractualist
  conception of, 163; blindsight
  experiences concerning, 134–35;
  contractualism and, 147–67;
  contractualist enfranchising of,
  165–68, 170; desire theorist
  views of, 125–27; free agent
  view of, 143–45; and Kant, 89–
  90; pain of, 137–42; Rawls's
  view of, 154–56; resource view
  of, 118–20; sentient experiences
  of, 35, 77; Stich's views of, 129–
  31
anthropocentrism, 11, 12; deep
  ecologists' view of, 95, 97; and
  grue paradox, 103–4; of Hume,
  94; optimal states and, 100
Aristotle, 63; moral patienthood view
  of, 90; and posthumous welfare,
  60
Austin, J. L., 44
Ayer, A. J., 143

benefit, 14, 20, 55, 68, 69, 78, 95,
  100, 169; and aberrant desires,
  85; of another, 101; comparative,
  53; and contractualism, 147;
  and deep ecology, 89–90, 104–
  09; of desiring but
  nonphenomenological being, 76;
  in experientialism and desire

theory, 47–50; and Hume, 94;
  and L. Johnson, 99; and moral
  patienthood, 15–16; being more
  than experience, 39; as objective
  occurrence, 22; as ordinary
  language term, 17; in
  perfectionism, 81; posthumous,
  59–66; in teleological centers, 91
  See also harm
Bentham, J., 170
Berkeley, G., 61–67
blindsight experiences, 134–35, 142
Butler, J., dictum of, 17

Callicott, J. B., 102
cambridge change, 19; and fictional
  characters, 20
capability. See capacity
capacity, 4, 9, 13–15, 35, 39, 43, 76–
  77, 101, 104, 106–7, 110, 118–
  19, 132, 145, 154, 156, 170; for
  belief and language, 127; and
  chauvinistic desire theorist, 125;
  chemical analogy for, 10–11; for
  conscious experience, 23; for
  desires, 46, 70–71; of direct
  moral object, 148; for higher-
  level thought, 129; of rare and
  unique, 17–18; of stoves, 109; to
  suffer, 27, 69
Carruthers, P., 140; and animal
  awareness, 133–37; and animal

Carruthers, P. (*continued*)
    as moral patients, 160–62; and
    blindsight experiences, 135–36;
    and language acquisition, 137;
    and rule rejections, 161–62
chauvinistic desire theory, as
    Cartesian legacy, 133; as
    conceptual thesis, 132;
    introduction to, 122; as only
    toward humans, 124–25
chauvinistic experientialism, 144–45;
    as Cartesian legacy, 133
chauvinistic perfectionism, 120–21;
    definition of, 123; and potential
    properties, 124; problems of, 12
Clinton, B., 63–65
conceptual thesis, between desires and
    sentience, 69–78
constitutive/identificatory distinction,
    43–45, 47
contractualism, 5, 15–16, 169;
    altruistic form of, 162–64; and
    animals' moral status; and
    character-expressive account, 166;
    as philosophical moral theory,
    149–51; as requiring reciprocity,
    167; Scanlon's view of, 158

Da Vinci, L., 85
deep ecology, 4, 84, 89; disrepair of
    104–5; and Moore, 110; and
    Hume, 95; of Leopold, 102; of
    Taylor, 90–93; as test case for
    perfectionism, 88
Descartes, R., 5, 16; and animals, 133;
    and dream argument, 35, 37–39;
    and evil genius, 136–37; as
    experientialist, 35–36; and mind/
    body, 139–40; compared to
    Nozick/Kane, 42–43; and
    privileged access, 47, 51; and
    transcendental ego, 143; as
    transparentist, 33–34
desire theory, 68, 84, 86, 169; and
    aberrance, 85; and animals, 118;
    and conceptual thesis, 75; and
    constitutive account, 45; and
    deep ecology, 105; definition of,
    4, 46–47; evaluation of, 114; as
    extrinsic theory, 50; and Freud,

55–57; ideal representation of,
    54; as limited case of
    perfectionism, 83; and
    metaphysical problems, 53; and
    nonconscious events, 49; and
    nonmental values, 87–88; in
    opposition to Taylor, 92; and
    perfectionism, 79–82, 112;
    posthumous results of, 59–66;
    and privileged access, 51–52;
    relational character of, 48, 58, 78;
    restrictions to, 67; and self-
    consciousness, 129; and
    subjectivity, 110
Dostoevsky, F., 74

Everly brothers, 38
experientialism, 35, 37, 38, 67–69, 71,
    79–80, 86, 147, 160, 169; and
    animals, 118; as basic theory of
    welfare, 31; and Cartesianism, 34;
    and chauvinist conceptual
    theorist, 132–33; compares to
    conceptual theories, 75; and
    constitutive/identificatory
    distinction; and contractualism,
    169; and deep ecology, 89, 96,
    105; definition of, 4, 9, 22–23;
    and desire theory, 47, 49, 76;
    and Freud, 157; and intra-
    personal and interpersonal
    comparisons, 32–33; and as an
    intrinsic state, 40; limiting moral
    domain, 39; and nonmental
    values, 88; as opposed to
    Johnson, 99; as opposed to
    Taylor, 92; and pain, 24–29, 33;
    and perfectionism, 82–83; and
    posthumous existence, 66; and
    privileged access, 51–53; and
    sentience, 77

fiction, 19–20
free will, 41, 142–44
Freud, S., 56–57
Frey, R. G., 132; and self-
    consciousness, 125–29
functionalism, and phenomenology of
    pain, 26; and Taylor's theory, 91–
    92; and treatment of pain, 71

Gandhi, M., 40, 55
Goodman, N., and grue paradox, 103

harm, 20, 54, 68–69, 78, 95, 118, 169;
　of another, 101; comparative, 56;
　and contractualism, 147; within
　deep ecology, 89–90, 99–100,
　104–9; within experientialism
　and desire theory, 47–50; and
　Hume, 94; of infants, 136; more
　than experiential, 39; of
　nonphenomenological, persons,
　76; as objective occurrence, 22;
　as ordinary language term, 17;
　and pains, 27–28; conferring
　patienthood, 14–16; and
　perfectionism, 81; posthumous,
　59–66; and teleological center,
　91; and welfare, 13–14
Harrison, P., against evolution, 142;
　and animals not as free agents,
　143; and animals not as moral
　agents, 144; and human infants,
　145; and pain, 137–41
Hitler, A., 28, 83; and big lie, 104
Hobbes, T., 143; and state of nature,
　150
Hopkins, G. M., 23
Hume, D., 10; and causality, 93–96;
　and induction, 103; and is/ought
　gap, 13, 29; and objection to
　altruistic contractualism, 164; and
　projectivism, 97

intrinsic properties. *See* non-relational
　properties

Johnson, L., 98, 105; and Leopold,
　103; and optimal states, 99–100

Kane, R., 112; and constitutive/
　identificatory distinction, 44–45;
　and Descartes, 41–42; as
　introduction to perfectionism, 79;
　and key obscurity, 43; major
　moral of, 47–48; and thought-
　experiment, 40
Kant, I., 89–90, 165; and
　contractualism, 148; and

morality's good order, 151; and
　noumena, 143
Kennedy, J., 24
Kripke, S., and fixing the referent, 25;
　and necessary a posteriori, 21, 72
knowledge, 86, 161; analysis of, 30;
　of interior life, 52; as necessary a
　posteriori, 72; of neural
　structures, 138; of robots, 110; as
　perfectionist value, 82;
　transparency of, 33–34

land ethic, 102
last man arguments, 110–12
Leibniz, G., 61–62
Leopold, A., 102, 104–5
Lewis, D., 143
Locke, J., 22, 143

materialism, 37; as to enjoyment and
　suffering, 98
Moore, G. E., as inspiration to deep
　ecology, 110; and is/ought
　distinction, 29; and open-
　question test, 13
moral agents, Harrison's view of, 142;
　Knish as one of, 144; Leopold's
　view of, 104; and moral patients,
　10–11
moral enfranchisement, 9, 77, 160; of
　animals in contractualism, 148,
　165–67; and anthropocentrism,
　12; and desire theory, 46, 124–
　25; and Hume, 95; and
　individual's well-being, 15; and
　natural/artificial distinction, 124;
　of those with opposable thumbs,
　122; Rawls's view of, 155–58; of
　resources, 117; of teleologically
　centered, 92
moral patienthood, 3, 5, 17, 37, 165,
　169; of animals, 118–24; as
　capacity, 11, 15–16, 24;
　Carruthers's view of, 160; and
　contractualism, 145, 147; and
　deep ecology, 89, 95; definition
　of, 9; and desires, 46, 77, 132;
　and experientialism, 23, 35;
　Kantian view of, 90; Leopold's
　view of, 102–3; modal

moral patienthood (*continued*)
  characterization of, 13; as
  opposed to resources, 117;
  perfectionist conception of, 114;
  and Rawls, 154–57; and
  relational properties, 18–21, 69;
  Taylor's view of, 92–93
moral standing. *See* moral
  patienthood
Mozart, A., 114

Nagel, T., 23, 140–42
non-relational properties, 18, 19, 148;
  and desire theory, 48–49, 69;
  and experientialism, 23, 37–40,
  58; of fictional characters, 20; as
  motivating theory, 66–67; as
  necessary for welfare, 21–22, 35
Nozick, R., 47, 112, 180; and
  authenticity, 41; and constitutive/
  identificatory distinction, 44–45;
  and Descartes, 42; and
  experience machine, 40; and
  introduction to perfectionism, 79;
  and key obscurity, 43; major
  moral of, 48

optimal states, and Leopold's view,
  100, 102; and teleological
  centers, 99

pain, 68, as adaptation, 142; as
  anthropocentric projection, 97;
  and consciousness, 129; and
  conceptualist thesis, 70–73;
  control of, 140–41; and evil
  genius, 39; and experientialism,
  23–27; and Freud, 56; and Frey,
  128; and Harrison, 137–38;
  gratuitously inflicted, 165–66;
  immediate access to, 51–52; in
  infants, 136; as intractably
  mental, 138–39; as object of
  desire, 67; and St. Francis, 74; in
  teleological centers, 91–92; as
  worthy of avoidance, 28–29
paradigm-case argument, 12
perfectionism, 54, 78, 89, 81–82, 89,
  112, 169; and animals, 119–25;
  definition of, 4–5; as distinct

from experientialism and desire
  theory, 80, 83; as emanating
  from constitutive/identificatory
  distinction, 46; introduction of,
  79; metaphorical picture of, 86;
  and nonmental values, 87–88;
  and teleological centers, 90–91
Pitcher, G., 61, 66
Plato, 83; and myth of the metals,
  104
pleasure, 76, 83; aberrant, 28; and
  conceptual thesis, 71, 73; and
  desire theory, 48, 73, 85–86;
  produced by evil genius, 39; and
  experientialism, 23, 85–86; and
  immediate access to, 51 as object
  of desire, 67; as perfectionist
  good, 82; as welfare-diminishing,
  25
posthumous benefit/harm, 4, 69, 78,
  87; as a problem for desire
  theory, 58–66
projectivism, 96–97

Rawls, J., and animals, 155–57; and
  contractualism, 149; and
  criterion of personhood, 154;
  and cultural bias, 157–58; and
  reflective equilibrium, 150–51;
  and Scanlon, 159–63; and
  sentimental attachments, 153;
  and veil of ignorance, 152
Regan, T., 156–57
relational properties, and desire
  theory, 58; examples of, 18–19;
  of fictional characters, 20–21
Rembrandt, v.R., 39, 85, 114
representative realists, 14–15
retrocausation, 63–65
Ruth, B., 40

St. Francis of Assisi, 73–74
Sayre, K., 92
Scanlon, T., and Carruthers, 161–62;
  and contractualism, 158–60; and
  Hume, 163–64
Schlick, M., 143
sentience, 69, 132, 165, 170; and
  animals. 145; and contractualism,
  147; as criterial for moral

standing, 133; definition of, 24;
and deep ecology, 95; and
desires, 46, 69–71, 76–77, 125;
and teleological centers, 92–93
shallow ecology, 89
Stich, S., 129–32
Strawson, P., 128

Taylor, P., 96, 105; and deep
ecology, 90–96; and Leopold,
102–3; and teleological centers,
108
teleological centers. *See* Taylor, P.
Tintoretto, J. R., 86, 114

value, 20, 43; in deceived world, 44;
and desires, 51, 57, 84; and
experience machine, 40; and
perfectionism, 80–82, 86–87; of
rationality and well-
informedness, 55; relative and
non-relative, 44; and resources,
117

welfare, 4–5, 37, 58, 67–68, 112, 169;
of babies, 114; in Cartesianism,
43, and constitutive/

identificatory distinction, 45; and
contractualism, 147; for deep
ecology, 89, 92, 101, 105–6;
definition of, 3, 13–14; and
desire theory, 48, 84–86, 124;
132; of dolls, 109; of ecosystems,
111; and experientialism, 24, 31,
38, 133; of Freud, 55; and gung-
ho soldier, 54–55; intra- and
inter-personal comparisons of, 32–
33; and intrinsic properties, 17–
23, 35; introspection of, 34; of
life unlike ours, 107; and moral
patienthood, 15–16; and ontic
commitments, 26, as ordinary
term, 30; and pain, 27–29; and
perfectionism, 46–47, 78–83, 88;
posthumous, 59–66; and
privileged access, 49–53; of
resources, 117; of robots, 110
Wittgenstein, L., 19; and going on in
same way, 103–4; and learning
concepts, 72–73; and language
acquisition, 128

Yankees, N.Y., 48–49; 58